Australia's Golden Era of Social and Legal Reform 1965 -1995

The Memoir of a Participant

By Terry Purcell LLB

Director, Law Foundation of New South Wales 1973 - 1995

Connor Court Publishing Pty Ltd

Published in 2024 by Connor Court Publishing Pty Ltd.

Copyright © Terry Purcell

ALL RIGHTS RESERVED. Not to be reproduced without the permission of the Copyright holder. This book contains material protected under International and Federal Copyright Laws and Treaties. Any unauthorised reprint or use of this material is prohibited. No part of this book may be reproduced or transmitted in any form or by any means, electronic or mechanical, including photocopying, recording, or by any information storage and retrieval system without express written permission from the publisher.

Connor Court Publishing Pty Ltd.
PO Box 7257
Redland Bay QLD 4165
sales@connorcourt.com
www.connorcourt.com

ISBN: 9781922815941

Cover Design by Tim Purcell

Printed in Australia.

Contents

Foreword (Dr Peter Cashman)	v
Introduction	vii
1. Early Life	1
2. Getting into Law School	27
3. Winning a Churchill Fellowship	38
4. California: Learning from the Best	48
5. The Navajo Reservation: Learning from First Nations People	67
6. Chicago: The Good, the Bad and the Outrageous	77
7. Washington: Doors Open in Miraculous Ways!	86
8. New York: Power and Sophistication	102
9. Canadian Legal Aid: A Broad Acceptance of Reform	108
10. UK Legal Aid: A Uniquely Benevolent Concept	116
11. The Law Foundation and Me	139
12. Lift off for the Law Foundation	151
13. The Askin Government and Its Unlikely Reformers	163
14. The Whitlam Era: Colour and Light	182
15. The Whitlam Era: Inside the Reform Tornado	194
16. Wran's Surprising Election Result and His Reform Initiative	201
17. Wran's 1978 Big Win: The Green Light for Reform	213
18. Law Foundation's Contributions to Wran's Reforms	226
19. Increasing Community Access to Legal Information	246
20. Law Foundation: Modernising Courts	256
21. Law Foundation: Youth and the Law Projects	273
22. Law Foundation Grants Programme	283
23. The Hawke/Keating Era: Transforming the Economy	291
24. The Hawke/Keating Era: Law Foundation Opportunities	303
25. Constitutional Reform 1: An Interest from Childhood	313

26. Constitutional Reform 2: Time for Change — 320
27. Constitutional Reform 3: The Constitutional Commission — 328
28. Adapting to Keating's Micro-Economic Era — 349
29. Tomorrow's Legal Services: A Plan of Action — 356
30. Tomorrow's Legal Services: International Recognition — 363
31. A Politician's Assassination Changes My Life — 368
    Postscript — 371
    Acknowledgements — 374
    Index — 375

Foreword

Former Churchill Fellow, Law Foundation Director and solicitor in private practice Terry Purcell has written an informative and incisive historical analysis of legal and political change in Australia over a 30 year period: 1965-1995.

During this period Terry had both insight into and direct participation in many landmark reforms introduced by all sides of politics at both state and federal level.

The NSW Law Foundation itself, under Terry's direction, introduced a number of pioneering reforms, including in the areas of legal education in schools, community legal information, the evaluation of justice initiatives, including community justice centres, and empirical research into various aspects of the operation of the legal system and legal services.

Terry's analysis of the 'golden era' of law reform is well researched, balanced and devoid of party political bias. He rightly gives credit to the major political parties on both sides of politics for their significant legal reforms during their period in office.

At a personal level, I had the good fortune to be recruited by Terry from my professional and post-graduate sojourn in the UK to take a research position with the Law Foundation, to work on various law reform enquiries, to carry out various empirical research projects and to establish the Public Interest Advocacy Centre (PIAC) which continues to thrive. I was one of the many personal and institutional recipients of the Law Foundation's beneficence.

Leaving aside the major achievements of the NSW Law Foundation generally, and Terry in particular, this publication sheds much needed light on a multitude of law reform initiatives in Australia, many of which have either been overlooked or taken for granted.

It is essential reading for members of the public and the legal profession for its invaluable historical and political analyses.

Dr Peter Cashman

Barrister; Adjunct Professor, University of NSW

Introduction

"If ever a society needed the injection of new concepts and new policies, of theories and programmes, to replace the old, blind instinctualism, it is Australia at this moment." (*Profile of Australia* by Craig McGregor, Penguin, 1968, page 378).

This memoir includes my personal journey and the story of the Law Foundation of New South Wales (NSW) of which I was Director, and my dealings with four reforming governments, the Askin and Wran governments in NSW and the Whitlam and Hawke/Keating federally. The Foundation worked closely with all of them, giving impetus and credibility to so many of its achievements.

The election in December 1972 of the Whitlam government (1972-1975) heralded a much anticipated and much needed era of change and reform for the Australian nation which took off with all the colour and excitement of a giant Catherine wheel. In the typical uncontrolled manner of these much loved and often highly dangerous fireworks, the sparks of reform flew in all directions exciting many, but terrifying others.

This unprecedented 30-year era of reform provides a backdrop to the story I tell. The Law Foundation played an important role in this era, assisting successive governments, both state and Commonwealth in implementing their reform agendas.

The longevity of this remarkable period of reform arose in effect from a "relay", with the reform baton being handed over to successive governments which continued to complement each other in building the foundations underpinning Australia's modernisation and economic success.

While the baby boomer generation probably thinks the nation's golden era of reform commenced with the election of the Whitlam Government, I found that the reform race had actually commenced in NSW with the election in 1965 of the Askin Government. It had replaced a worn-out Labor Government, which "expired" after 24 years of heavy lifting through the difficult post war years.

Like all good sporting analogies, there needs to be a dark horse and, in this case, to many today, the Askin Government (1965-1976) was probably the most unlikely entrant. This unexpected and largely unheralded participant set the initial pace with a remarkable record of introducing reforming, innovative and wide-ranging legislation benefiting all levels of the community.

In the legal context, the NSW court system was dragged out of the 1800s into the late 20th century by the foresight of Attorney General Ken McCaw and his legal colleague, Minister for Justice John Maddison.

The later strong allegations of corruption on Askin's part tarnished most people's recollection of his government's achievements.

A week before Whitlam's election, I was appointed the first director of the recently established Law Foundation and held that role for the next 23 years, giving me a unique qualification to tell its story. It is interwoven with the politics of the time and also describes how, as a young lawyer, I brought the experience and knowledge gained via a Churchill Fellowship to my role. In early 1972, I had travelled for five months through the US, Canada and the UK learning about the advances in legal aid, law reform and the emerging role of computers to aid this work, all of which were of interest to the Board of this fledgling institution.

The Foundation was a relatively new statutory fund, another of the early reforms promoted by Ken McCaw with the support of the NSW Law Society, intended to undertake research, support law reform activities, provide assistance with legal education and offer greater community access to legal information and legal aid services.

During my time as its Director, the Law Foundation undertook many major projects which left indelible marks on the legal system and gradually changed for the better the way that system met the

INTRODUCTION

community's needs. In addition, the Foundation became the funder of choice for community groups seeking to promote reform and educational initiatives being undertaken to improve access to legal information and grassroots legal services.

The other governments with which the Law Foundation and I had close working relationships included the Wran Government, which unexpectedly defeated the 10-year-old Askin Government in May 1976, barely six months after the dismissal of the Whitlam Government in Canberra. This long serving government continued on successfully following Wran's retirement, with Barrie Unsworth as Premier. It was defeated two years later leaving behind a very impressive 12 year record of much needed good government and reforming legislation.

The other reforming governments which I was to deal with were the Hawke Government (1983-1991) and its successor the Keating Government (1991-1996).

While Hawke inherited a government in serious financial strife, nevertheless he moved forward with implementing the Prices and Income Accord negotiated with the unions prior to the election, backed up by a commitment to implement Medicare.

Keating's dominant responsibility initially was re-building the economy by structural changes rather than by creative legislative responses to major issues. His solution to funding new initiatives was to sell off government owned assets such as Qantas and Telstra.

The first part of this memoir covers my early life in Cabarita on the banks of the Parramatta River, which ultimately leads me to gaining a law degree from Sydney University and becoming a solicitor. However, when married and in my late twenties, my professional life took an unexpected turn when I was awarded a Churchill Fellowship enabling me to investigate legal aid services in the US, Canada and the UK.

This fortuitous award brought me to the attention of the leadership of the NSW Law Society who were in need of help to bring their new initiative, the Law Foundation, to life. I was honoured by their invitation but also enthusiastic to replicate the roles of similar foundations in the US.

The Law Foundation's role in injecting new concepts, policies, theories and programmes into the Australian landscape would have been music to the ears of the earlier quoted Craig McGregor and other social commentators.

However, I take pride in noting that the Foundation's groundbreaking work was being observed, recorded and brought to the notice of the wider legal profession by J G Starke QC, editor of the illustrious *Australian Law Journal*, who noticed and approved when he commented in the Journal in 1988:

> In the two decades of its existence the Foundation has become indubitably the outstanding institution in Australia in the area of its statutory functions. No other body in the country has such a measure of achievement to its credit or pioneered so many new initiatives to serve the legal needs of community or to ensure that the laws in the community will be administered so as to improve the public welfare.
>
> In the field of legal innovation, it has a record not surpassed by any other institution in the nation. Moreover, but for the flexibility of the Foundation's approach in the making of its financial grants, some of the finest research projects ever undertaken in Australia would never have seen the light of day.

This quotation was included in a special edition of the Foundation's 1992 Annual Report, which was released at a function held at the Law Society to mark the 25th anniversary of the Foundation's establishment in 1967.

1

Early Life

I came into the world in Sydney on 29 June 1942 at the nadir of the Second World War, with the Nazis largely unchallenged and rampant in Europe and the Japanese spreading out across Asia and the Pacific, even bombing Darwin for the first time earlier that same year. Sydney itself had been under attack a few weeks before my birth when Japanese midget subs entered the harbour and sank a vessel, killing 21 sailors.

Under the steady leadership of the new Prime Minister John Curtin, the situation was starting to look better for Australia. At his request the United States (US) was coming to our aid. In fact, in May 1942 the American and Australian navies had stopped the advance of the Japanese navy in the Battle of the Coral Sea, the first battle fought by aircraft carriers.

Still, for my parents, Daniel and Edna Purcell, a couple of factory workers raising a family in a time of war, those first years of my life must have been difficult. The papers would have been filled with doom and gloom. Everyone would have known someone with a son fighting in the war or worse missing, presumed dead. Almost at the same time as my arrival, butter began to be rationed, followed soon after by tea, then sugar, eggs, and later petrol, meat and tobacco.

I was my parent's third child. I had an older sister Colleen and an older brother Michael. I would soon be followed by Denis and another sister, Pat, then 10 years after my birth a surprise baby brother, Brian. That was a lot of mouths to feed. However, despite my father's modest wage, my parents provided well for their children. My parents had both seen times much worse than those they were facing. By contrast, they felt themselves well off.

My father's early childhood was difficult to comprehend by the standards of my generation. He was born in 1902 in Leonora in the Western Australian goldfields, 800 kilometres north-east of Perth, where his Irish immigrant father had taken his family in search of work and the hope of striking it rich. My grandfather, Patrick Purcell, had migrated from Ireland in the early 1880s and quickly married a 16-year-old bride, Catherine Clancy, newly arrived in Sydney from Ireland herself. Birth records show the newlyweds moved about quite a bit – from Sydney to Kiama on the south coast, then north to Ballina, then west across the continent to Fremantle, in Western Australia, then to the goldfields at Kalgoorlie, then north to Leonora where Patrick found work at the nearby Sons of Gwalia mine in the latter part of the 1890s.

By the time my father was born my grandmother was 33 and already had six children, aged between four and 16, to look after. What her life must have been like, travelling here, there and everywhere, with her six children, in what couldn't have been very pleasant conditions, I can only imagine. My father's childhood was spent not in Leonora where he was born but in nearby Gwalia on the edge of the mine in a whitewashed corrugated iron shanty with a hessian curtain for a door. Curiously, my father was never heard to complain about the conditions of his childhood, nor of the cold or the heat, or the dirt floor, the isolation, nor the crushing poverty, no doubt because it was all he knew.

These two small towns, Leonora and Gwalia, only 12 kilometres apart, clung together amidst a vast wasteland of red dirt and low grey green shrubs. My father told me that he and his siblings used to catch a tram across the desert to Leonora to go to a school run by nuns. Gwalia is a tourist attraction now, for when the gold mine first closed in the 1960s the inhabitants of the town left overnight, the buildings deserted, abandoning most of their belongings, leaving a veritable ghost town. From current photos I can see the place is littered with tin shacks just like my father described. It would have been a hard life.

Incidentally, my grandfather worked at the Sons of Gwalia mine when it was managed by Herbert Hoover, later the 31st President of the US. However, Hoover's time there was a period notorious for industrial unrest caused by his importation of cheap European labour. This, in hindsight, was an early indication of his policies which unnecessarily prolonged the devastating effect of the Great Depression on working people in the US. Perhaps my grandfather's firsthand experience of injustice filtered down to me in some way, leading me to fight it wherever I found it.

When my father was about eight years old, the family set off for Sydney, leaving behind their eldest daughter, Mary Ann, who was already married, an aunt I was never to meet. My grandparents settled in Burwood where my father was sent to the Christian Brothers School. However, tragedy struck the family ten or so years after making a home in Sydney. The First World War was finally over, but the Spanish Flu epidemic followed hot on its heels, with my grandmother Catherine's hard life ending at the age of only 51, when my father himself was only 16. The same epidemic struck her son Patrick's young wife as well and they were just two of the estimated 50 million people worldwide to lose their lives, more indeed than the war itself.

As both of my father's parents died before I was born and my father wasn't much of a storyteller, I am ashamed to admit I know little about them. One lasting relic of my father's family's time in the goldfields of Western Australia was a white cockatoo the family brought back with them. It was my grandfather's pet. He bequeathed it to his son Thomas on his death in 1937, but I knew it as my father's brother Uncle Mick's family pet. How my grandfather first acquired the bird, no one seemed to remember, but I remember Mick saying that as kids they had trained the clever cockatoo to walk with a stick under its wing like a soldier in the First World War marching with his rifle on his shoulder. Though I never saw it perform tricks, this cockatoo was still entertaining several generations of our family in the late 1970s, including my own children.

My mother Edna's childhood was not as colourful. Her father, John Griffin, born in 1877 to a poor family, grew up in a small town north-west of Orange in NSW called Molong. Somehow, he managed to get a job with the Post Master General and progressed from being a linesman up poles fixing and extending telegraph wires to being a superintendent working in the Blue Mountains. In 1908 he married Annie Marie Kerr, with whom he was to have seven children, all of whom lived to ripe old ages. The family settled in Campsie in Sydney. However, in the late 1920s, after years in the harsh Australian sun, John developed skin cancer which forced him to give up work and caused his early death at only 54 in 1931.

Born in 1911, my mother Edna suffered from poor eyesight as a child growing up in Campsie. This was never detected, and she finished school with a very limited education, not unusual for girls in the early 1920s. However, once she left school it didn't take long for a workmate in her first job to see the cause of her difficulties and told her in frustration that she was blind and needed glasses.

Glasses transformed my mother's life, and she was soon going to technical college at night to learn dressmaking at which she excelled. This skill meant that during the depression of the 1930s she kept her job as a piece worker at Lustre Hosiery in Rushcutters Bay making women's underwear. Thus it was that, though still a young woman of 20, my mother became the breadwinner of her family made up of her recently widowed mother, Annie, and a team of younger siblings, the youngest Josephine being only two or three years old.

By the mid-1930s my father Daniel was considered to be a confirmed bachelor who was a smart dresser and a regular at Randwick Racecourse where, because of his outgoing personality, he mixed in circles not normally frequented by persons whose weekday job was a semi-skilled worker in AGL's Mortlake Gas Works. However, he was also good friends with some cousins of my mother and it would seem that they became matchmakers and introduced them to each other, recognising that they would be a good couple, and it was not long before they were headed for marriage, Dad being 35 and Mum 26, in August 1937 at St Mel's Catholic Church, Campsie.

Largely through my mother's determination, my parents somehow were able to borrow enough to build a new home in 1937 at Putney after their marriage, a significant feat for a couple of factory workers with modest earning capacity. As I got older, I realised my mother was a home economics genius. She looked after the family on my father's very modest wage and made sure her six children were well fed, well dressed, largely due to her being a highly skilled and efficient dressmaker, and, above all, for the times, that they were well-educated.

Both of my parents were raised in Catholic families and were educated by religious brothers and nuns respectively, in Catholic schools. But the education they received in the early decades of the 20th century had been modest, and this had placed limitations on them. Both were determined that no such limitations would be placed upon their children. To be really free to choose a path in life, they realised, one would have to go on to university and so they ensured that all their children had the opportunity to attain their Leaving Certificates with five of their six children doing so.

This focus on higher education was not abnormal in our neighbourhood as a majority of families had children who aspired to tertiary education which was in part because it was, by today's standards, a largely middle-class enclave, with children either going to Catholic high schools, private high schools or selective public high schools.

Our Catholic education, of course, was supplemented by attending Sunday Mass at the local St Patrick's Catholic Church in nearby Mortlake. As children all this was taken for granted and complemented the religious education we received during our school years. However, we met our obligations without any great involvement in Church activities, not that there was a lot going on as during my time our parish priests were old Irishmen at the end of their careers and cranky old men to boot.

Though the son of an Irishman, my father, like many children of immigrants of his generation, had no interest in the old country. When his father had emigrated to Australia in the 1880s Ireland was still ruled by the United Kingdom, not gaining their partial independence until 1921. Life was hard in Ireland, opportunities scarce, so there had been good reason for my grandfather to leave. My father in turn was immensely proud to have been born in Australia not long after the Federation was proclaimed in 1901, and like all others of his generation was taught Civics at school. This compulsory subject was devoted to ensuring all Australian children learnt about our new national Constitution and government, and Australia's status as self-governed nation.

When the Second World War came, despite Dad having steady work at the Gas Works, which, being a protected industry meant he would not be called up for military service, other problems loomed. While he could get to and from work from the house they built in Putney, via the Mortlake vehicle ferry, wartime demands meant that he was regularly required to work longer shifts which finished after the ferry stopped for the night. It must have been frustrating for my tired father, because the lights of Putney were only a few hundred metres away across the Parramatta River, swimming distance really, but by road, crossing the newly built Ryde Bridge, it was seven kilometres. Ever the pragmatist, my mother gave up her new home. It sold quickly and they bought the only family home I was to know, an older 1920s cottage in Stamford Avenue, Cabarita, the suburb next to Mortlake. Now my father only had a short walk to work.

Both my parents had a strong interest in current affairs in the early post-Second World War years. Coming from a working class background my father believed it his civic duty to become involved in the union movement and I can recall him attending meetings regularly in the evening, meetings usually concerning the need to keep the Communist Party from taking over the union to which he belonged. The 1940s and the early 1950s saw strike action in many industries but in time the more moderate unions with government support prevailed.

My father read *The Sydney Morning Herald* daily and while he usually disagreed with its political views, he could not stand the alternatives and appreciated the *Herald's* overall quality. Like many of his era the ABC news was the other daily staple. Needless to say, I followed in his footsteps and became a lifelong reader of the *Herald* and an ABC listener. He was a good, caring father and a gentleman as well as being a teetotaller, a term rarely used now but meaning someone who abstained from drinking alcohol. That, combined with not being a smoker, meant that, unlike many of his workmates, 100% of his modest wage found its way home to my mother who took responsibility for managing the household accounts.

The modest 1920s cottage in Cabarita they had bought was a tight squeeze as our family grew. When we were young, Michael, Denis and I slept in one room while Colleen and Pat shared another. It was really a two-bedroom home but my parents turned a dining room into a bedroom for the girls. Later, when Brian was born, things got even more cramped. When Michael was 16 and already attending university, my parents decided to add a small room to the back of the garage for him. It was a reasonable size with windows on two sides. I am sure we all envied him his private little kingdom. Not long after this, Colleen, the eldest, left home leaving younger sister Pat with a room of her own, too.

Cabarita, a Kids' Paradise

As small as our family home was, it was in a pleasant established neighbourhood surrounded by water with a park with play equipment at the bottom of the street and Cabarita Park, the big park as we kids called it, with the public swimming pool, boat shed and an old wharf to fish from, five minutes away.

There was very little traffic as Cabarita was effectively a peninsula, jutting out where the Parramatta River meets Sydney Harbour. There was only one main road which serviced the local BALM paint factory and along which the number 81 tram and later buses ran, terminating at Cabarita Park before heading back to Burwood.

Everyone had bikes and few people had cars. Kids rode everywhere and as a number of nearby properties had full-size back yard tennis courts, my siblings and I all became competent tennis players. It was a great place to grow up.

My first real memory of leaving Cabarita and heading into the city of Sydney was on 1 January 1951, when Dad, in a suit, tie and hat no less, took Michael and me to see the Commonwealth of Australia Jubilee Celebrations. There was an enormous parade with floats and marching bands called the Cavalcade of Jubilee that started in Farm Cove and snaked through the city before heading out to the show grounds via Anzac Parade. It was billed as the biggest event ever held in Sydney.

Later that same year, in May, there was a minor replay when officials held a ceremony in Cabarita Park to mark the 50th anniversary of the opening of the Australian Parliament. The event was held in the park's bandstand because it was one of the two buildings used at the original Federation ceremony 50 years before in Centennial Park. Our local council had bought it in 1903 and it had been used as a bandstand ever since. So the park down the road from where I grew up had a direct connection to Federation, the bandstand being the place where the proclamation was read out and signing of the Constitution documents took place. Some 30 years later, while involved with the Constitutional Commission, I would participate in another re-enactment of the proclamation of Federation, this time back in Centennial Park. It would appear some childhood experiences have a direct influence on one's adult life.

By 1952 my mother had saved enough through her clever economies for them to buy their first car, a 1939 Chevrolet, which my poor father at the age of 50 then had to learn to drive. Having a car transformed our lives. We were now able to head to Sydney's much famed beaches, formerly out of reach, as well as follow Dad's Rugby League team, Wests, and see their games at various suburban grounds, and even at the Sydney Cricket Ground.

Another advantage of having a car was that I would get used to going into the city every couple of weeks on Saturday mornings. Dad would take Michael and myself shopping for fruit and vegetables, sometimes in bulk, at Paddy's Markets followed by a walk up to Anthony Hordern's Brickfield Hill store to buy items Mum needed for sewing or knitting. Wandering around the cavernous department store was a real adventure for us children.

We also had family visits each year to Moore Park for the Royal Easter Show on Holy Thursday, a real highlight for kids each year, topped off by getting our favourite show bags. Dad also had an old footy mate in Burwood, Bob Hedges, who had a 1928 Hudson soft top tourer in which we would be driven to Moore Park to see Rugby League games at the Cricket Ground. There was so much space in the Hudson's back seat that the tallest of us couldn't reach the back of the front seat.

When growing up in the 1940s and 1950s, not unlike kids today, my main source of knowledge about the wider world, outside my immediate neighbourhood and home, came mostly from the then comparatively primitive electronic media. Initially, it was the ever-present radio, particularly before and after school, and later in the evening. This in turn was, in those early post-war years, complemented by a regular visit via the tram on Saturday afternoons to the Ritz cinema in Wellbank, as the nearest shopping centre was known locally, referring to the number 81 tram stop at the corner of Wellbank Street and Majors Bay Road.

Going to the pictures with my older brother and sister, a standard Saturday activity for most young pre-baby boomer Australians, exposed me to a much wider world than the radio offered. The programme usually included newsreels which often told us stories about dramatic events overseas, complemented by cartoons followed by a mix of Hollywood B grade westerns and endless black and white English movies re-telling stories from the Second World War, most of which, as a little boy, I found frightening.

These trips to the pictures led me to conclude at an early age that everything exciting in the world was happening elsewhere, in a different universe to the one I inhabited with my family. That world I saw up on the big screen was always far away. Nevertheless, at about this time the bigger world was suddenly being talked about down at the local Cabarita swimming baths with the prospect of some local swimmers being selected for the 1952 Olympic Games soon to be held in Helsinki.

I was probably about eight or nine at the time these rumours started, and I had no idea what or where Helsinki was, or for that matter what the Olympic Games were. So, for the first time in my short life it seemed that not all the exciting events were on the other side of the world, and I had a direct connection to those who would end up becoming Australian Olympic legends.

My connection to those being talked about, namely local swimming club champions Jon Henriks and Lorraine Crapp, was tenuous but very real to me. Real life sports stars were swimming in the pool just down the road from my house. I watched them in awe as they trained, won races and broke records against other club members who also competed at state level.

This connection also flowed from the fact that I had not only been taught to swim by their coach Harry Cremer, but that I was also a member of the same swimming club. However, my connection soon ended as I was a hopelessly uncoordinated swimmer, unlike my older siblings who showed real promise as elite swimmers, so much so that my brother Michael was sought out by the swimming coach to undergo intensive training.

Overcoming Dyslexia and Learning to Read at Last

Not being able to swim as well as Michael wasn't my only source of shame in this period. I couldn't read.

While others in my year were reading books and winning prizes, I was struggling to read a simple sentence aloud. I can't say how deeply this failure to read affected me. Perhaps it encouraged me to keep in the academic shadows. I don't remember thinking myself stupid, as I could keep up verbally with my peers. I felt frustrated more than anything, that something which came so easily to others was impossible for me. It was difficult at times to hide my inability to read. And occasionally I felt a great shame at being the dunce of the family.

However, my mother had experienced similar learning difficulties because of her poor eyesight as a child, so she knew I wasn't a dunce and that there had to be another factor at play. After I was made to repeat fourth class, my mother enlisted the help of Brother Barnes at the Christian Brothers Burwood Intermediate School. In doing so she ensured that I had a chance of overcoming my reading difficulties. I am certain, if I was a child at school now, I would have been diagnosed with dyslexia, but back then such diagnoses didn't exist. You were simply thought an idiot if you couldn't read and were expected to drop out of school and work with your hands. I was very lucky to have the support of my mother and to have Brother Barnes as a teacher as he changed my life, an experience many people have when they are lucky enough to have a teacher who cares.

Mastering reading led me to explore the resources of the Burwood Municipal Library and my knowledge of the wider world opened up via yet another medium, namely books and magazines. I quickly discovered the joy of being transported into the more adventurous lives of others through Enid Blyton's *Famous Five* books and Captain W E John's *Biggles* series. I also discovered fascinating American magazines such as *Popular Mechanics*, *Popular Science*,

National Geographic and the *Readers Digest*. A natural by-product of this was that, from then on, I happily coped with my school studies while not attaining a starring role.

In hindsight, my love of books, which continues to this day, complemented by quality newspapers and magazines, has always been my most enjoyable means of gathering new information. Neither of my parents seemed to read books. There were certainly no books in the house other than those required by school and university, but in both their cases this probably reflects the fact that books were expensive, their education was modest and both left school at around 15. My parents' love of a good newspaper and interest in current events suggests they might have been big readers given the opportunities they had been proud to give their own children. In fact, I feel certain they would have been.

We didn't get a TV until about six months after transmission started in 1956 when I was already in my mid-teens. I wonder whether I would be the reader I am today had I been born five or 10 years later. Initially TV wasn't much competition, but as programming matured it became hard to ignore, especially as the whole family might gather in front of it of an evening.

Learning to be a Caddy

Books weren't the only thing broadening my horizons. Becoming a caddy at Concord Golf Club, one of the oldest and, at the time, most exclusive golf clubs in Sydney introduced me to a world I had up until then only ever glimpsed. Members were men and women with successful careers in business or the professions. These were the sort of people my parents wanted us to become, educated, well-off, free to associate with whomever they wanted. Not bound by their class or education.

Initially, for Michael and me, it was a way to make a bit of pocket money on the weekends while at high school. Though we never felt poor, largely due to our mother's clever home economics stretching our father's moderate pay packet, we always needed spending money and in our teen years we took jobs in the school holidays. But the golf club was different.

To succeed as a caddy, you had to adapt to members' different personalities and individual idiosyncrasies while at the same time watching their ball and keeping count of the shots played. There was also a certain etiquette required from both the members and their caddies and, as time went on, if you were any good you ended up having a semi-permanent caddying gig with a particular member which meant a modest yet steady income.

In time, this experience meant that both Michael and I picked up the rudiments of the game with some help from the club golf professional, Bruce Jackson. One of his assistants was the big hitting Frank Phillips who, during the time we were caddying, soon became famous for winning the Australian Golf Open. Another small window into the bigger world.

This experience led us to save up and acquire sets of second-hand golf clubs following which we started to play golf at the new Massey Park municipal course not far from where we lived. This meant that, when we were in our late teens, we were competent enough to join Concord Golf Club as junior members with some help from a member whose father was one of Dad's fellow gas workers. Michael still plays at Concord regularly and is probably heading towards joining a select few having Club membership for over 60 years.

Of course, besides becoming competent golfers, being a caddy exposed us to the conversation and manners of the wealthy members. It is hard to judge the effect this had on us both, but I can guess it made us feel more comfortable in the company of successful men, something school couldn't teach you, nor something we could learn at home. Perhaps it helped reduce the distance between them and us giving both Michael and I the confidence to chase our dreams.

But I am getting ahead of myself. In the early 1950s I didn't have any dreams about careers, unlike Michael who always knew he wanted to be a doctor. In the early 1950s I was just a kid hanging around Cabarita exploring the sandy beaches around Hen and Chicken Bay or fishing down off the wharf. Not that I was lonely. Being a member of a large family meant there was always something to do and I was never really allowed to be lonely. I was in awe of my brother Michael as a child and teenager as he was just so good at everything and seemed to know what he wanted out of life. So did my older sister Colleen, come to think of it. But Michael did things I wanted to do and did them well while Colleen's life as a young, would-be woman of the world was completely alien to me.

I don't want to paint a picture of me as some kind of wimp. Although not the sportsman my brother was, I could swim, I played tennis reasonably well, could play cricket, kick a footy, row a boat, and became a competent golfer. Once we got the car, Dad would drive us to the beach in Dee Why and Mona Vale where we would body surf. With the parks, the tennis courts, the swimming club and the Parramatta River at our doorstep, we all led very active lives and were very fit and healthy.

Most years we would go on holidays. From 1947 to 1949, we went north to the Central Coast for the summer holidays. We got there by cab to Strathfield Station, steam train to Gosford and then on a large burgundy coloured bus to The Entrance. We all loved the lake where there were row boats for hire, etc. In the 1950s our parents took us on holidays to Kiama where we camped right above the beach, choosing the same spot for maybe seven or eight years in a row. Dad had a large tent made with several rooms. I remember we had all camping mods and cons – gas cooker, small refrigerator, lights.

When I finished primary school my brother Michael was completing his Intermediate Certificate. Though less than two years older than me, because I had been forced to repeat a year, Michael was three years ahead of me at school. Our parents wanted all of their children to continue on to obtain their Leaving Certificates. However, schooling at Burwood Christian Brothers ended with the Intermediate Certificate, so my parents managed to get Michael,

Denis and me moved from Burwood to Christian Brothers High School Lewisham. I imagine it was down to my mother repeatedly writing to and then visiting the school to persuade the Brothers in person. She was a very persistent woman who usually got her way in things when it concerned her children's education.

Going to High School

Lewisham was much further from home than Burwood. Her three boys would have a couple of minutes' walk to the bus stop, a 20 minute ride to Burwood station and then a 20 minute trip on the train to Lewisham but she considered the trek there and back worth the reward. The move enabled Michael to obtain his Leaving Certificate and opened the door for both Denis and me too. Lewisham had an excellent reputation dating back to the 1890s for producing engineers, doctors and priests. Curiously, compared with the other disciplines, very few lawyers seemed to have been educated at Lewisham, perhaps because of its strong orientation towards maths and the sciences.

Looking back there was little in my formal schooling to indicate any great potential. The only exception was winning an Intermediate Bursary via a public examination, the reward for which was that my school fees were paid for my last two years of high school. Curiously, that spike in my results coincided with a vocational guidance assessment carried out at the time by the NSW Department of Labour and Industry which indicated I had little prospect of obtaining a university degree.

The Catholic education system played a key role for many Australian families as it enabled children of working class parents to attain the Leaving Certificate and university matriculation. The only way to gain the Leaving Certificate in the public school system was to qualify for entry to state selective high schools such as the nearby Fort Street Boys High School. But the places were limited and the competition for them was fierce. The majority of those who sat for their Leaving Certificate with Michael and later me at Christian

Brothers High School Lewisham would not have qualified. We were very fortunate that Irish religious leaders like Edmund Rice, the founder of the Christian Brothers in the middle of the 19th century, took it upon themselves to devote their lives to providing affordable, safe educational opportunities to the children of poor and working class Catholic families.

The contribution such religious teaching orders made to the development of Australia has never been fully appreciated, with so many of their students going on to obtain degrees as well as fill the ranks of the public service, particularly in Canberra in the second half of the 20th century.

My father-in-law, Jack Wright, was a typical example of a bright child getting the Leaving Certificate at 15 in the mid-1920s thanks to De La Salle College, Ashfield. On leaving school he got a job as a junior clerk in the Commonwealth Bank where his high intelligence and capacity were soon recognised. He spent the next 20 years of his career in the Exchange Control section of the Bank's central banking department. Ultimately, after gaining an honours degree in Economics from Sydney University part time after the war he ended up in the top echelons of the Reserve Bank. There were thousands of others like him, many with migrant family backgrounds, expanding the pool of much needed highly qualified Australians capable of making major contributions to Australia's post war development.

Decision to Leave School and Get a Job

At 15, I decided it was time to leave school, get a job and become financially independent. This was just before the summer holidays and just after I had sat for the Bursary exam, and in which I felt I had little hope of being successful. Knowing my mother wouldn't approve of my decision to leave school I decided prove to her I had what it took to be independent. On the first day of the summer holidays, I decided to see if I could get a job in a shipping company. I went to the city and sat in the GPO getting numbers from the Pink Pages and started making calls.

I wanted to work for a shipping company because I had read a prescribed book for English that year, *Pattern of the Islands* by Sir Arthur Grimble, which was about his experiences in the British Colonial Administrative Service. In 1914, despite having a Cambridge degree, Grimble took on the role of a British cadet administrator on the Gilbert and Ellice Islands in the western Pacific. The Gilbert and Ellice Islands were a long line of islands crossing the equator and running northwest from Samoa to just below the Marshal Islands. Apparently, Grimble had chosen this post because, a born adventurer, he noticed it was the furthest place on the globe from Britain, and therefore a great place to start.

The author told an interesting and, to me, exotic story of life on this remote set of islands in the early years of the 20th century on the eve of the First World War. Little was Grimble to know that his career in such a role would be one of the last as the war would mark the beginning of the end of Britain's hold on various colonies and protectorates.

The book also brought to my attention the important role shipping played in the lives of those on such remote islands. To a 15-year-old, the way Grimble told it, life there, was idyllic as well as both colourful and adventurous. Not only that but the life of a ship's officer seemed very attractive compared with that lived by my parents, both of whose working life, like so many of their relatives and friends, had consigned them to low paid factory work.

This was an outcome my mother was determined would not be the lot of her children who, through education, would have the opportunities she and my father were denied. Needless to say, my dreams of being a ship's officer in the face of such determination were doomed to fail.

I made my first call to Burns, Philp & Co and was surprised to be put through to the staff manager who invited me to come down for an interview immediately. I duly made the short journey from Martin Place to Bridge Street and entered Burns, Philp & Co's beautiful sandstone building whose interior had not changed since it was built in the late 1800s. The most notable feature to a 15-year-old was its lift, which unlike the big department store lifts, had no electric controls but was propelled by the operator pulling on a rope which passed through the lift. I should have realised then that the world of shipping was different.

After a short interview in which I explained why I had decided to approach them for a job I was hired and spent the next six weeks of the school holidays working in the ground floor shipping department as a junior clerk answering to Captain Sharp, the manager. My duties included occasional errands such as taking papers to the various company ships then in port or taking arrival and departure updates to the offices of *The Shipping News* in North Sydney, which were a welcome distraction from what was a pretty boring job.

One of my daily responsibilities stands out in my memory and left a lasting impression. It was my job to place a very large and expensive Japanese jade vase in a prominent spot on the front counter. This was done as a sign of respect whenever a ship of the Japanese NYK line was in port. Apparently, Burns Philp were the commercial agents for NYK, and the vase had been a gift from them many years before. I remember thinking it odd that the relationship and the vase had survived the war considering the horrors inflicted on Australians by the Japanese during the Second World War.

For a relatively young person it was difficult to understand the ways of diplomacy and commercial reality. It seemed strange that a longstanding commercial relationship could survive a war during which Japanese atrocities towards Australian POWs, let alone to the millions of civilians in all the countries of South-East Asia and China, could be so readily overlooked. I decided that some relationships are more complicated than others.

However, these issues were soon to become just another part of my life experience as towards the middle of January, much to my surprise, my parents received notice that I had won a State Bursary which meant I was going on to do my Leaving Certificate. This bit of good luck, as my parents saw it, torpedoed my seagoing ambitions. Nevertheless, I felt pleased that I had taken the initiative and had shown that I could get a job of my choice, not all that difficult at a time when I learned later that unemployment was running at a low of 1%.

I was also pleased, however, to have had the experience of working for such a long-established company. Subsequent events meant that, had I stayed with Burns Philp, my career would have been curtailed because of the introduction of container ships and the arrival of large passenger planes such as the Boeing 707 and later the 747. In less than 15 years from my time at Burns Philp, it had disposed of most of its ships and slipped into relative commercial obscurity, and I would be flying to the US as a passenger on the inaugural Qantas 747 flight as a Churchill Fellow.

Off to University: Attempt No 1!

When I completed my Leaving Certificate, my results, while good enough to matriculate for entry into Sydney University, were not good enough to win a Commonwealth Scholarship which would have covered my university fees. University was out of reach again. I had won my right to be there but couldn't afford to attend. Not that this mattered much to me at the time, as I, unlike my brother Michael, had no idea what I wanted to study and so no burning ambition to go to university. Once again, I was at a loose end.

However, the NSW government intervened again and, in mid-January 1960, I received a scholarship to study for a Science degree at Sydney. The end of the Second World War had resulted in a global baby boom and governments everywhere were trying to adjust to accommodate this unexpected jump in population. The NSW Education Department was desperately trying to find enough teachers to teach the wave of new students coming through the education system. As my best results were in science and maths, without stopping to consider whether I would make a good teacher, or even if I wanted to be a teacher, I was earmarked for the role of science teacher.

The experience of that year was scarring. I quickly discovered a major gap between what I had learned in Physics, Chemistry and Maths for the Leaving Certificate with what I now needed to know to even understand the lecturers. I realised that not having studied those subjects at Honours level at school, I was seriously out of my depth. At great cost to my self-esteem, I dragged myself through most of the year until I couldn't take it anymore. Much to the distress of my parents, I applied to be released from my contract with the Education Department. The Department had invested in me and were reluctant to let me go. The thought that I might have to continue for another two years was depressing, so I restated my case for release. The University Medical Officer, Dr Wilkins, referred me a psychiatrist, Dr John Ellard, who assessed me. He concluded I was unsuitable to be a teacher and in the interests of my health my scholarship should be cancelled. I was free. But I had lost a year. Incidentally, Dr Ellard was later to play an important role in my life as a Board member and Chairman of the Law Foundation. But that was far in the future.

Needless to say, following this personal debacle and facing no immediate prospect of gaining a university education my self-esteem was severely bruised. I then tried several jobs but nothing appealed.

Winning a Bravery Award

In January 1961, while on the family's annual camping holiday in Kiama, a tragic event occurred which paradoxically helped restore some of my lost self-belief. One morning, when the weather was unseasonably foul, I was reading on my camp stretcher when I heard a commotion outside. I got up and walked to the edge of the camp overlooking the beach where I saw a bunch of young children caught in a rip. I later learned they were from a nearby church camp and had rushed down to the beach unsupervised and jumped into the water, unaware that the beach had been closed due to rough seas. As I made my way down to the water, I watched as a man, one of our campsite neighbours, jumped from the rocks and with difficulty managed to drag the kids back to shore. But then, to everyone's astonishment, their saviour, probably exhausted after his efforts, got caught in the rip and was being washed out to sea before our eyes.

My younger brother Denis and I, much to our mother's horror, dived off the rocks into the rough sea and swam to the man who was by then unconscious. We managed to get hold of him and together we started to swim him out of the rip and back to safety. The sea was very reluctant to let us go but Denis and I fought back. Thankfully a lifesaver appeared and helped us all back to the shore. Denis and I only realised the danger we had been in and the risk we had taken after we got back to the beach. We had put our poor mother through a terrible time thinking she had lost two of her sons. This was brought home when we learned the man we had saved, after attempts to revive him, had been pronounced dead on the beach.

The dead hero was a holidaying police officer, Francis Laurel Burke. The traumatic incident taught me something about duty. This man enjoying his holiday saw others in danger and didn't hesitate. In uniform or out of uniform he had dedicated his life to others and saw it as his duty to risk his life to save the lives of strangers. He had saved the children but, in doing so, had sacrificed his own life. My brother and I acted in the heat of the moment. I don't think we weighed up the dangers in the way a trained police officer would. We were typical male teenagers, being good swimmers from an early age with every confidence in our ability. We didn't really assess the danger; we just dived into the water. We were sure we'd be alright, but that was not how it looked to my mother and other witnesses.

There were several significant outcomes of this tragedy, the first being that a few days later we packed up camp and returned home to Cabarita. I learned that my parents had decided to attend Mr Burke's funeral, my mother having provided support to Mrs Burke at the campsite after the incident. During the funeral service, which was attended by a number of senior officers, his death was referred to as a tragic accident while on holiday leave.

After the service, my parents spoke to one of the senior officers and pointed out how Mr Burke had died and that he was, in fact, performing his duty as a policeman. This in turn resulted in Mr Burke's widow receiving a full police pension – I was very impressed by my parents' taking this initiative.

The second outcome was that Denis and I were subsequently required to attend the coronial inquiry at Kiama Court House during which the presiding magistrate commended us for our bravery. It was my first visit to a court.

This led to us being awarded Royal Humane Society Medals and Certificates for Bravery and in one of life's strange twists, the proceedings were managed by my old boss Captain Sharp of Burns Philp who was President of the Society. The medals were bestowed upon us by Sir John Northcott, NSW Governor, and the following day a photo of Denis and me featured in an article on the ceremony in *The Sydney Morning Herald*.

The experience went some way towards restoring the equilibrium of my self-esteem, but at the cost of the life of the brave holidaying policeman who left behind a widow and young children.

Working in a Creative Environment

On returning from this dramatic holiday, I obtained a job with the venerable old printing company, John Sands Pty Ltd., as a clerk in the merchandise planning division of the Greeting Card department. It operated from an old, small two-story warehouse across Day Street from the John Sands main printing plant which was in between Druitt Street and Bathurst Street, now the site of the Parkroyal Hotel. Despite the run down, quaintly rustic and unusual working environment, it had two advantages. The people, including the senior managers, were all pleasant, relatively cultured and interesting, and we were largely left to get on with our jobs without being troubled by visits from the General Manager or the Managing Director.

John Sands was the Australian market leader in greeting cards and at the time they were very popular. My job involved routine clerical work and keeping sales records, etc., as well as taking approved artwork and film across to printers or to the art studio. It was an interesting place with around a dozen full-time commercial artists headed by a colourful artist and character, Syd Penny. The team included artist Judy Cassab, who, the previous year, was the first woman to win the Archibald Prize. In 1967 she would go on to be the first woman to win it twice.

The staff I worked with were largely responsible for the creation of new ranges of cards; it was an interesting atmosphere in which to be working. Most of the staff had completed the leaving certificate at good schools, with some being university dropouts, and they made me welcome. They also introduced me to different aspects of culture from discussions of the latest book to art movies and theatre. I became a subscriber to Hayes Gordon's newly established Ensemble Theatre in a boat shed at Kirribilli and overall was being exposed to new ideas. It was still relatively boring work, but I found the atmosphere and colleagues pretty stimulating as well as helping broaden my view of the world.

I was also lucky enough to work closely with another lost soul, John Seale, who was my age, and we had endless discussions about how we might get some momentum into our careers. He was keen to become a TV cameraman and after a while he left to work as a jackeroo on a relative's cattle property in Queensland, taking a small movie camera with him to make experimental movies. He subsequently returned to Sydney and got a job with ABC-TV as an assistant's assistant and from there rapidly progressed to becoming a camera operator.

When I knew him, John was a decent young bloke from Mona

Vale with a dream. His father was Clem Seale, war veteran, friend of photographer Max Dupain, and at the time Australia's preeminent commercial black and white artist. Clem obviously passed the artistic gene on to his son because John went on to have an enormously successful career as a cinematographer in Hollywood, working on some of the most iconic films of the last 50 years, including *Rain Man*, *Dead Poet's Society*, *The English Patient*, *The Talented Mr Ripley*, *Harry Potter and the Philosopher's Stone* and *Fury Road*, just to name a few. He won an Academy Award for Best Cinematography for *The English Patient* and was nominated another four times. Quite a career.

John Sands was an interesting place in which to work, but I saw little prospect of developing a career there. So, after about 18 months, I resigned, but took with me a lot of new knowledge and interests and a broader perspective on the world.

The John Sands I left had an incredibly talented workforce and seemingly impregnable market positions in a variety of fields. However, I remember thinking at the time that the management, largely still family run, was inhibited by out-dated traditions such as senior managers needing to be master printers and that the younger generation of the Sands family who were my age showed little promise. The lesson I took away was that in the second half of the 20th century no business could survive while treating its marketing and sales teams as just another cost of doing business and ignoring the market intelligence gathered by those teams.

Also, the company was facing the disruption of being forced to relocate to new premises as their current building had been resumed by the State government to allow for the building of the Western Distributor.

The new plant was built at considerable cost in Herbert Street, St Leonards, but, like Burns Philp, changing market tastes, rapid developments in new printing technologies, rising overheads and growing competition from Asia meant that the old ways were largely doomed. It was no surprise to me that within five or six years of my leaving, the Sands family sold out to a US conglomerate which broke up the then 130 year old business. SBS now operates from the Herbert Street premises.

Joining the Commonwealth Public Service

My next career move was to seek employment with the Commonwealth Public Service, a common path amongst Catholic high school leavers at the time. This resulted in me being assigned to the Commonwealth Department of Works as a Third Division accounts clerk, not quite the outcome I had hoped for. The positives were that, once in the public service, there were opportunities to apply for jobs in other departments, a steady reasonable wage and assistance with part time study.

The negatives were that the clerical job I found myself in was exceedingly uninteresting and, unlike the people I worked with at John Sands, my new colleagues could do nothing to alleviate the boring repetitive work.

In my first few months I worked at three different locations, the first being the beautiful, art deco Queensland Insurance building in Pitt Street, the second the then new Commonwealth Centre on Phillip Street, which the department moved to in June 1962, while a few months later I was relocated to an old barracks type building located beside the Hawthorne Canal in Leichhardt, which was the department's stores depot.

I realised that this had to be the nadir of my working life and as such I had to make a change. This is where the idea of studying law arose, not from some altruistic reason or driven by an iron determination to see law as the path to making a fortune, but simply as a way of getting away from this awful environment.

I had somehow become aware that the Commonwealth Public Service imposed an obligation on the employing department to relocate an employee wanting to undertake a part time tertiary course to the location nearest to the place of study.

As the Sydney University Law School was in Phillip Street, this offered a way of being relocated back to the Commonwealth Centre. I had already made inquiries with the Law School and at the time there were no quotas, and as I had matriculated, I was entitled to entry provided I could pay the fees. An attraction law had over other part time University courses was that lectures were held in the morning and late afternoon so there were no night lectures, a system tailored around students who were articled clerks in law firms.

A short time later the system worked, and I was relocated to a new job back in the city in the section handling workers' compensation claims, largely because of my forthcoming law studies. This, in itself, was a considerable improvement over my previous tasks.

2

GETTING INTO LAW SCHOOL

Deciding to study part time for a law degree was daunting. It became even more so when, during the welcome to new students, the lecturer pointed out that, in every likelihood, only one out of three would progress to year two. This prediction proved accurate when about 30 of us, a majority being mature age public servants, were fortunate enough to pass.

The bonus for me was that I was awarded a Public Service scholarship and no longer had to save like mad to pay my university fees, or make up the time lost from work by attending lectures, by starting work at 7.00 am. Passing also allowed me to apply for a job in the Commonwealth Deputy Crown Solicitor's office which was also located in Phillip Street at the time. My application was successful meaning I had taken another step towards a legal career by working in an office full of government lawyers.

During my third year at Law School, I decided that I wanted to move into a private law firm as I found the current work atmosphere stifling and, while the lawyers there were competent, they were, by and large, a discontented group who seemed to look enviously at those in the private sector. Also, the office was responsible for prosecuting conscientious objectors who had been called up for war service in Vietnam, something I did not agree with. A further reason was that I was getting no practical legal experience, simply doing another type of relatively boring and inconsequential clerical work.

Joining a Law Firm

A little later someone mentioned that a litigation firm, Maxwell Connery & Co, was looking for an articled clerk. I immediately called and, after being interviewed, was offered the opportunity to gain articles of clerkship, the ancient prerequisite for qualifying for admission as a solicitor for law graduates. In my new role I would be representing the "bad guys", the employers and their insurers – in my defence, purely out of necessity and not preference!

At that time, to gain admission as a solicitor, a law graduate needed to have completed the required number of years as an articled clerk in a private law firm where the clerk worked under the supervision of their master solicitor. One slightly daunting aspect of my new job was that the person I was replacing was another aspiring young lawyer, Mary Gaudron, whose career shortly after took off. She ended up as a Justice of the High Court of Australia!

My master solicitor was to be Max Connery Jr and the firm was headed by his father Max Connery Snr. They specialised in representing insurance companies. Here was my opportunity to do real legal work which involved me initially taking personal responsibility for managing an endless stream of workers' compensation claims under the supervision of one of the Maxes! The only reason I could afford to take this position was that, unlike many law firms, the partners were fair and pragmatic and prepared to pay a decent salary to articled clerks who were productive rather than the normally low wage most articled clerks then received.

Max Jr early on colourfully explained to me that a litigation solicitor's role was like the director of a play. It meant ensuring that all the relevant "actors", such as the barrister to conduct the hearing, the doctors, other expert witnesses, and any lay witnesses, were all formally notified of the court hearing date several months in advance.

On top of this, the law clerk needed to ensure that all the necessary court documentation had been filed in the court registry and served on the opposing law firm, along with any requests for additional information. Also, a brief had to be prepared and delivered in a timely manner to the barrister retained to conduct the case for the defendant, in most cases nominally the employer but in actual fact, the employer's insurer. In our matters, the opposing firm was, invariably, a very experienced union-aligned law firm. In addition to having these new responsibilities, I was also studying and heading off to lectures most days.

I was soon responsible for a continuous stream of cases each week which required me to be organised and constantly planning ahead while managing a large individual caseload. I also learned that besides getting good diary systems and procedures in place, a good memory was a prerequisite for successful case management.

This was when modern technology meant IBM "golf ball" electric typewriters and the introduction of the very first Xerox dry copier which thankfully the firm had just acquired. It was still nearly 30 years before law offices were revolutionised by computer technology.

One afternoon, late in 1965, I rushed out of the building where I worked in Bridge Street near the corner of Pitt Street, to head up to the Law School in Phillip Street for my 4.00 pm lecture.

As an articled clerk I typically spent most mornings in court trying to settle workers' compensation or personal injury claims brought by union lawyers on behalf of their injured worker clients. On this particular day, I was running late, as usual, due to my heavy workload. Suddenly I realised that instead of the usual traffic noise there was a lot of shouting and singing. I looked down to Pitt Street and was confronted by a huge crowd of mostly young people in colourful garb with large placards blocking my path. I realised that I was in the midst of a protest march, one of the first anti-war demonstrations, heading down to protest outside the US Consulate.

I was aware of the growing discontent about conscription amongst young people, particularly the baby boomers, through news stories and from having worked briefly in the Deputy Commonwealth Crown Solicitor's office whose lawyers were daily challenging conscientious objectors in court and prosecuting others objecting to being conscripted.

Fortunately, unlike many other families, mine was not impacted by the birthday lottery introduced to select those who were being conscripted for war service in Vietnam. My older brother and I were just too old, and my younger brother Denis won the reverse Lotto in that his number did not come up!

The demonstration was my first personal exposure to the growing community pressure for radical social, political and legal change which the now rather maligned baby boomers were largely creating. At that stage, perhaps regretfully, I was not part of it and my road to Damascus conversion had to wait until I achieved my immediate goal of completing my degree and establishing a foothold in the legal profession.

However, there was little or no recognition of the need for massive changes by our political leaders in the mid-1960s and many Australians, particularly the young, were angry and frustrated by our national leaders such as Menzies, McEwen, Evatt, Calwell and McMahon, and their NSW counterparts such as Cahill, Heffron, Renshaw and Askin.

Our leaders' thinking, actions and policies had been moulded by the searing experiences of the depression in the 1930s, bookended by two World Wars, which meant they were totally unprepared for the demands and expectations of this new generation of post-war young adults.

Most baby boomers came of age looking enviously at visionary American leaders such as John Kennedy, his brother Robert and Martin Luther King. Unlike their Australian counterparts, these ill-fated leaders had the ability to communicate messages outlining a better future and also hope of a better life for all citizens. Where was our War on Poverty like the one initiated by President Lyndon Johnson?

That such an initiative was taken at the highest level of the US government was simply incomprehensible to most Australians, particularly those like me living in NSW under state and federal governments both of which had been in office far too long.

Not only did they these governments seem impervious to the changing aspirations of many Australians, they also ignored a growing restlessness and desire for policy changes shared by many, particularly the young. Australians of all ages were also rightly unhappy that their country was being tarnished internationally by the overt support given to the South African government's apartheid regime by our governments.

An equally important source of provocation to many young people and their families was the decision by the old men in Canberra to happily consign a half a generation of young men to the prospect of an early death in a pointless war in Vietnam. As we now know, they also exposed those who were lucky enough to survive this war to the risk of long-term suffering and deadly psychological injuries and scars. Embarrassed, the government then ignored the bravery of the young men on their return from this failed intervention in a war which could not be won.

By the late 1960s, to the relief of many, Gough Whitlam emerged as a potential national leader and showed promise of being our own visionary communicator equal to the Americans. His election in December 1972 brought new hope to young Australians who were particularly excited by the prospect of his government dealing with the myriad of problems and issues which had been too long ignored by his conservative predecessors.

However, such was the political and social context of my working life for the next few years before Whitlam was elected, I had little time to get excited by the big picture. During this time, I graduated, was admitted as a solicitor and began married life. These events gave me both a reasonable income and a happy home life and the opportunity to take tentative steps towards carving out a long-term legal career.

Fortunately, I was able to function as an efficient litigation lawyer, but it was a job and not a passion! My experience led me to ponder on the difference becoming a lawyer had made to me in terms of the knowledge and legal experience, seemingly quickly acquired through study and undertaking legal work, and the power that knowledge gave me. It seemed almost as though I had joined a secret society with its own rules and rituals to which the lay community was excluded unless invited in as a participant in a case. I also thought about my own previous ignorance about the law and the legal system. This was a fog I had escaped from, but which still enveloped my family, friends, neighbours and a large part of the rest of Australia, all living with the relative powerlessness which resulted.

I began to realise that while most of my fellow Australians were supposed to be law abiding citizens, they were pretty much in total ignorance of the laws they needed to abide by. Yet this power disadvantage made them vulnerable, not only to unscrupulous employers and landlords, but also to officious representatives of the state they dealt with, such as the police and local authorities.

In addition, there were commercial organisations, major and minor retailers, banks, which ordinary Australians had to deal with on a daily basis, all of whom had lawyers advising them as to how best to exploit their rights and power for personal, financial or political gain. This nagging concern did not leave me the older I got. Doing something about it started to become a personal challenge to find a way to change this imbalance.

Life Other than Work and Study

I always felt that studying law and passing exams started to have an immediate benefit in terms of meeting more people and allowing me to start to think more about a future with possibilities and a social life outside work and study.

The social life aspect initially came through joining a local tennis club with some former school friends, which also included some of their sisters and their friends. At the same time, I had also become a junior member of Concord Golf Club and most weekends played several rounds of golf, managing to earn a competitive handicap.

When I was working at the Deputy Crown Solicitor's office, one of the lawyers there, Michael Maher, who lived in Five Dock and later became its local MP, suggested I come along to a tennis club he frequented at Roseville Park. Here I met a whole new group of young people, most of whom had been to North Shore Catholic colleges, earlier students of which started the club some 10 years or so before. They were a nice friendly group, many of whom were also studying at university or had recently completed their studies. I soon got to know most through Sunday afternoon tennis and regular club social events.

Joining this tennis club, on top of my being recently accepted as member of an excellent golf club, plus making reasonable progress in fulfilling my professional ambitions meant that for the first time I was becoming a grown up. It also meant that I felt confident enough to start asking some of the girls out.

To me one girl in particular stood out and that was Pat Wright who, when I joined the club, was finishing the last subject of her Arts degree part time while working as a secretary. Getting to know her better was accelerated on Good Friday in 1966 when, both having been invited to spend the Easter weekend at Bateau Bay with a group of other members at the holiday home of one of them, I was designated as the driver to take Pat up on the Friday morning.

So, early that morning, I headed from Cabarita over to Pymble, where Pat and her family lived. Pat was the eldest child with two younger brothers. After meeting her parents, we headed off in my old cream FJ Holden on what was intended to be a quick journey to Bateau Bay.

Pat and I rapidly became acquainted with each other while sitting in a hot car in a queue of traffic on the recently opened F3. Arriving at the Mt White exit three or so hours after leaving, we found the cause for the long holdup to be a lorry laden with fruit and vegetables which had tipped on its side at the point the expressway turned into one lane.

Some weeks later I invited Pat to partner me at a ball and to my surprise she agreed. We both had a good enough time for us to start going out regularly and we eventually became an item.

Shortly after the F3 debacle Pat gained employment in the NSW Department of Labour and Industry as a Vocational Guidance Officer because of her psychology qualifications, a role she found satisfying and useful, particularly in advising young people on their career options.

She was surprised at the advice I had received as a 15-year-old but pointed out that, in the 10 years or so since then, the tests used had improved significantly. To prove the point (or to reassure herself?), shortly after we were married, she had me complete a current test and the results apparently reassured her she had not married an idiot!

As a true professional she did not share the actual results with me but said it was in line with someone capable of obtaining a degree. As this was in my final year of the law degree, it was a self-evident truth as far as I was concerned.

Married with Children

Pat and I bought our first home, a semi-detached cottage, in Neutral Bay, just prior to the birth of the first of our five children and, as was the practice those days, we attended Sunday Mass at the Neutral Bay Catholic Church. Not long after joining the Parish, Father Ted Kennedy was appointed administrator and he imbued the parish with a strong sense of social concern, strongly influenced by the new theology flowing from Vatican II.

Like many of the younger generation of parishioners, Father Kennedy's message opened up for us a range of new possibilities as to what it meant to be progressive Catholics in the early 1970s. Ted Kennedy, as he was known to his parishioners, later devoted his life to caring for the Aboriginal community in the Catholic Parish of Redfern.

Exposure to someone like Ted was extraordinary as he was so different to all the other priests I had ever been exposed to, largely because they were invariably old, charmless, irascible Irish priests. There must have been some charming charismatic Irish priests in Australia, but they never found their way to St Patrick's Mortlake where I went to Mass with my parents for most of my first 25 years.

Ted Kennedy was able to motivate and mobilise the younger parishioners like us and it had a magical effect on the whole parish in that we became involved directly in a range of social concerns and activities – comparatively speaking the place was jumping!

Sadly for us fired up parishioners, Ted's vocation soon took him to Redfern where he felt he could do something to help the local Aboriginal community, the most neglected and poorest Australians, and his replacement, while a decent well-meaning man, could not maintain the magic Ted had created.

Getting Involved with the Law Society

As a solicitor, who spent most days in court, I met a number of other lawyers who were to play a part in my professional advancement. They were mostly union lawyers who represented injured workers in workers' compensation or common law damages claims cases I defended on behalf of employers' insurers. Amongst these was Terry Sheahan who later, as NSW Attorney General, played a large role in ensuring the success of the Law Foundation.

Terry's employer, well known union solicitor Roy Turner, was a member of the Law Society Council and later an MLC, and I had discussions with him regarding my concerns about the lack of legal aid, a concern I was aware he shared. In 1970, on Roy's recommendation, I was appointed to the Law Society's Associate Committee, forerunner to the Young Lawyers Section, by the Society's President.

As a golfer, the name of this committee seemed a bit odd as "associates" in golf clubs were the women members. However, in its wisdom this was the name given to a committee by the Society's

Council and it was made up of younger solicitors who were under 35 years old. As I recall there were relatively few women members of the committee.

Mobilising the Committee

At an early meeting, the committee discussed its plans for the year and I suggested that besides organising social functions for young lawyers, the committee might do something socially useful. I suggested we could try to find out more about the shortcomings of legal aid currently provided by the Public Solicitor's Office. This service had been a significant innovation in the early 1940s, but by the early 1970s it was seriously under-resourced and its hard working staff had little to offer for ordinary working class people as they were limited to helping the very poor.

I proposed that the committee conduct an experiment to gain a better understanding of the scope and nature of the unmet need for legal aid by establishing a legal advice service conducted by volunteer solicitors.

Eventually, as is the way with all committees, this proposal found its way onto the agenda of the Law Society Council which eventually approved of the initiative. Thus, armed with the endorsement of the Law Society, the project got underway in February 1971 in inner city Redfern. The South Sydney Council also supported us by providing accommodation at Redfern Town Hall to conduct a weekly after-hours clinic for local people.

Little did I foresee that such a comparatively modest initiative would quickly be recognised as a much needed and ground-breaking pro bono service soon replicated by young lawyers throughout the state. It was also the catalyst and the first of many steps I was to take towards increasing access to legal services and legal information for the community.

Within a comparatively short period of 12 months, this led to me being awarded a Churchill Fellowship which allowed me to study legal services delivery programmes in the US, Canada and the United Kingdom during the first half of 1972.

Having the opportunity to take such giant step for a young litigation solicitor from a traditional Australian working class background was nothing short of amazing. Nevertheless, I have always felt having no legal pedigree behind me, unlike most of the other members of the Law Society Committee, was a considerable advantage as it helped me appreciate the consumer's side of the law and the widespread lack of awareness on the part of many ordinary working families of the rights and protections offered by the law, limited as they were.

However, none of this would have been possible without the support of open-minded and thoughtful senior members of the committee. Many were from long established city firms, including John Mant, Russell Stewart and David Castle. They were soon to be joined by dozens of other young lawyers who volunteered to take part in the new service, many of whom were later to be leaders of the profession and holders of judicial office.

They became the trail blazers who gave the concept of pro bono legal services a much higher profile and legitimacy to the long tradition of most solicitors quietly helping needy individuals.

It was John Mant who urged me to apply for a Churchill Fellowship which was to be the catalyst that in many ways transformed my career. The original idea of opening the free advice service in the then poor inner-city suburb of Redfern was in part influenced by what young lawyers had been doing in the US. Not long after, John also stepped away from legal practice and was later an adviser to Gough Whitlam when Prime Minister and later became an expert on the role of local government and more recently served on the Sydney City Council. My subsequent involvement with the Law Foundation represented my own movement away from legal practice into a role which was something of a blank canvas.

3

WINNING A CHURCHILL FELLOWSHIP

Despite friends on the Law Society's Associate Committee encouraging me to apply for a Winston Churchill Memorial Fellowship, there was, of course, no certainty about whether my proposal would be accepted. Further issues were whether I could afford to give up my legal career to undertake such an expedition and be away from my wife Pat and young daughters Anne and Jane for many months.

Fortunately, both sets of parents were encouraging and supportive. Pat's parents, Jack and Nan Wright, who had twice been posted overseas by the Commonwealth Bank and later the Reserve Bank, were aware of the career opportunities and benefits which could flow from being awarded a Churchill Fellowship. Their support, plus learning that an award carried with it a modest stipend to allay some of the normal living costs of family members left at home, meant that, if I was lucky enough to win a Fellowship, it would be financially viable.

Of course, the most immediate benefit of being awarded such a prize was that it would allow me to undertake a study tour of the three countries with comparable societies and legal systems to ours, namely, the US, Canada and the UK. These countries were also extremely relevant as reports emanating from them indicated that there were movements in each, at both formal and informal levels, aimed at improving access to legal services and legal information.

The Churchill Fellowship programme has enabled many thousands of Australians to travel overseas over the past 50 years and bring back and apply a vast array of knowledge which has contributed so much to the improvement of our nation.

The programme's initial funding via a national "door knock" in

1965, with the support of the RSL, was a huge success and raised over £2.3 million, the equivalent of $4.6 million, which, in turn, translates into about $35 million in today's dollars.

I remember the door knock well as my parents made a donation. We all liked the idea of a trust which would democratise the concept of travelling fellowships which had been limited historically to those with high academic qualifications. Like most people we thought the idea of the trust fund allocating fellowships to those who want to make a contribution to the community was an attractive idea and, for the era, strikingly innovative.

Applying for a Churchill Fellowship

In the middle of 1971, after discussing the implications of applying for a Churchill Fellowship at length with my wife Pat, we decided that I should apply for an award in 1972, which was the seventh intake of applications. I approached the task with a degree of trepidation as I had, in only a matter of weeks, to settle a research agenda and itinerary of sufficient quality to justify me being awarded a Fellowship.

This was long before internet and the worldwide web, let alone the wonders of Wikipedia. I had to rely on library research reviewing the journals of overseas Bar Associations and Law Societies, looking for relevant articles and references to recent reports of developments in the countries I proposed to visit. The journals collected by the libraries of the NSW Law Society and the Sydney University Law School were my main source of information, as well as correspondence with a number of overseas legal organisations.

Once I had mapped out a preliminary itinerary and list of institutions I would be visiting in the US, Canada and the UK, I needed to finalise an application by the imminent closing date in late July 1971. So, having made the decision to apply, we needed to finalise my application and, fortuitously, I had recently been offered the use of a cottage in Katoomba by a grateful elderly client for a short mid-winter break. Knowing time was running out to submit the application, Pat's parents kindly offered to mind our two young daughters to allow us to head to Katoomba so we could use the opportunity to finish the task without distraction.

Child-free, we drove up to the mountains and, happily working as a team, formulated what we hoped would be a winning pitch. Pat's editing and typing skills, gained as a research assistant in the library of the Reserve Bank, and her experience of overseas travel ensured that the document submitted in late July 1971 was of an acceptable standard. The application was completed and posted off just before 6.00 pm from Katoomba Post Office a day or so before the deadline. Feeling like celebrating this feat, we decided to have dinner out but, to our bitter disappointment, in the early 1970s in July nothing was open in either Katoomba or Leura and we had to settle for take away hamburgers and chips!

With my application in the post, I was by then quietly hopeful as my inquiries revealed that no other Australian at that time had been awarded a Churchill Fellowship to investigate this area of interest.

The applications from NSW were reviewed by the Trust's NSW committee which included the head of the Public Service Board, Sir John Goodsell, who chaired the interviewing committee. The committee included me in their short list to be interviewed, were very helpful in their comments and seemed to like the purpose of my proposed study tour. They suggested that my itinerary, as submitted, would prove very difficult because I had allowed only three months for the trip and, in their view, I had included too many cities. They suggested that in their experience I should visit fewer places and stay longer in major centres. They invited me to reconsider my itinerary and submit a revised programme and itinerary.

This advice proved invaluable and, as a result, I limited the number of places to visit, particularly in the US, and concentrated on visiting organisations in or near the larger cities. I realised that this revised programme meant that there was less travel time needed and more time to acclimatise in larger centres. I felt it was likely to be more productive, which in time proved to be the case. It did however mean that I would be away a bit longer, but Pat and I agreed that it was likely to lead to a more beneficial study tour and a more comprehensive report of my conclusions.

My Program and Itinerary

As noted earlier, the catalyst for me applying for a Churchill Fellowship was news of the establishment in the US of neighbourhood law offices providing legal aid in poor city neighbourhoods staffed by bright young lawyers. I realised that I needed to visit the US to learn about the impact these young lawyers were having on social change in this new "war".

During his State of the Union Address on 8 January 1964, following his recent election, President Lyndon Johnson had stated his intention to launch a War on Poverty by submitting to Congress the *Economic Opportunity Act*, the purpose of which was to alleviate the lot of the 19% of the population living in poverty in the US.

Johnson's groundbreaking initiative was influenced by Michael Harrington's 1962 book, *The Other America*, of which one review noted:

> When Michael Harrington's masterpiece, *The Other America*, was first published in 1962, it was hailed as an explosive work and became a galvanizing force for the war on poverty. Harrington shed light on the lives of the poor – from farm to city – and the social forces that relegated them to their difficult situations. He was determined to make poverty in the United States visible and his observations and analyses have had a profound effect on our country, radically changing how we view the poor and the policies we employ to help them.

Harrington's revelations spurred President Johnson and his administration to respond to what had been revealed and what had for too long been hidden and ignored.

President Johnson's *Economic Opportunity Act* quickly passed through Congress and came into effect on 20 August 1964, and so commenced the formal implementation of Johnson's War on Poverty. It was seen at the time as an extension of President Roosevelt's New Deal initiatives in the 1930s. For such a radical piece of legislation to become law in such a short time was remarkable, aided by the fact that the Democrats controlled both houses of Congress.

Legal services were identified as having a unique role in providing indigent persons with representation against unequal treatment under the law.

Confirmation of this was made by the late Robert Kennedy, when Attorney General of the US, in his 1964 Law Day Address at the University of Chicago:

> We need to begin to develop new kinds of legal rights in situations that are not now perceived as involving legal issues. We live in a society that is a vast bureaucracy charged with many responsibilities We need to define those responsibilities and convert them into legal obligations. We need to create new remedies to deal with a multitude of daily injuries that persons suffer in this complex society simply because it is complex.

The views of the founders of Office of Economic Opportunity (OEO), as confirmed by Robert Kennedy and also stated in the OEO Guidelines, show clearly that the Legal Services Program was never intended to be limited to merely providing legal aid to the poor.

Those responsible for setting up the OEO programmes included Sargent Shriver, appointed by President Johnson to head up the programme, and Clinton Bamberger, a prominent left leaning Baltimore lawyer, whom Shriver appointed as the first director of the OEO Legal Services Program. I was told that Clinton Bamberger was a must-see person and his generosity with his time meant that I had a "general's view of the War".

Shriver and Bamberger both realised from the outset that War on Poverty would be merely a token effort, having regard to the extent of the unmet need among the poor, unless the law was used in the way referred to by Robert Kennedy.

It was accepted in the US that the legal profession's new awareness of its duty to all members of society, rather than merely those who could afford their services, stemmed in part from an address delivered by Mr Justice Brennan of the US Supreme Court. This address, delivered in 1967, at the 150th Anniversary of the Harvard Law School, exhorted lawyers in private practice to devote a part of their professional time to some project involving the public interest.

As will be seen later, this relatively small part of the President Johnson's War on Poverty far exceeded the expectations held for it and proved to be a long lasting and highly influential part of the OEO legacy assisting the poor by enlisting the support and active intervention of both the Federal Courts and the influential major Bar associations.

Included in my goals were to explore how these new programmes interacted with local bar associations and whether changes were required to ethical rule and professional regulatory standards; to investigate the concept of preventative law relying on community education to lift awareness of legal rights and ways of dealing with legal problems; and to see whether computer technology was assisting in the delivery of legal services.

In Canada I intended to visit a relatively new legal aid programme operating in Ontario, involving the private profession, and which appeared to be largely based on the UK legal aid programme in that, while it was funded by the Provincial government, both civil and criminal legal services were provided by the private profession.

The final leg of my itinerary would take me to London where I had plans for visiting and learning at first-hand about the long-established government funded programme with services provided by solicitors and barristers in private practice with overall management being delegated to the Law Society of England and Wales. It was part of the Britain's welfare services and as such was a potential model for Australia to follow.

After submitting the revised programme and itinerary, I was advised that I was included on the list of NSW applicants recommended to the national selection committee. I then discovered that the majority of national selection committee were senior members of the judiciary from other states, and I was moderately hopeful that such leaders of the legal profession might well be concerned about the state of legal aid and access to the law in Australia.

Notification of Award of a Fellowship

Fortunately, my plan met with the approval of the national selection committee and, late on the evening of 29 October 1971, I answered the doorbell to be confronted with a "telegram boy" handing me a telegram. I opened it to find that I had been awarded a fellowship.

I was not sure what surprised me the most, the fact that in 1971 there were still telegram deliverers who worked at night or the bizarre message on traditional yellow paper which I still have, and which said:

> STRICTLY CONFIDENTIAL CONGRATULATIONS ON BEING AWARDED A CHURCHILL FELLOWSHIP PLEASE DO NOT DISCUSS EXCEPT WITH PRESS RADIO OR TELEVISION PENDING RELEASE OF NAMES BY TRUST CHAIRMAN LETTER FOLLOWING
>
> ... MEDDLETON CHIEF EXECUTIVE OFFICER WINSTON CHURCHILL MEMORIAL TRUST.

While naturally overjoyed by this news, I found the direction regarding confidentiality highly amusing. We did immediately call our respective parents who we figured could keep a secret for a couple of days until the official announcement of the 1972 Churchill Fellowship winners. When the names were announced I saw that I was not the only winner who was raised in Cabarita, as Jeff Peterson, a contemporary of mine was named as winning a fellowship to study the wine industry overseas. Jeff and I became re-acquainted at the NSW Fellowship awards ceremony.

Having the cachet of being awarded a national travelling fellowship carrying the Churchill name somewhat camouflaged my limited qualifications for carrying out such a significant research project. This was amusingly evident when I consulted the Law School's eminent Professor Julius Stone. On reviewing my dismal mark in Jurisprudence, the subject he lectured in, he seemed to roll his eyes and wonder why I had this unique opportunity when those who won prizes in his subject were now applying their brilliance in tax and corporate law.

Nevertheless, he was kind enough to give me an introduction to his good friend and former colleague, Dr Erwin Griswold, former Dean of Harvard Law School and the then current US Solicitor General. His more junior colleague, Dr Upendra Baxi, was particularly helpful at a practical level in terms of carrying out my investigation. He was genuinely interested in the issue of legal services and knowledgeable about the US, having studied at University of California, Berkeley.

Being awarded a fellowship set in train a number of challenges, not the least of which was that Pat was pregnant with our third child which meant that we now had to decide as to the timing of me undertaking the Fellowship. We decided that it was probably best if I went away sooner rather than later and be back for the baby's birth. When I raised this issue with the Churchill Trust they were understanding and arranged for me to start my travels in mid-January 1972.

Of course, another major issue related to my employment on my return. Pat and I felt confident that opportunities might well open up because of the Fellowship, and that happened much sooner than we could have hoped. It came about through me making an appointment to meet with Norman McDowell, a senior member of the Law Society Council, who had provided me with a reference for the

Churchill Trust on behalf of the Society. I was keen to advise him of my success in being awarded a fellowship and, once I had conveyed the good news, he asked me what I was planning to do on my return.

I responded that I was not keen to return to being a solicitor specialising in insurance litigation and was proposing to review the situation on my return from the trip. He then said that the Board of the Law Foundation was looking for someone to assist it with the management of the Foundation's affairs and advised me that the Board was seeking a lawyer to take up the role of Part-time Temporary Executive Officer. Although the Law Foundation had been established for a few years it had no administrative staff as yet, as funding was limited. Norman inquired whether I might be interested in that role on my return and I immediately indicated I would. He then arranged for me to meet with the Board to take the matter further.

I met a few days later with a number of the Foundation's Board members and was interviewed. The end result was that they put a proposal to the full Board recommending I be appointed for a six-month full-time appointment on my return. My role included assisting the Board by managing the Foundation's administration while also making recommendations for an operational strategy as to how best to implement the Foundation's charter. I was to use the balance of my time during the consultancy completing the report for the Churchill Trust.

This was an opportunity and potentially one which might allow me to leave, at least for a while, my career as a litigation solicitor, a decision which resulted in my employers being very much disappointed.

The support and encouragement of those involved with the committee's Redfern advice service was later matched by leaders of the Law Society, including Norman McDowell, Ken Smithers, John Bowen, Allen Loxton and John Broadbent, most of whom were on the Law Foundation Board. They were to provide me with the opportunity to continue what started in Redfern on a larger stage through entrusting me with the development of the Law Foundation of NSW's role and activities.

This opportunity would involve me drawing on the knowledge and experience gained during my travelling fellowship and applying that by recommending a number of initiatives which the Board could take to implement the Foundation objectives. Fortunately for me, the Board members recognised that I could be the key to opening up the Foundation's full potential of other statutory objectives, a significant honour but also a daunting one.

However, with these several steps I began to realise that the Churchill Fellowship had the potential to transform my career, with the Board's likely invitation offering me the space, time and income on my return to consider an alternative career to that of a personal injury solicitor or barrister.

With the excitement and promise of playing a leading role in the Law Foundation's development spurring me on, I headed off on a five months odyssey with the blessing of my pregnant wife Pat, leaving her and my two gorgeous little daughters behind at home. At that point in time, it was positively scary. However, it was matched by the excitement of travelling to interesting places for the purpose of gaining the knowledge and experience I needed if I was to live up to the hopes of the Foundation's Board and to the expectations of the Churchill Trust.

My future was largely dependent on acquiring the credentials to justify the faith shown in me by the Law Foundation Board and, indirectly, to the constituencies to which they were accountable.

Another stroke of good fortune came via a call from the Town Clerk of South Sydney Council, Frank O'Grady. Frank was so appreciative of the assistance being given to local residents with legal problems by the advice service I had helped set up in Redfern, that he had organised a collection from local businesses to assist with the costs of my trip. It was a very generous gesture and meant that while travelling I had a little extra money with which to defray expenses and meet additional travelling costs.

4

CALIFORNIA: LEARNING FROM THE BEST

I had never been to the US before. I knew the Vietnam war was dividing Americans but, tragic to admit, like many of my generation, my expectations of life in the US were also framed by years of watching US movies and television. While later in my trip I experienced the world of the movies and the tourist brochures that I had expected, much of what I saw and heard in California told a very different story.

What I did discover was that innovative academics, lawyers and social activists in California were first responders to the funding opportunities coming out of Johnson's War on Poverty and I was in the right place at the right time.

I soon discovered that California was the perfect place to start my journey. Yet coming from an Australia that was provincial and where overseas travel was rare, I felt like the proverbial stranger in paradise!

When I contacted Qantas to book my departure flight I did so in person by visiting the Qantas Building in Phillip Street to discuss a departure date and ticketing. When I indicated that I was hoping to leave in the second half of January the woman assisting me asked me if I wanted to depart on the inaugural flight of the airline's new Boeing 747. This was flying out on 19 January 1972 to San Francisco which was my first destination. I readily accepted the invitation to participate in such an aeronautical milestone.

When I boarded the flight, I found to my surprise that it was only about half full and that on board were a number of VIPs and politicians. Despite the Jumbo being the newest plane in the fleet, it still made stops for refuelling in Fiji and Honolulu, which made the journey five or six hours longer than current non-stop flights.

However, I was in a beautiful state of the art, spacious, comfortable and quiet plane and the experience was beyond my wildest dreams as my only previous flying had been in much smaller Fokker Friendships flying to Canberra and back.

Reaching the Californian coast during the day and then flying in over San Francisco Bay gave me a great thrill. Seeing the iconic Golden Gate Bridge and then the city of San Francisco itself, made me realise that, after all the planning and decisions made, I was actually about to arrive in America. About to take the first steps of a five months journey, I was also very much unsure as to how it would change my life, but obviously hopeful that it would create opportunities and so justify leaving Pat and our growing family at home.

Eventually I was safely deposited on the tarmac at San Francisco Airport where I passed through immigration and customs with no great delay. I had arrived! I was met by Milton Cook, a friend of my sister Colleen, who seemed a nice guy and fitted the Hollywood stereotype of being tall, good looking and charming.

Besides being very welcoming, Milton had an immediate surprise for me. Rather than heading to the car park he took me to another part of the airport for another aeronautical first. As he lived in Berkeley on the east side of San Francisco Bay, he had arranged for us to fly across the bay via a large twin engine commuter helicopter to Oakland Airport where he worked for an air transport company. The idea of flying in such an icon of the Vietnam war brought out the little boy in me. It was such a surprise, having seen the troop-carrying version regularly in the news coverage of the war. I was very excited – what a welcome to the US!

However, the reality of flying in such a beast was another thing. While being in such a large helicopter was an interesting first, it was noisy and vibrated somewhat disconcertingly. As an interesting twist, it was to be the first of a number of weird aircraft I would fly on in North America, not only on that trip but also on later visits to the US. It was a bit like their cars. Having seen so many US television programmes and movies you might think everyone drove a shiny new Ford Mustang or a Buick, but the reality was that most of the people I met had cheaper models or imports such as Volkswagens, Volvos or Hondas.

On arriving in Berkeley, I discovered that Milton had not been joking when he told my sister that he lived in a pretty hopeless place. It was a small flat at the back of a house which he had moved into recently following his divorce. It was on the edge of a black neighbourhood but had the advantage for my purposes of being near the Berkeley campus of the University of California, home to a number of programmes I was to visit, as well as being free, comfortable and well situated.

I arrived in California at a time when ex-movie star Ronald Reagan was Governor, an office he had held since 1967 and to which he had been re-elected in November 1971. Since coming to office, he had reversed many of the progressive social programmes introduced by the previous Governor Edward (Pat) Brown, a Democrat and father of recent Governor Jerry Brown. Reagan also had defunded many state government agencies previously established by the Californian legislature to protect the rights of workers and consumers.

As I was to learn, this led to various local legal services programmes funded by the OEO successfully challenging many of Reagan's anti-welfare decisions in court. The success of these programmes in the courts put them under siege both by Governor Reagan and President Richard Nixon. Nixon's 1972 re-election campaign, he being another Californian like Reagan, was heavily supported by the agri-businesses and farming interests which had long hated the "socialist" legislative measures introduced by former Governor Pat Brown.

Of course, much of this was unknown to me on my first day in California, Thursday 20 January 1972. It started later that day with a visit to Professor Richard Buxbaum of the Law School at the

University of California Berkeley, with whom I had corresponded when planning my itinerary and he had arranged several initial meetings for me.

San Francisco Neighbourhood Legal Aid Foundation

I was very keen to visit the San Francisco Neighbourhood Legal Aid Foundation, the major OEO funded programme in the area where the director John Stewart, who had arranged a meeting with Tim Hoffman, the deputy director Pacific region of the OEO Legal Services Program, who happily agreed to see me at very short notice, and not the first time this would happen in the coming months. I was quickly learning that the Americans I was dealing with were more than happy to arrange introductions to assist someone who had a genuine interest in what they were doing.

At 28, Tim was a veteran legal services lawyer, and he briefed me on the current circumstances the programme found itself in due to funding restrictions imposed by the Nixon administration. It was no secret that funding limits were imposed for political rather than fiscal reasons, which meant there had been no increase in funding for the previous three years, commencing as soon as Nixon took over the office of the President.

It was a very helpful briefing, particularly as Tim had extensive knowledge of the Californian projects of the Legal Services Program which were some of the best funded. This funding was in part due to the role that leading academic lawyers and sociologists took in putting together coalitions of local organisations to apply for grants. No doubt due to the experience the academic members of the coalition had with seeking grants, their applications included large yet, in hindsight, realistic budgets. These budgets reflected the need to establish major legal services programmes based on the neighbourhood law office model operating throughout the city or targeting particular communities such as oppressed rural workers.

My two hours with Tim were well spent and his detailed briefing and recommendations as to people to contact meant that my remaining time in the Bay area would be utilised fully. My meeting with him was one of a number of similar meetings with OEO officials over the next couple of months. These all proved invaluable as they enabled me to gain such a comprehensive overview of virtually all aspects of the Legal Services Program, including funding issues, which would be a key focus of my report to the Churchill Fellowship Trust. I was very impressed with the openness of these meetings and how generous most of those I met with were with their time.

Equally valuable was the willingness of everyone I met to alert me to other people, not only in their city but in other places I was to visit, whom I should meet. In almost all cases, when contacted, they responded and set aside time to see me, often at short notice. It became a feature of my stay in the US that, even though I usually had a list of people I had already contacted in a new place, within the first couple of days my available time became readily filled with more "must see" locals drawn to my attention.

Once those I met realised that I was seriously interested in learning as much as possible about legal services programmes from a range of points of view, they were very co-operative and shared information, ideas and materials generously. I later learnt that the further East I travelled, the more time I spent bringing people up-to-date about what I had learned in the West. Being quick off the mark with requests for substantial and successful funding, Californian programmes almost immediately had a huge impact which delighted their Washington DC funders and quickly gained much national prominence as well as media and political attention.

I also soon found myself getting to know my way around the San Francisco downtown area and did so by walking between meetings as it was a reasonably compact area. San Francisco was fun because everything was so different and yet interesting to an Australian.

So, happily, at the end of my first two days in California, I felt I had hit the ground running and had met some great people whose advice would serve me well during the rest of my stay in the US. I was tired but energised, now having a better understanding of what to expect as I moved across the country and who were those I must talk to. Looking back, it is an interesting reminder of how dependent I was on strangers being interested enough about my plans to share knowledge, which ensured I got the most out of the visit and of the precious time I had available. How that has now all changed with the wonders of emails and Wikipedia! Although I still feel that being on the spot and soaking up the ambience was of inestimable value.

The First Weekend: Visiting San Fran's Famous Fern Bars

With a sense of accomplishment, I was also looking forward to being a tourist on the weekend soaking up the Californian vibes with Milton's help! That happened sooner than I expected as that evening Milton took me on a bar tour in San Francisco. He was keen to show me a bar called Henry Africa's which had opened some years before and had become known as "a fern bar". Henry was credited with inventing this style when he decided to open a bar but did not have enough money to decorate it. His solution was hanging baskets with ferns in them from the ceiling, which worked a treat attracting a lot of interest and thus business. Soon fern bars popped up all over San Francisco. After a drink there – I thought it seemed a bit quiet that evening – Milton suggested we walk around the block to another bar.

This was located on the corner diagonally across the city block on the opposite corner from where we had the first drink. There I found myself entering an identical bar decorated with an old pianola and lots of bric-a-brac and hanging baskets of ferns. Unlike the first bar, this was full of people and really hopping. Milton then explained that Henry Africa had fallen out with a business partner and walked away from the original bar, came around the corner and opened this new bar with him as the sole owner.

It was a fun evening seeing San Francisco at its liveliest, We spent the next few hours following the crowds as people moved from one bar to another. It was only a couple of days since I had left my family and usual daily life in Sydney, and suddenly I was in one of the coolest places on the planet being shown around by a local who knew what was then "in"!

After spending Saturday settling in and getting to know the local Berkeley neighbourhood, on the Sunday Milton generously decided to show me the sights with my afternoon spent being quietly terrified while driven by Milton at breakneck speeds in his tiny Saab on the vast Californian expressways.

His initial destination was Sausalito down the bottom of the San Francisco Bay, an interesting artists' colony tucked in a little bay which looks out across the water to the Oakland Bay Bridge. It was a beautiful day to be in such a charming spot, surrounded by gay bars and what at the time seemed to be some very "way-out people". We had a late lunch, a steak sandwich, looking over the bay from a restaurant above the water and it was another of those moments when I needed to pinch myself to check it was really happening. The steak was quite enormous but not all that expensive. Afterwards we drove across the Golden Gate Bridge back into San Francisco and then across the Bay Bridge which had two five-lane decks and a lot of traffic.

We spent the evening with friends of Milton who lived in an apartment complex in the hills behind Berkeley. Amazingly, on the way there we saw two rather large deer on the roadside as we drove to their home. During the evening I was shown a copy of a local rag, *The Berkeley Barb*, a radical counterculture product of the 1960s which they pointed out had a few ads for swingers!

California Rural Legal Assistance (CRLA)

The new week was back to serious business. It started with my catching a bus to San Francisco over the Bay Bridge for a series of meetings. The first was at California Rural Legal Assistance, the legal services programme which had become nationally famous for using the courts to enforce the legal protections and entitlements of the thousands of low paid farm workers whose labours made the vast Californian agribusiness so profitable. There I met Marty Glick, the director of litigation, who briefed me on the background of the programme and its modus operandi and also arranged for me to visit a branch office in Modesto, a farming area, later in the week.

I learnt that CRLA was probably the most successful OEO funded "impact" litigator, which aggressively used the courts in pursuit of law reform. From the outset it achieved an impressive list of successes, mainly against agribusinesses and the state government for failing to enforce workplace safety and consumer laws. I came away enormously impressed by such programmes and their role in pursuing the public interest against well-funded defendants.

One of CRLA's earliest victories, which set the seal on its position as a leading advocate for the poor, was winning a suit against the State of California. This successfully prevented the state from reducing its medical benefits commitment to Californian citizens by $250 million despite it having received the funds from the federal government. Soon after, another of its cases resulted in stopping the importation of low paid Mexican labourers locally known as "Braceros". For years, many American itinerant farm workers known as "Chicanos", who were US citizens, had been denied employment opportunities on Californian farmlands because of the importation of cheap Mexican labour.

My last appointment that day was with Carol Silver, a law teacher, recommended to me by Tim Hoffman because of her previous involvement with a legal aid project conducted on the UC Berkeley campus. She had not only successfully managed the Berkeley programme, which serviced predominantly the local black community, but was a leader in the development of a systematised method of drafting pleadings in matrimonial matters. I had been advised that matrimonial matters were soaking up too much of the resources of the local legal services programmes which should have been devoted to impact litigation and her work offered a partial solution to the matrimonial problem.

When I called to confirm our meeting, it being my last meeting for the day, after which I was heading back to Berkeley, she suggested that she was heading over to nearby Oakland where she volunteered at the Synanon Foundation's drug rehabilitation centre. She thought I might find it interesting to meet her there. Synanon was an interesting, if somewhat radical programme, which operated from a very beautiful old building that had formerly been the males only Oakland Athletic Club. One of its facilities was an impressive full size swimming pool on the fourth floor and, as she was going for a swim, I joined her swimming some laps, after which we had a light meal in the cafeteria.

I learnt that Synanon also operated as a community centre which provided residential accommodation, with most of the residents being young people there for drug rehabilitation. While the place appeared to have a very relaxed atmosphere, the rules imposed on those there for rehabilitation were quite strict, but it apparently worked. I understand Odyssey House in Australia operated on a similar basis.

My host drew my attention to recent letters in the press from indignant parents whose children had been reclaimed from drug addiction by the project, which were pinned on a notice board. The writers were responding to claims by a young man that the restrictions were too harsh. As my new friend was intending to participate in a group therapy session called "the game", I decided I was not ready for "the full Californian thing" and left her to it as gracefully as I could.

San Mateo Legal Aid Society

The next day I headed off via a Greyhound bus to see Simon Rosenthal, director of the San Mateo Legal Aid Society in Redwood City, an hour's ride south of San Francisco and in the heart of what later became known as Silicon Valley, then a very nice rural environment. Meeting Simon was an important opportunity as he had a lot of experience in service delivery with various early OEO funded programmes and had spent time in Washington working with the Legal Services Program administration.

My three hours with him were extremely valuable as I learnt a lot about the mechanics of operating a successful legal services programme and the problems of finding enough lawyers with litigation experience to undertake the types of cases which would make an impact for clients. He had chosen to return to this smaller programme in which he had previously worked because it had lost its momentum and he felt he could help it get back on its feet.

Coffee with Legal Services Guru Jerome Carlin

Later in the day I telephoned Jerome Carlin, a prominent UC Berkeley sociologist, whose research Professor Julius Stone used to refer to in his Jurisprudence lectures. I was aware Carlin had been a key player in establishing the San Francisco Legal Assistance Foundation, but when I arrived in California, I was told he had retired to the hills behind Berkeley to paint. When I explained why I had called we arranged to meet for a coffee that evening in Berkeley.

Rather than being a superannuated academic Jerome was in fact far from retirement age and very unassuming. You would never have guessed that he was an internationally renowned sociologist/lawyer and author of several much-cited books about the legal profession. He had moved to Berkeley in the early 1960s to teach and undertake research at the University's Centre for the Study of Law and Society. While in that role he became involved in a group putting forward an early application for a grant from OEO to fund a legal services programme and, on being awarded it, the group prevailed on him to take up the role of the new programme's first director in 1966.

After our coffee he was happy to continue talking and, as the coffee shop was closing, we returned to Milton's flat and conversed for quite some time. I learned a lot more about the practicalities of running a major legal services programme. In time, funding issues and the sheer size of the demands on the Foundation to provide routine legal services, as against engaging in law reform, wore him down and he resigned in 1970 to work as an artist at home. There was a lot to admire about Jerome. He had given up a brilliant academic career to be a co-founder of the biggest legal aid scheme in San Francisco which he then set on track and headed successfully for four years.

In our discussions that evening, and after hearing me talk about the Australian situation, he made the surprising comment that a mix of pre-paid legal services and group legal services might be a better path for us to follow. This comment coincided with my initial impressions that the needs in the US far outweighed those in Australia at the time. I noted in one of my first letters home:

> I have met a number of people so far, all very intense, but very helpful. I feel almost ashamed of my expedition when I realise the enormity of their problems. In retrospect, Australia has little wrong with it compared to the urgent needs here.

Meeting Jerome was another giant step in my education. I had what amounted to a private seminar with one of the most experienced figures in both the theory of lawyers' role in legal services delivery in the common law world and the practice of establishing and managing one of the largest legal services programmes established by OEO. I was immensely privileged and to cap it off he invited me to come to dinner on the following Friday evening to be followed by an evening at the theatre.

My meeting with Jerome was very timely as the next day I met with John Stewart, San Francisco Legal Assistance Foundation's current director. After being briefed by him as to the current situation with the programme, he suggested I visit several of the Foundation's neighbourhood law offices. I later walked around the poor part of the town visiting neighbourhood legal programmes under the guidance of the Foundation's administrator, Len Casanares.

At the Central City branch of the Foundation, I met Larry Curtis who explained how they operated and their typical clientele, being "skid row" alcoholics, landlord and tenant issues in old hotels run by "slum landlords", which housed many welfare recipients who lived precariously. Resolving such issues soaked up resources and the time of lawyers working on such cases which usually got settled. Also, the clients were normally fearful and worried that the lawyers would not be around in six months. This office had four lawyers supplemented by students and volunteers under the VISTA programme initiated by John Kennedy when President.

It was one of many such visits I would have over the coming months which highlighted the challenges facing the young lawyers working at the coal face. They were helping the poor but at the same time were expected by OEO to be challenging the laws and processes which made the poor powerless. I now understood the frustration of activists such as Jerome Carlin.

Another Taste of the San Francisco High Life

After another long day I called on David Phillips, a lawyer I had been in touch with before I left home, who immediately invited me to join him for dinner at the University Club. He was a young man of about 35 years. He was joined by his girlfriend, Marilyn Waldron, who taught art and lived in Sausalito. We were also joined by another couple who were David's friends, Dwight Simpson and his wife Harriett, both academics and both very charming people. Dwight was a Political Science Professor whose specialty was Middle East politics. They were all very interested in learning about what I was doing. I was wryly amused by what the fellowship was exposing me to – wandering around "skid row" and discussing "slum landlords" a few hours earlier, only to be dining in an elite establishment with Americans at the other end of the economic scale.

After dinner we went to the cocktail bar in the Carnelian Room at the top of the Bank of America building, then the tallest in San Francisco with 52 floors. It was eerie. The clouds actually passed us by and were sometimes lower – a very luxurious place and far beyond my modest daily allowance. I really appreciated the opportunity to meet such interesting people who at the end of the evening were thankfully heading across the Bay and dropped me home on a very cold night. It snowed in downtown San Francisco later that night for the first time for 10 years or so, another first on this amazing journey and another full day.

Modesto: a CRLA Frontline on Behalf of Underpaid Chicano and Okie Farm Workers

The next morning it was raining and very cold due to the overnight snow and, after a short bus ride to Oakland, I was on another Greyhound bus taking an hour and a half trip to Modesto, a small city which was in the midst of a large farming area about 140 miles east of San Francisco. On the way I was able to see snow on all the nearby mountains, which provided much needed water for the farmers. While I did not know it at the time, I later learned that George Lucas had lived and gone to high school in Modesto as a teenager. He later based his 1973 hit move *American Graffiti* there, recalling his teenage years cruising and hanging out downtown and reviving interest in the 1950s pop culture. It was also inspiration for the equally successful spin off TV series *Happy Days*.

My purpose for this trip was to visit a branch of the CRLA programme in the field. The Modesto branch had a team of five lawyers, supplemented by two community workers who filled multiple roles as investigators, lay-advocates in welfare hearings and process servers. These community workers were, in many ways, the most interesting people in the office. One was "an Okie", while the other was a Chicano and each had links with their respective communities

It was fascinating to hear that the local Okie population were the descendants of the reported million people who left the Midwest during a long drought in the 1930s, having been lured by the promise of work by California farmers and growers. Having been forced to leave their own farms in the "Dust Bowl" in places like Oklahoma, they moved with their few possessions in old cars or horse drawn carts, as recorded by famed photographers, and headed west where they became a cheap source of farm labour. Due to low pay and small prospects, many such families ended up being marginalised and living in poor parts of the towns. This was still the case when I visited Modesto.

The Chicanos, I learnt, were descendants of either original Spanish speaking inhabitants of the area dating back to when the Spanish controlled California or were descendants of later Spanish speaking immigrants, probably mostly from Mexico, who settled and worked as farm labourers. However, their families eventually became American citizens who then traditionally worked as an underclass of itinerant workers moving from one farm or crop to another. They were abused and marginalised by the growers with their children never being properly educated – a vicious poverty cycle.

During my visit I also met with Gene Livingston, CRLA's former director, who now conducted a technical assistance unit for CRLA and was temporarily based in Modesto. He generously gave me a detailed briefing and also provided various reports and statistics on the programme's operations. This contributed greatly to my later being able to prepare a very detailed report on CRLA's operations which greatly enriched my Churchill Fellowship report.

Gene also briefed me on the problems during the office's early years when it faced attacks from local Bar Associations. They attempted to use the courts to force them to close and constantly harassed them for alleged breaches of so-called ethical rules. Those involved in the centre were also harassed and threatened by the local District Attorney. Eventually higher courts intervened, and such challenges were overturned on appeal and effectively stopped.

Because of these politically inspired attempts to shut CRLA down, aided and abetted by Governor Reagan's administration, the OEO administration in Washington, to ensure CRLA's survival, decided to make an exception to the normal funding rules and directly fund the programme on the basis that its role covered a large part of the state and various towns. Later during my visit to Chicago, I learned how the political interference came from the city administration of the infamous Mayor Richard Daley and that a similar funding approach had to be adopted by OEO to avoid corrupt political interference with its legal services funding.

The work practices and victimisation of the low paid itinerant farm workers, which CRLA successfully overturned in the courts in the late 1960s, had long been in place and had been vividly documented in John Steinbeck's 1939 Pulitzer Prize winning novel, *The Grapes of Wrath*. It was also chilling to learn about the power and reach of the agribusiness interests, which I felt had a distinct *Soviet* flavour. I noted:

> The environment was aptly described by John Steinbeck in *The Grapes of Wrath* which incidentally as late as the 1960s was absent from nearly all libraries and banned in most schools together with the rest of Steinbeck's works in the lush farming valleys of California – so much for it being 'the land of the free'!

I came away with the clear impression that the towns in California's rich farming areas were dominated by powerful farming interests. To avoid local political interference, the normal process of funding passing through representative city-based Community Action Programs (CAPs) did not apply. After visiting this office located only a few hours from San Francisco I thought that I might have been in another country! I shared my thoughts in a letter home:

> From my discussions in Modesto, there appeared to be many Americans who are narrow minded, bigoted and mean. The young lawyers at the CRLA office had so much opposition from the 'silent majority' that the silence was almost shattered by their violence. The champion of these narrow minded people is Governor Reagan who does 'nice things like cut thousands off welfare' and has tried to shut down some of the programme. The majority like him because he is cost conscious and home owners pay very high state property taxes.

CALIFORNIA: LEARNING FROM THE BEST

On my return to Berkeley, Jerome Carlin picked me up and drove me to his home which was right on top of the hills above the University. It was a mock Tudor style home, very big and comfortable with a magnificent view of the bay, San Francisco, the Golden Gate Bridge and the ocean. It was a clear evening with the winds blowing off the snow-capped mountains clearing the air. All the lights of the cities on both sides of the bay were like sparkling crystals.

I met his wife Joy who was a delightful person, and I had an enjoyable evening, relaxed and in very good company. They had three children who were all away in college at that time. Jerome showed me his studio, which he had built in the attic right at the top of the house and showed me some of his paintings which I liked. However, he was apparently not interested in selling them.

After dinner, Joy, who was an actress, invited me to come to with her as her guest to the theatre where she was playing the leading lady in a Victorian play by Pinero called *Dandy Dick*. She was a member of the American Conservatory Theatre which was the major group on the west coast. Jerome urged me to go, so I had the unusual and pleasant experience of being driven to the theatre in an ancient Morris Minor convertible by the leading lady of a play. Joy was very nice and down to earth.

Joy told me that she had studied at the Yale Drama School and later in New York with Lee Strasburg, but after she was married didn't take much part in the theatre until recently. The show was very funny, with all these American actors playing such parts as corny Guards officers and a strait-laced vicar. I am sure many in the audience didn't catch on to some of the Victorian English phrases which I thought were very funny. Joy was terrific and a very good comedienne.

Having the Carlins take me under their wings added to the richness of my experiences and, as I moved across this amazing continent, my fellowship was greatly enriched by many other generous and caring people who went far out of their way to ensure I was nurtured and encouraged to maximise this opportunity I was given.

On my last weekend in San Francisco, I decided to see the tourist sights, e.g., the cable car, Fisherman's Wharf, etc. So, after doing some housework and getting my washing from the laundromat, I headed over the Bay to visit the tourist areas at Fisherman's Wharf. After catching the famous San Francisco Cable Car along with hundreds of other tourists, I arrived at Fisherman's Wharf where there were thousands of tourists.

Having played tourist exploring the sights offered by San Francisco, it was time to prepare for my next stop, Los Angeles. However, before heading for the airport I took the opportunity on a quiet Sunday afternoon to start a procedure I followed for the next few months and that was to write thank you letters to all those I had met. Later when back home I again wrote to everyone, in some instances, sending material they requested. I later followed up by sending copies of my Churchill Fellowship report to the main organisations I had spent time with.

The Western Center for Law and Poverty at the University of Southern California

My final stop on the West Coast was Los Angeles where I visited two university-based programmes. The first was the Western Center for Law and Poverty at the University of Southern California where I spent some valuable time with Professor Terry Hatter, the Centre's executive director.

The Center was established in 1967 as a central resource and training agency on poverty law in Southern California and some 50 years later is still a major force for reform and equity for millions of poor citizens in one of the richest states in the world.

When I visited the Center in January 1972 it had already carved out an impressive record in supporting local legal services programmes and law schools in the first joint venture of its kind to:

- train and involve law students in poverty law through the development and supervision of clinical poverty law at the

University of Southern California, the University of California at Los Angeles, and Loyola University;

- offer research and back-up facilities for the neighbourhood law offices in Los Angeles; and
- provide professional recruiting, training, technical assistance, and general support for all the legal services programmes in Southern California.

As noted above, it was only five years old when I visited. It had, during its brief life, made a significant impact on the oppressive conditions under which many of the poor in Southern California lived, although I noted that much still needed to be achieved.

As many objective observers have noted, the conditions under which many poor Americans live have not greatly improved since my first visit to the US. However, the fact that this Center has continued to be a force over the past half century is a tribute to the three supporting Law Schools which still underpin this remarkable and much needed institution.

Professor Terry Hatter was a much-respected black leader who later was appointed by President Jimmy Carter to a seat on the Federal District Court for Central California in 1979 and continued in that role till he retired in 2005.

When I met him, he had had a distinguished role in legal services having served as chief counsel at the San Francisco Legal Assistance Foundation. He had been Regional Legal Services Director, Office of Economic Opportunity in San Francisco before taking up the appointment in Los Angeles with the University of Southern California in 1970.

My visit to California had started with excitement and hope, which masked some basic concerns about my capacity to survive for the next five months without my usual safety net of family, friends and an established career path. However, any such risk soon evaporated in the face of the welcome I received, not only from those few

I had contacted before leaving home, but also from all the others those initial limited contacts had so readily introduced me to.

It also helped that, fortuitously, California was the home of the most mature, well-funded and successful of the OEO legal services programmes, and that the induction I received there gave me the expectation that rest of my trip would be similarly successful, not the least because Johnson's War on Poverty had attracted a special group of brilliant American lawyers, both young and old, to its just cause.

5

THE NAVAJO RESERVATION: LEARNING FROM FIRST NATIONS PEOPLE

My visit to Arizona was all about visiting the Navajo reservation. I was interested in learning how legal access for Indigenous Australians might be better met and my inquiries prior to leaving home revealed that it would be instructive to see at first hand the well-funded OEO legal services programme which was tailored to meet the needs of the Navajo people. I was keen to see if the work done on the Navajo reservation by young OEO funded lawyers might provide me with some insights to take back home to Australia.

My visit was coloured by the friendly dedicated people I met, and by the amazing scenery and the stories of concerted efforts by the sources of power on the reservation, the Bureau of Indian Affairs and the Navajo Tribal Council, to de-rail the good work and the important and gratifying wins in court by the good guys, being the young OEO lawyers,

A visit to the Navajo reservation had been included in my itinerary following a meeting with several young lawyers with the Public Solicitors Office in Sydney. One of these was Peter Hidden and we discussed the type of legal services provided by the Public Solicitors Office. During our meeting, Peter inquired as to whether I was proposing to visit any services dedicated to assisting Indigenous communities in the US.

My interest in this important issue raised by Peter was also piqued by the then recent announcement by the Minister for Social Security, Billy Wentworth, of funding for the establishment of an Aboriginal Legal Service in or near Redfern. This was a project recommended to The Poverty Inquiry established by the minister and undertaken by Professor Henderson. I like to think that this outcome flowed from representations Professor Ron Sackville and I had made to the inquiry urging it to include the need for such a specialised legal aid service.

As a result of this important development and my conversation with Peter, I decided that I should include a visit to the Navajo reservation which I learnt had an OEO funded legal services programme. The growing recognition of the need for specialised legal service to assist members of the Aboriginal community in both urban and country areas was another factor in my decision.

After applying for a Churchill Fellowship, I also discussed my trip and the proposed new Aboriginal legal service with Professor Hal Wootten QC, the Dean of the new University of New South Wales (UNSW) law school and chair of the committee appointed to establish the new legal service. I later wrote to Hal and told him of my conversation with Peter Hidden and I suggested that he contact Peter, as in my view, he was not only well qualified to take up the new role, but genuinely interested in this special need.

On my return home in June 1972, I was pleased to learn that Peter had been hired to lead the new Aboriginal Legal Service. Peter did an excellent job, giving the service great credibility and creating a road map for his successors and similar services in other states to follow. Peter was later admitted to the Bar and had a distinguished legal career, ending up a Justice of the NSW Supreme Court.

A Few Initial Hiccups on Arrival

My arrival at the Navajo reservation to meet with the leaders of the Navajo run legal services programme immediately presented several conflicting challenges. The first was that I had contacted the wrong legal aid service, which was a legal aid service funded by the Bureau of Indian Affairs and the Tribal Council, and not the OEO funded service Dinebeiina Nahiilna Be Agaditaher Inc (DNA) which I had intended to visit. DNA's name in the Navajo language means

THE NAVAJO RESERVATION: LEARNING FROM FIRST NATIONS PEOPLE

Attorneys who Contribute to the Revitalisation of the Economic Circumstances of the People.

The second challenge was that I had been advised to let the Bureau know of my visit as they could facilitate my time there and it quickly became apparent that neither organisation was enthused about me meeting with the OEO funded legal services programme.

The programme had been funded by OEO in February 1967 and operated under a board made up of Navajo representatives, practising lawyers and several law professors. Its first director was a white lawyer, Theodore Mitchell, who I was told was pretty aggressive in pressing the rights and interests or ordinary members of the Navajo people against both the Bureau and the Tribal Council.

I soon made contact with the DNA head office and met with Peterson Zah, a Navajo who was the assistant director of the programme and a former teacher at the local high school. Apparently, the director, Navajo lawyer Leo Haven, was also an educator who initiated DNA's very effective community education programme. When I arrived, Pete Zah was helping install a new hot water heater as he could not get help from either the staff of the Tribal Council or the Bureau. He said plumbers from Gallup would not take the time to come out, so he had to be a jack of all trades. It was a quite unexpected but, at another level, a down to earth introduction to this interesting man.

During my meeting with Pete Zah, he explained the structure which followed the model of other legal services programmes. It received a grant of around $1 million and employed 23 "Anglo" lawyers, as the Navajos referred to them, most of whom were young and from the best law schools all over the States. The rest of the staff were Navajos, with the lawyers being complemented by 30 Tribal Court advocates. These were spread over five offices (although a new one in Utah was about to be opened) and these branch offices were where all the lawyers and advocates worked. The latter appeared in the Tribal Courts, a network of which operated throughout the reservation.

Besides the branch offices, DNA had a law reform unit, a Navajo law development and litigation unit, a preventative law and community education unit and an administration unit. There were also plans to open an economic development unit.

Following my initial meeting in the Window Rock office with DNA's leadership group and with the assistance of the guide and driver provided by the Bureau, Cato Sells, an itinerary was settled. This itinerary enabled me to meet with young lawyers and to see how the various branches on the reservation operated while at the same time travelling around to see the sights and programmes the Bureau wanted me to see.

Both aspects of the itinerary gave me the chance to see some of the most spectacular, unique scenery and vistas on the planet – the mesas, canyons and deserts familiar to me from my Saturday afternoons spent seeing "Cowboy and Indian" movies at the local Ritz Cinema. I was like a kid in a candy store recognising scene after scene from the movies of my childhood with the added advantage that, being February, it was sunny but quite cold so I avoided the searing summer heat.

When DNA started, one of the first activities was to set up local committees in almost all the 101 chapters or sub-districts of the reservation. This network apparently was very effective in alerting DNA to specific problem in their areas. The Tribal Council which governed the reservation was openly hostile to the establishment of DNA and provided no support for its establishment so DNA staff had had to fit out their own premises. It also soon became apparent to me that both the Tribal Council and the Bureau had a long history of making decisions in relation to the tribal lands which were not in the interest of the tribe as a whole.

One then current example brought to my notice when I visited was the Council's decision to waive the tribes' water rights to the Colorado River, the reservation's main source of water. DNA challenged this decision which appeared to be the latest in a long list of corrupt ones. This challenge resulted in Ted Mitchell being thrown off the reservation by the Council, a decision soon overturned in court. This in turn led to the removal of the chair of the Council and a partial reform in the way the Tribal Council operated soon followed.

DNA was also soon challenging the Bureau of Indian Affairs whose authority in every realm of Navajo life was absolute, both in legal and practical matters. In 1944 the Bureau illegally transferred ownership of 5,000 acres which it held as trustee for the tribe and evicted the tribal people from the land. This action was challenged in the Federal Court by DNA on the basis that the Bureau acted without the approval of the federal government. Ownership was restored to the Navajos. The presiding judge noted in his judgment that:

> Representatives of the Bureau of Indian Affairs, or the Bureau of Land Management of the Department of the Interior, have allowed this cruel hoax to be perpetuated.

Other high-profile cases where DNA intervened to force changes included a court decision requiring the Bureau to stop its policy of removing children from the reservations and relocating them to boarding schools. At that time the Bureau was still mirroring the experience of young Aboriginal children who made up the Stolen Generations in Australia, by taking over the education of Navajo children who were frequently removed at an early age from their parents and placed in boarding schools, often miles and sometimes thousands of miles away from their homes, e.g., from Alaska to Oklahoma. A variety of social, local political pressure and economic issues, rather than legislative intervention, have reduced the number of native American children being educated in boarding schools by the time I visited, thankfully.

DNA also intervened to require the Bureau to meet one if its core legal obligations which was to make sure Navajo children were properly clothed, while another intervention resulted in a US Court of Appeal order requiring the Bureau to use its authority to protect the Navajo people by regulating traders and trading posts on the reservation. The court found that the Bureau oversaw "a system of unregulated monopolies" imposed on the Navajos by government officials.

The third "enemy" of the people identified by DNA was the state of Arizona which, in DNA's view, had illegally imposed state income tax on Navajos living and working on the reservation. In *McClanahan v Arizona State Tax Commission*, the appeal against this decision to the Arizona Supreme Court was unsuccessful at the initial hearing, the Arizona Appeal Court rejecting the appeal arguments put forward. DNA then made its first appeal to the US Supreme Court which upheld it in a unanimous landmark decision delivered by revered black Supreme Court Justice Thurgood Marshall. This decision came down after my visit and it held that Arizona had no jurisdiction to impose a tax on the income of Navajo Indians residing on the Navajo Reservation, whose income was wholly derived from reservation sources.

In my Churchill Fellowship report, I noted that possibly the most significant contribution by DNA was in the field of community education. Its main role here was to educate the Navajo people about their triple citizenship status under tribal laws, state laws and federal law. Having this knowledge shared with ordinary members of the tribe was greeted with great enthusiasm, with the number of people attending DNA meetings in the various chapters increasing significantly.

The most obvious contrast with the Californian OEO programmes was that while they operated in very large metropolitan and highly dense urban populations, or major rural towns, DNA existed to serve a population of approximately 130,000, most of whom lived well under the poverty line and eked out subsistence livings. The reservation covered an area of almost 65,000 square miles and was mainly situated in the northeast quarter of Arizona, with small areas overlapping into Utah in the north and New Mexico in the east.

The Navajo population was spread thinly over this very large reservation which was mainly desert and known to the world at large by its spectacular scenery. However, I soon learnt that, despite its services being stretched, DNA was the only legal service trusted by tribal members.

The contact between the lawyers and the "Dinee", as the Navajo people preferred to be known, was very effective with DNA being kept continually informed of problems confronting the people. One constant problem when I was there were unregulated "rogue" traders illegally coming onto the reservation despite the previous court order directing the Bureau to stop such traders.

As well as visiting DNA's branch offices to meet with its mostly young lawyers, I was taken on a tour of the obligatory "good things" the Bureau had done for the tribe since the middle of the 19th century. These visits took me to dams, oil fields, power stations and forests. The opportunity to spend five days in this amazing place was one of most memorable outcomes of my trip.

The Extraordinary Sights of the Reservation

Cato Sells was also responsible for guiding me to some of the reservation's more familiar sights such as Monument Valley with its amazing flat top mesas, the backdrop of many John Ford Hollywood westerns. By strange coincidence, on one of the first nights back home, one such movie was on television and the spot where I was photographed by Cato was the scene of the inevitable shoot-out between "the goodies and the baddies". For some reason my wife Pat was not quite as excited as I was. In retrospect, the fact that she had recently come out of hospital after giving birth to our son John was probably the reason. Or, possibly, I am a bit eccentric in getting excited about such things!

Cato was an excellent tour guide as I visited the various DNA branches which operated in small settlements, all of which had names straight out of old cowboy movies such as, Shiprock, Fort Defiance, Tuba City, Crownpoint, Chinle and Mexican Hat. Each such settlement seemed then to have little more than the obligatory motel, petrol station and café and a few relatively ordinary houses, as few Navajos seemed to live in such places.

Reaching such outposts provided constant opportunities to make short diversions to visit legendary places such as Canyon de Chelly and its amazing cliff-side dwellings inhabited for over 5,000 years by the ancient Pueblo peoples. We also visited the Snake River which carved its way through the famous Four Corners where Arizona, Utah, Colorado and New Mexico meet, the only place in the US where four states meet in this way.

While in that part of the reservation, and after visiting the new Mexican Hat DNA branch, Cato took me to Gooseneck State Park in Utah where you can look down on the San Juan River as it weaves its way to the Colorado River in a very tight series of "S" bends. The difference between the canyons it creates, and the Grand Canyon, could not be more extreme.

Window Rock itself was unique, not just because it was the capital of the Navajo nation and home to the Bureau, the Tribal Council and DNA, but it also had its own movie worthy natural feature in the form of a very large rock sitting above the small town which it dominated. It had a large wind-carved hole in it, yet another memorable and spectacular natural phenomenon.

Another unusual sight, which I did not recall ever seeing in movies, were traditional Navajo homes known as "hogans". Tourists from outside the reservation are not welcome to visit these hogans and the closest Cato was prepared to take me was to view them from a distance, probably about a half a mile from the road. They were quite difficult to see because of the way they blended into the background, as they are relatively small structures with domed roofs made of mud, supported by low log walls and with blankets hanging at the entrances.

Despite my misgivings about the Bureau, I was very appreciative of the generous provision of a car and the assistance of Cato Sells as my driver/guide, a font of knowledge about the tribe and the reservation and a very interesting man. He was a delightful person and more than happy to take me wherever I wanted to go.

Some Bureau Staff Held Different Views from their Superiors

Through Cato I discovered that there were Bureau staff who took a different view from the view I had heard in Window Rock. This occurred when Cato drove me to Chinle to meet the young lawyers there. He suggested we make a courtesy call on the Bureau superintendent, Paul Hand. It turned out that Paul's wife had spent some time visiting friends in Sydney the previous year so, on discovering that I was from Sydney, he invited us to come over to his home to meet his wife. During an interesting discussion about my US experiences so far and his wife's Sydney experiences, Paul expressed the view that he thought that DNA was doing a much-needed job for the community, and he seemed to be someone who was there seeking positive outcomes through his role and felt that greater efforts should be being made to promote the interests of minorities.

They have around 200 official visitors a year, with the 1971 quota including a number of judges and diplomats from a range of countries. It appeared that some were keen to assess the US government's approach to Indigenous minorities while others were keen to learn more about the Navajos as a surviving tribal race.

From my own perspective, the visit was an opportunity to learn whether what was happening on the Navajo reservation held any relevance for the Indigenous communities which were similarly spread thinly over large areas of western, central and northern Australia and whether they could similarly benefit from access to legal services tailored to their needs.

Of all the OEO funded programmes, largely because of the unique legal status of reservation-based Navajos, DNA had a more immediate and lasting impact on its constituency than any of the other legal services programmes I visited. For the relatively limited funding it received, the return in personal, social and economic terms was totally disproportionate to OEO's outlay.

My visit to the Navajo Reservation ranks high in my life experiences.

6

Chicago: the Good, the Bad and the Outrageous

I had been deeply impressed by the innovation and enthusiasm of young lawyers on my first stop on the West Coast. My next visit to the young legal aid lawyers on the Navajo Reservation highlighted the special needs of remote Indigenous communities and was highly relevant for the plans to establish the Aboriginal Legal Service. By contrast, my time in Chicago was like being rolled over by a tsunami of glaring inequality, corruption, poverty, and violence, quite outside the experience of someone from Australia.

My hosts in Chicago arranged for me to live on the University of Chicago campus which, besides housing the renowned Law School, was also home to the American Bar Association (ABA) and its research centre, the then much vaunted American Bar Foundation research team.

While there were many good reasons for visiting this city, its violent reputation, which I had been alerted to having picked up a recently published paperback exposé of Chicago's infamous Mayor Richard Daley by famed Chicago journalist Mike Royko, made me apprehensive. Reading his extraordinary revelations about the Daley machine, as I travelled towards this important fellowship destination, I was having second thoughts about the wisdom of the decision.

Making an Important Washington Connection Mid-flight

With all these negatives about Chicago running around in my head while on the flight from Albuquerque, I was luckily distracted by the passenger in the seat next to me who, on hearing my Australian accent, inquired as to what I was doing in the US. I briefly told him of my Fellowship, my itinerary and where I had been and what I had seen so far. He introduced himself as Tom Carr, a senior official in the US government's Office of Management and Budget, who was returning to Washington after visiting New Mexico trying to coordinate the various local agencies receiving federal funds in the south-west States.

What excited him about my fellowship was that he had, until recently, been the Director of the White House Fellows Program which had been initiated by President Johnson, whereby 20 of America's brightest and best young adults were selected to spend a year in Washington as special assistants to the President's Cabinet secretaries. Each year thousands of young people were nominated by their city's Mayor or their state Governor to be considered for this honour. The aim was to expose to national government at its highest level a small group of the brightest and best of young Americans, who had not previously been involved in politics.

According to Tom, those chosen were mostly young professionals about my age, although several places were reserved each year for officers serving in the defence forces. He thought that it would be mutually beneficial for me to meet with some of the current appointees when I was in Washington and said the concept of the Churchill Fellowship appealed to him greatly. My chance meeting with Tom enabled me to open doors in Washington at a level I would never have dreamed possible.

Prior to leaving Australia, I had contacted the National Legal Aid and Defender Association, the professional association of lawyers involved in legal aid and in the American justice system, which was based on the campus of the University of Chicago. I had contacted them seeking advice and assistance with planning my US programme, as well as advice about relevant people and organisations in Chicago. A senior administrator there, Mayo Stiegler, had been very helpful with advice about my programme. After arriving in the US, I had contacted him and did so again prior to leaving Arizona, as I had sought his assistance with finding affordable accommodation during the three weeks I had planned to be in Chicago.

On my arrival at O'Hare Airport, having given clear instructions about which bus to catch from there to Evanston where he lived, Mayo gave me the good news that he had arranged my accommodation, having booked me a room at the University of Chicago's International House (IH) at a very reasonable and affordable rate. He and his delightful wife Sheree invited me to stay the weekend and organised a very enjoyable dinner in my honour that evening – what a great welcome to Chicago.

Staying at IH was a considerable privilege. It also had the great advantage of being close by the campus and the legal precinct which also conveniently housed the Law School, Mayo's office, the ABA headquarters and the American Bar Foundation. My visit to Chicago was significantly enhanced by Mayo's generosity, assistance, and advice.

A Taste of College US Style

Living in IH during my stay in Chicago was as close as I would ever get to "going to college" in the US context and I soon discovered that there were four Australians already in residence, two guys and two women. My room was on level 8 in the men's wing and Mike Jones, an Adelaide medical graduate doing research in theoretical biology, lived on my floor and we soon met and from him I learnt about the facilities and how the place operated.

Once settled in, I met with Mayo who gave me names of people I should meet at the ABA and the American Bar Foundation, then an internationally respected research organisation focusing on the operation of the US legal system. This initial visit to Mayo's office coincided with a visit from the then President of the English Law Society, to whom I was introduced. He said he was aware of my proposed visit to the UK because of a letter of introduction sent by the NSW Law Society. He was interested in what I had learnt so far and said he was keen to see me when I reached London so I could share my conclusions about the US situation with him, which I had the pleasure of doing when I later visited the Law Society and the legal aid programme which it then conducted for the government.

Mayo also put me in touch with the dean of the University Law School, Professor Norval Morris, a Melbourne Law School graduate and a leading criminologist, and co-author with my old criminology lecturer, Professor Gordon Hawkins, of the highly influential and best-selling *The Honest Politicians Guide to Crime Control*. With Mayo's assistance, I made contact with key legal aid figures and was soon visiting downtown legal aid programmes.

Later, I also visited several outer suburban legal aid offices, one of which involved travelling to a southern suburb called Harvey which was one of three neighbourhood offices of the Cook County Community Assistance Foundation. This office of four lawyers saw over 3,000 people a year, although only about 20% required more than advice and, like the other neighbourhood offices I visited, there was no need for a means test as everyone there was under the poverty line. The office had developed a good relationship with local lawyers and was building an effective referral process for the few locals who could afford a lawyer.

One of the more interesting aspects of their operation was that, unlike in some other offices, they had developed a good working relationship with the local Municipal Circuit Court judge and the supervising lawyer had arranged for us to have lunch with the judge. The judge was relatively young and yet had been appointed some 10 years previously. It was fascinating to hear them talking about the operations of the court and the process of appointments to the bench. I was left with the strong impression such appointments in Chicago were governed by different principles than those at home.

Political patronage seemed to rule, whether it was appointments to a court or getting a hole in your street fixed. In Chicago the black communities had no access to the levers of power and were ignored by government departments. These only seemed to act on the intervention of a local ward boss.

CHICAGO: THE GOOD, THE BAD AND THE OUTRAGEOUS

My return journey from Harvey was not good, as the office was a mile and a half from the nearest train station and my host misunderstood the departure time of the train so I missed it by two minutes. I had to wait 58 minutes until the next one. I spent the time thankfully not freezing because for some reason the station I had been dropped at was new and had an indoor heated waiting room. I spent the time writing a long letter home describing some of my recent experiences and recounting some of the scandals in the city administration which had recently come to light.

These scandals included the attempt by Mayor Daley to sack his Attorney General, a fellow Irish American named Hanrahan. Hanrahan was supposedly involved in the killing of two Black Panthers in the aftermath of the riots during the 1968 Democratic Convention. The victims were later found to have not resisted arrest as claimed. Another current scandal was the arrest of a doctor in a state hospital for the killing of over 200 people by prescribing the wrong medication as a form of mercy killing.

During my last week I visited the Legal Aid Bureau's Woodlawn office, which was a few blocks south of IH, and I decided to walk over to the office. In a letter home my shock was obvious. I recorded:

> I went there yesterday on foot, suicidal literally at night. If you recall pictures of cities in war torn Europe, then that is 63rd Street. The worst slums I have ever seen. It is the subject of urban renewal in Chicago which in local terms means urban removal. I was told that it was in reality a way of removing the black tenants who lived there on the promise of rehousing elsewhere which did not happen.

I recorded in my diary that, in recent years, violence on the campus and in nearby areas had become extremely prevalent due to marauding gangs of black youths. In a recent one-month period prior to my visit, two students were murdered and a number of others assaulted. When I was in residence at IH every night there were police, ambulance and fire truck sirens constantly heard. In the face of the University threatening to leave and move the campus to a safer place, the city promised the urban renewal project if they stayed.

The lawyers I met in the Woodlawn office worked closely with a number of local organisations which were fighting a losing battle to keep the area alive. The office operated with seven lawyers from a storefront but most of the other shops were empty and the local bank branch had recently closed. The office provided a range of services to the local community and had a good track record of successful litigation in a range of courts.

Exposure to Chicago's Infamous South Side Ghetto

On leaving, as my next meeting was downtown in the Loop and somewhat on the spur of the moment, I decided to take advantage of the fact that outside the Woodlawn office was a station for the Elevated Train, known locally as "the El" which would take me there.

I was not particularly apprehensive about taking the train as my fellow passengers appeared to be obviously decent black people who probably had more to fear from police violence and victimisation by their own youth gangs than the white community did. The trip took me to the Loop over 50 blocks north through an endless number of poor black areas, initially made up of identical three-story narrow apartment buildings, many of which had been burned out, particularly between the 51st and 44th blocks.

The train rode on a trestle type structure which meant that the travellers looked over the top of these suburbs which were as desolate as they were depressing. Some of the buildings were inhabited but their condition was invariably very poor. The decision to construct an elevated rail line was because Chicago was established on a swamp and building a subway was simply not feasible.

My last working day in Chicago included a visit to the Legal Aid Bureau's Grand Boulevard Office, East 47th Street. Fortunately, I did not have to find my own way to this infamous heart of the South

Side ghetto as was I given a ride by the office's supervising attorney, Marthe Purmal, in a shiny blue Karmann Ghia coupe which, for a car enthusiast like me, was an excellent way to start the day. After this bright start the reality was that the office operated from a boarded-up shop front in one of the most notorious sections of this infamous ghetto and my notes of the visit make grim reading.

The office was located in Chicago's worst area for poverty, unemployment, violence and crime. After being introduced to the staff, I was told that their approach to gaining credibility was to try to get across to the community that their type of law practice was not there to lead or dominate, which was the traditional view of lawyers held by blacks. Its aim was to guide and assist them by being technical assistants, particularly to community and tenant organisations.

Apparently, the challenges of operating in such a neighbourhood were made worse for white lawyers trying to help by the insularity of the local black residents. Nevertheless, some saw the office as a resource. When I was there a call came in from a mothers' group at a nearby high school who were worried about their kids being "ripped off" and raped by a local youth gang known as the Blackstone Rangers. This gang, which apparently originated in a youth group in the Woodlawn area near the University of Chicago, now specialised in standover tactics and protection rackets. I was told that they were known to murder dissenters, which was the recent fate of two local youths whose mothers were then threatened with similar consequences if they assisted the police.

According to the legal aid lawyers, the local people were not only subject to such gang violence but frequently suffered at the hands of the Chicago police with little relief in sight. In fact, Marthe assured me that she had been accosted and stopped by the police many times since coming to Chicago. This in turn led to another problem for the legal aid lawyers. There was a lack of co-operation from the police, and they had many examples of petty corruption by the police who victimised drug addicts.

The lawyers tried to promote community education by working closely with community groups, with Marthe being the legal adviser to a tenants' council of a local high rise community housing project. However, the common feeling amongst the local people was a pervasive one of apprehension. This was compounded by the lawyers not getting the co-operation of city agencies responsible for a variety of community codes. I suspect this was because of the history of the legal service programmes being removed from the control of the city administration some years before.

Attending a Catholic Anti-War Peace Rally

An equally unforgettable experience occurred one evening in Hyde Park, a middle class neighbourhood adjacent to the university, following evening Mass. I learnt that a Catholic Anti-War Peace Rally was taking place in the neighbouring Church Hall, so I decided to look in on it. It was being held to mark the release from gaol of Catholic activist and editor of the *Catholic Worker*, Karl Meyer, who had been gaoled for having refused to pay taxes as an anti-war protest. He was a colleague of the left wing American Catholic activist icon and founder of the *Catholic Worker*, Dorothy Day, who was also in attendance but did not speak while I was there.

The main speakers were Father Jim Groppi, a leading militant Catholic priest, and Dick Gregory, the black comedian turned anti-war activist. They both spoke at length, with Gregory initially being highly amusing before getting more serious and starting to criticise the Nixon administration's attempts to suppress anti-war protests and views. Father Groppi did likewise, going into considerable detail about the abuse of citizens' rights by both the FBI and the CIA.

As an experienced litigation lawyer, I had developed a reasonable level of scepticism, but the stories they told seemed utterly fact-driven and believable. It was another experience that one could only have had in America. After several hours of high intensity political speeches, the emotional impact on me was simply too much and I left totally drained by the experience. As I walked back to IH, I felt very despondent about America's future under the Nixon administration.

I came away from Chicago deeply impressed with what I learned from these national legal bodies as well as from the local legal aid lawyers who fought the good fight in the nearby notorious South Side ghettos.

7

Washington: Doors Open in Miraculous Ways!

Washington offered a colourful palette of personalities who played various important roles in the capital besides those involved in the OEO programme. These included government officials like US Solicitor General, Dr Erwin Griswold, and a number of lawyers in large law firms and public interest law firms who ran landmark cases on behalf of the poor and oppressed.

The opportunity to have a front row seat at the trial of anti-war protesters, the Harrisburg Seven, and to meet and mingle with both defence and prosecution lawyers in such a high-profile trial, was a once in a lifetime experience.

Later, another similarly rare opportunity was to meet some of the best and brightest young Americans who were selected each year as White House Fellows and to be personal assistants to each of the 20 Cabinet secretaries. They in turn led to other extraordinary doors in Washington being opened to me.

Washington was simply dazzling for a political neophyte like me!

Visiting a Legal Services Legend

Before arriving in Washington, I had already accumulated a long list of people who had been recommended to me during the earlier part of my programme. However, the one person everyone involved in OEO funded programmes recommended I meet in Washington was the founding director of the OEO Legal Services Division, Clinton Bamberger.

As noted previously, Bamberger and Sargent Shriver immediately saw how an activist legal services programme could supplement other OEO activities, as their research told them that many poor people were locked into the poverty cycle by the lack of legal rights. Bamberger had immediately got moving on several levels and had promptly been endorsed by the leadership of the ABA.

Bamberger quickly went around the country speaking to state and local bar associations and was often met with outright hostility with some local Bar leaders claiming "it was the first step towards socialising the practice of law". He told me that even some of his lawyer friends and other legal contemporaries in the law, whom he had known for many years, were worried "that he could become a tool of the communists".

There was a similar reaction from the leaders of the profession in Australia when the federal Attorney General Lionel Murphy QC announced the establishment of the Australian Legal Aid Office in July 1973, and I recall being invited to a meeting at the Law Society to discuss this new development. I was shocked and surprised to hear absurd claims being made by senior lawyers, many of whom came from large city firms, like those made by US lawyers only a few years before.

I soon decided that I could add nothing to the discussion with my senior colleagues and, making my apologies, left the meeting. Eventually, cooler heads prevailed, and the profession soon realised, as their US counterparts had done, that this new service would be complementing seriously underfunded services provided by state legal aid agencies, particularly in the family law area.

When I met Bamberger in 1972 he was a law school dean, having decided after his OEO role not to return to his earlier career as a partner in his Baltimore law firm, Piper & Marbury. I had a number of meetings with him discussing my experiences to date and he was kind enough to say that I had met the right people and acquired an excellent understanding of the history, purpose and achievements of the legal services programme.

According to Bamberger, those charged with establishing

the legal services programmes soon realised that, to make a real impact, the programmes needed to engage in "law reform", which meant establishing binding legal precedents through challenging administrative decisions by state and local officials who were refusing to protect the rights of workers and consumers. These challenges were soon being mounted in courts at both state and federal levels in order to achieve greater progress at lower cost than handling matters on a case by case basis.

This approach was possible through the engagement of a mix of bright young lawyers working at "the coal face" supported by experienced specialist lawyers from large firms volunteering their time and expertise. These were supplemented by legal academics who combined to win groundbreaking superior court orders requiring such agencies to provide the services and offer the protections they were set up to do by legislation.

Meeting Clinton Bamberger resulted in a long-term friendship with him and his wife Katharine, who took me under their wings with great generosity.

Meeting the US Solicitor General

Armed with my letter of introduction from Professor Julius Stone and organised prior to leaving Australia, I had called the office of the US Solicitor General, Dr Erwin Griswold, a former Harvard Law School Dean and a close friend of Professor Stone, to arrange a meeting. He seemed very happy to see me.

I was particularly keen to get Dr Griswold's view of the legal services programme as he was a well-placed official in the Nixon administration. Dr Griswold happily spent an hour and a half discussing these and related issues with me. He suggested that the administration's views of the OEO programme related to whether the expenditure was justified and that the programmes had become too political.

Other issues he mentioned as causing him concern was the increasing reliance on the courts by OEO lawyers and the subsequent heavy workload this imposed on the court system to obtain remedies which, in his view, could have been obtained by other means. He noted in passing that the use of the courts was in fact encouraged by several Supreme Court judges, particularly Justices Brennan and Black, which he did not seem to agree with. We also discussed the increasing use of class actions, and he gave me some briefs of cases he had argued in the Supreme Court seeking to limit the right to bring actions based on this novel concept of the courts recognising that an action on behalf of a large class of people affected by decisions mainly by government agencies.

When the Law Foundation established the Public Interest Advocacy Centre in the early 1980s, its initial director Peter Cashman successfully used class actions in US courts on behalf of many Australian women, who had suffered injuries through various forms of US developed contraceptive devices, to recover substantial damages on their behalf.

Meeting Dean Griswold was a definite highlight of my visit to Washington. It was a great opportunity to be able to spend so much time with one of America's leading lawyers, particularly as he had such an important role close to the Nixon administration.

Ultimately, the gods shone on the Legal Services Program following first Vice President Agnew's forced resignation and later Nixon's own resignation. These resignations slowed the defunding process and allowed a number of leading legislators in the Congress to save the programme via the establishment of the Legal Services Corporation in 1974 which still operates today. Its current budget is in excess of a billion US dollars, but, according to its website, the legal aid programme only meets around 50% of the need for legal services amongst the poor.

My agenda in Washington in 1972 included talking to various former directors of the Legal Services Program, who included several recently sacked directors of the Program, to get a better understanding of what they saw the Program having achieved and whether it would survive.

When planning my stay in Washington, I learned that two of these former directors were both in Harrisburg, the capital of Pennsylvania. One was the recently sacked director, Fred Speaker, a former Republican Attorney General for Pennsylvania, who was back working as a lobbyist in the state congress building. The other was Terry Lenzner, who was working as a part of the defence team representing the so-called Harrisburg Seven, the defendants in the latest high-profile trial of anti-war protesters being mounted by the Nixon administration.

The FBI and the Justice Department were prosecuting the defendants in a trial which had begun a week previously in the US District Court for the Middle District of Pennsylvania, located in Harrisburg. The defendants were accused of having conspired to blow up the heating tunnels of Washington and to kidnap Henry Kissinger.

Having read in the press that getting access to the courtroom was extremely difficult, with hundreds lining up each day to gain entry to the few seats available, I decided to raise the matter with Dr Griswold. He thought it was a good idea for me to try to attend it as an observer. He immediately wrote a short letter of introduction to the US Attorney for Harrisburg who was prosecuting the case and wished me luck.

A Front Row Seat at the Harrisburg Seven Trial

On a Tuesday in March 1972, a few days after meeting Dr Griswold, I drove from Washington to the State Capitol building in Harrisburg, Pennsylvania, which took me a little over two hours. My initial meeting was with recently sacked Fred Speaker and when I caught up with Fred he was in the extraordinarily large and gilded Pennsylvania Capitol building where he was supervising the passing of a piece of legislation for an oil company client. To me this was another unexpected experience, getting behind the scenes and being able to observe, not only the legislative process of a State Congress in operation, but also to see it in the context of the exercise of the power and reach of big business.

However, while waiting for the law to pass, we had time to discuss his experiences as director of the OEO Legal Services Program. Apparently, he had resigned, contrary to what I had been told, because he had been promoting the establishment of a separate statutory corporation to conduct the programme, but the administration had rejected the proposal.

Having seen Fred Speaker, I was keen to meet Terry Lenzner, another sacked former director of the Legal Services Program, who was a member of the Harrisburg Seven's legal team. Lenzner later achieved further fame as chief investigator employed by the Senate Committee appointed to investigate the Watergate conspiracy and was famously photographed by the press heading into the White House to deliver the committee's subpoenas requiring production of the tapes recording all President Nixon's meetings.

The Harrisburg Seven were an unlikely group of defendants who included three Catholic priests, one of whom, Father Philip Berrigan, was currently in gaol for earlier protest activities, a Catholic nun, Sister Elizabeth McAllister, a Pakistani born US academic Eqbal Ahmad, and a married couple Anthony and Mary Scoblick. Sometime later Berrigan and McAllister would leave religious life and marry and continue to be a thorn in the side of many subsequent national governments for many years through the Plowshares Movement. This was an anti-nuclear weapon and mostly Christian protest group. The name derives from the biblical direction attributed to Isaiah about giving up warlike ways and beating their swords into plowshares.

Meeting the Prosecution and Defence Teams

My next appointment later in the day was in the Federal Building where I was to meet John Cottone at the US Attorney's office. He was the assistant prosecutor for the trial and, in light of my introductory letter from the Solicitor General, he said that getting access to the court could be arranged and gave me directions as to how to gain access to the building the next morning, which had intense security with armed service personnel in each lift and on most corridors.

I was introduced to his colleague and chief prosecutor, William Lynch, and I explained my background and the purpose of my fellowship as well as my interest in sitting in on such a high-profile trial. Both seemed pleasant, well-educated and highly qualified American lawyers, but I came away with the impression that they thought that the behaviour of the religious defendants was inappropriate. As both were conservative Catholics, this trial seemed like a throwback to the 16th century tradition of the Church persecuting heretics, an assertion they would, of course, deny.

Later that evening I visited the defence team who, all being volunteers, were living in a terrace house in an older part of Harrisburg not far from the Capitol, which reminded me of inner Sydney suburbs like Chippendale or Erskineville. I must say that I was somewhat worried, in light of what I had learned about the FBI, that this place could have been under surveillance and I might lose my chance of attending the trial the next morning. I felt I had to take that risk.

The welcome I received from both the defence team and some of the defendants who were there that evening was well worth the risk. It was an extraordinary experience to be able, not only talk to Lenzner, but also to talk about the case with other defence counsel, including former US Attorney General Ramsay Clark, Leonard Boudin, a prominent New York civil liberties trial lawyer who also famously represented Daniel Ellsberg when he was prosecuted for leaking the Pentagon Papers, Father Cunningham, a Jesuit priest and lawyer, and prominent liberal New York trial lawyer Paul O'Dwyer.

I also had a discussion for some time with one of the defendants, Father Joe Wenderoth, about the liberalisation of the Catholic Church in America.

WASHINGTON: DOORS OPEN IN MIRACULOUS WAYS!

The next morning, when I returned to the Federal Court Building, the security measures were incredible. Outside the court there were armed officers and crowd restraint barriers holding back the hundreds of protesters and those queueing up to try to get access to the court. In the building foyer there were more uniformed federal police with everyone required to check in, show identity and the purpose of the visit and, in my case, my credentials provided by John Cottone.

I was then taken to a desk where I was given a pass. I was then escorted to the lift lobby and taken to the 10th floor where John Cottone had his office. As he had already headed to the court his assistant took me down in the lift and I was told that all the security and court personnel had some form of communication device so they could call the person who had manual control of lifts which did not respond automatically. On every level there were several armed officers.

The court building was new, and the courtroom was a large friendly room with a high ceiling and well furnished with green leather chairs for counsel at a large, elegant bar table designed in a classical style. It was immediately familiar to me, having seen many American films and television programmes featuring court hearings.

There were only a small number of members of the public who were able to get seating as half of the public seating was taken up by press reporters and court artists. One significant visitor that day was Philip Berrigan's brother, Father Daniel Berrigan, a Jesuit priest and academic and another long-term anti-war advocate who had only been released from prison the day before. He had completed his term arising from the protest he and Philip carried out in 1968 in Catonsville, Maryland. They had entered the Knight of Columbus Building and taken away draft cards and, in front of the press in the carpark adjacent to the building, they had poured napalm over them and set them on fire. Daniel was the first priest to be on the

FBI's "most wanted" list before eventually being caught and gaoled in 1969.

Daniel Berrigan was an intellectual and while serving his sentence for the Catonsville protest in Danbury prison, he wrote the play *The Trial of the Catonsville Nine*. He continued to be an activist for the rest of his life which ended in April 2016 at 95. During the latter part of his life he was arrested many more times for protests, this time against America's role in the arms race in the name of the Plowshares Movement established by his brother Philip.

I had a wonderful position in the courtroom being seated immediately behind the bar table used by the prosecutors. I was introduced to the others assisting Lynch and Cottone, including several FBI officers. My seat was in front of those observing the trial in the gallery and on a bench behind the bar table.

The defence team, whom I had met the night before, were seated at the other bar table. I felt especially privileged as I was able to move freely in recesses and talk to the lawyers on both teams during the breaks.

There were 12 jurors, nine of whom were women and included an elderly black lady. In addition, there were six standby jurors ready to replace an ill member of the panel.

The presiding Federal judge, Judge Herman, came into the court at 9.15 am very informally and before the jury were empanelled. O'Dwyer and Cunningham made submissions arguing for mistrial on the basis that the prosecution had not produced evidence a jury could convict on, while Boudin made a separate and very strong submission about evidence and material the FBI had not produced because of a claim of privilege. These submissions were all readily dismissed by the judge.

The trial had been running about three weeks at this point and, once the jury was brought in, Boudin recommenced his cross examination of Boyd Douglas, the prosecution's lead witness. This took most of the day with Boudin relentlessly exposing Douglas as a conman with a long history of fraud, whose alleged close association and contact with the defendants was of someone obviously trying to ingratiate himself with them. At one point, Boudin put the question to Douglas asking, was he not surprised when the defendant Ahmad – someone he hardly knew – was prepared at their first alleged meeting to share with him their plans about a proposed kidnapping of Kissinger.

He later put to Douglas that his claims of contact with several of the defendants were not possible because they were not in the places at the times he claimed. This produced considerable laughter from the public gallery which caused the judge to admonish it.

Boudin also produced records of Douglas receiving cash payments from the FBI and parole records from Wisconsin revealing his long criminal record. With Douglas's credibility as a witness seeming to have been demolished, having completed his task at 4.15 pm, Boudin handed the discredited witness back to William Lynch for re-examination.

Later published reports of the trial credited Boudin's demolition of Douglas as a turning point of the trial, which ended a week or so later with the jury being unable to reach agreement on a conviction, resulting in a hung jury. It was yet another failed high-profile prosecution by the Nixon administration, alleging conspiracy by anti-war protesters.

Catching Up With Private Sector Public Interest Lawyers

After my trip to Harrisburg, I had noteworthy meetings with young lawyers in large firms who were undertaking major public interest litigation. One, John Ferran, was the public interest partner with a leading firm, Hogan & Hartson, while another was Harry Huge, a partner at the establishment firm of Arnold & Porter.

John Ferran headed up a then recently established section of the firm aimed at providing advice and representation for community organisations largely as a public service to ensure that they could get quality assistance. Initially it undertook criminal appeals and civil liberties cases while, subsequently, the priority had become urban zoning representing local community groups challenging planning decisions to encourage public housing. They also assisted those lobbying for changes in the law on behalf of groups such as migrant farm workers, native American groups and organisations as well as tax and corporate work for community organisations. One matter they were then involved in was a high-profile school tax case.

The firm's commercial clients, while probably aware of this part of the firm's work, apparently realised that this work was in the public interest and being undertaken by a special group of lawyers in the firm. They were very conscious of the risk of conflict of interest and, as they had banking clients and major retailers, they did not undertake cases in the consumer credit area.

The services they provided to community organisations were not just representation in litigation but extended to assisting clients develop and prepare legislation and assisting them with getting such legislation passed and implemented.

According to its current website, Hogan & Hartson was the first US law firm to establish a separate practice group devoted exclusively to providing pro bono legal services.

Harry Huge, like John Ferran, spent his time at Arnold & Porter on public interest issues, with his main activity from the late 1960s being a class action against the trustees of the United Mine Workers of America Welfare and Retirement Fund, alleging maladministration of the fund by the alleged corrupt union management. The case was successful and a small part of the bigger struggle to oust the corrupt management. It was ultimately successful in recovering substantial damages of $11.5 million for the Retirement Fund. According to Harry, the backlash against the reformers triggered the murder of leading reformer Jock Yablonski, his wife and a daughter, in their home. Yablonski had stood for election against the corrupt leadership of long-term incumbent union president Tony Boyle.

Just a few weeks prior to my meeting with Harry, those responsible for killing the Yablonski family were convicted and later that year the union's election held in 1969 was cancelled by the US government and the Boyle leadership was beaten by the surviving members of the reform team in a new election. Eventually Boyle was convicted of the Yablonski murders. He successfully appealed, but on a re-trial he was again convicted and gaoled. Like many things in the US, there appear to be few halfway measures at any level.

Harry also told me of his association with Robert Coles, the eminent Harvard child psychiatrist/social commentator, who wrote *The Children in Crisis* series and *Uprooted Children* subtitled *The Early Life of Migrant Farm Workers*, based on his research on the health of children of poor families in the south. Prior to studying law, Harry had worked as a journalist and apparently was inspired by Coles to investigate the lives of children of migrant workers in Florida. As in California, they were not immigrants but an underclass of low paid workers. His special focus was on hunger amongst their children.

He carried out research undertaking a grassroots investigation and used his journalistic skills to publish his results which showed an enormous number of hungry people and children in the US. Harry told me that, following his revelations, the FBI went around interviewing many of the people who had spoken to Harry trying to get them to say it was not true. Tipped off to this, Harry then followed the FBI officers around, taped some of the interviews and then exposed the attempted cover-up.

He did so because he was horrified by the condition of the migrant workers' children, causing him to be widely denounced and labelled a publicity seeking "nut" by the Florida Governor at the time.

He responded by issuing a challenge for the authorities to select a bus load of such children at random and have them taken to hospital by a nurse selected by the Governor. The challenge was taken up and it was found that most suffered from at least one serious disease with many suffering from multiple conditions.

In both the work he did for the mine workers previously, and for the children of migrant workers, Harry, in my view, deserved a medal. The risk he faced from the murderous miners' union leadership and the risk of death he faced as a young northern activist coming to the South to expose abuses of minorities was enormous.

These cases were further examples of abuse of power, which seemed a common theme in this part of my Churchill Fellowship report, counterbalanced by the good done by lawyers such as John Ferran, Harry Huge and their colleagues, and those in the OEO legal services programme. Recent Black Lives Matter protests lead one to believe that little has changed for many of those stuck in the minority underclasses.

Introduction to the White House Fellows Program

Shortly after arriving in Washington, I made contact with Tom Carr, whom I had met on the flight to Chicago. He was pleased to hear from me and promptly arranged for me to meet the current director of the White House Fellows Program, Gene Dewey.

Founded in 1964 by President Lyndon B. Johnson, the White House Fellows Program is one America's most prestigious programmes for leadership and public service. White House Fellowships offer exceptional emerging leaders first-hand experience working at the highest levels of the federal government. Selected individuals typically spend a year working as a full-time, paid Fellow to senior White House Staff, Cabinet Secretaries, and other top-ranking government officials.

Gene organised for me to meet with a number of the current fellowship holders. These were Deanelle Reece, Martin Seneca, Henry Cisneros and Terry McCann, who were Special Assistants to the Secretaries of Labor, Housing and Urban Development, Health Education and Welfare, and the Attorney General, respectively. They were very interested in the idea of the Churchill Fellowship programme and in the selection process. However, they spent most of the time asking me about my experiences and observations gathered during travels across America and some were keen to meet up with me before I left Washington.

One of the Fellows I met, Deanelle Reece, later arranged a lunch in her boss's very impressive private dining room (one of her perks for being his special assistant according to Deanelle) for me to meet a number of her colleagues. Bill Goff, a young Australian journalist in the US on the exchange programme, whom I had met recently on a visit to the Congressional Recorder, was also invited.

Deanelle later had a successful legal career, followed by an appointment as a federal judge in California, and on her recent retirement was appointed a law school dean. Henry Cisneros, after later serving as the Mayor of San Antonio, Texas, was appointed Secretary of Housing and Urban Development by President Bill Clinton, while Martin Seneca was appointed in 1978 as Deputy Commissioner of Indian Affairs.

A notable White House Fellow in 1973 was Colin Powell, who in 2001 became US Secretary of State. President Johnson's goal of attracting young leaders outside the country's political elite seems to have proved successful.

The First Cracks in the Nixon Administration

I later caught up with White House Fellow Terry McCann several times as his boss, John Mitchell, had resigned as Nixon's Attorney General to head up the ill-named Committee for the Re-Election of the President (known as "CREEP"!), soon to be deeply implicated in the infamous Watergate break-in which ultimately led to President Nixon's resignation on 9 August 1974, a little over 18 months into his second term. For his role in the Watergate affair, Mitchell's fall from grace was completed in 1977 when he was sentenced to 19 months in gaol.

McCann's background was unlike most of the other fellowship holders I met as he was a little older than the others and was a highly decorated New York policeman who had served in a variety of frontline roles. At the time we met, he had no boss as Mitchell's deputy and nominated successor, Richard Kleindienst, was then the subject of Congressional approval hearings.

Kleindienst's appointment had been approved some weeks before I arrived. However, following the sensational release of a memorandum prepared by ITT lobbyist Dita Beard, Kleindienst requested that the approval process be re-opened so he could clear his name.

It was an interesting time to be in Washington. The coverage of the hearing, with a young Ted Kennedy being one of the Democrat senators on the committee, was fascinating. To see the committee exploring Kleindienst's knowledge of a criminal collusion between ITT and the White House, involving a very large donation to the Republican re-election campaign, was eye opening

Ultimately, in the absence of any provable wrongdoing on Kleindienst's part, the committee, by a majority, approved his appointment as Attorney General, not without some misgivings on the part of the Democrat members of the committee.

For me, being in the US at the time, it was an extraordinary opportunity to witness the pressure on Nixon gain momentum like a tsunami. It began while I was in Washington watching the first subterranean cracks appear in the Nixon administration with Dita Beard's role being exposed in a congressional hearing a few weeks earlier. This tsunami not only obliterated Nixon's Presidency and legacy, but also claimed all his closest advisers and allies, many of whom were later gaoled, a fate Nixon avoided.

During my visit to Washington in 1972, it seemed that Nixon's war on the OEO Legal services programme would succeed, with his announcement later in 1972 of the withdrawal of funds for all anti-poverty programmes, including OEO. At the time this move would bring an end to the Legal Services Program and seemed to confirm the fact that few governments will tolerate criticism levelled at its inadequacies, or at inequities caused by its policies, coming from bodies which depend on it for funds.

Fortunately, however, politics was on the side of the Legal Services Program as Nixon's announcement caused Congressional leaders to step in and legislate to create the Legal Services Corporation and negotiate continued funding. History was also on the side of the legal services programme as Spiro Agnew was forced to resign in October 1973 over tax fraud and bribery allegations. These events had occurred during his long career in state politics in Maryland where he was Governor before being appointed Nixon's vice-presidential running mate in the 1972 election.

Nixon's own resignation in August 1974 removed the major threat to the Legal Services Program, at least until the Ronald Reagan Presidency commenced in January 1981.

I have no doubt that, if Robert Kennedy had survived to be elected President in 1968 – instead of Richard Nixon – not only would the US have been far better served, but the Legal Service Program would have survived. It would have justified better funding which, in turn, would have meant that more significant victories in the War on Poverty would have been won.

This could well have resulted in a very different and better US which might have avoided the generations of Americans who since that time have been consigned to living in poverty. Probably a far less politically divisive country, than the one we have observed over the past 40 years, or so may also have emerged.

8

NEW YORK: POWER AND SOPHISTICATION

And so on to New York, the epitome of what was exciting about America to most Australians in the 1970s: Broadway Theatres, fabled hotels like the Waldorf Astoria, the Rockefeller Center, Carnegie Hall, the huge and tiny art museums, Central Park, Yellow Cabs, and yet a terrifyingly high murder rate and an epidemic of muggings.

Although jaded from a couple of months of travelling and the information overload, the buzz in New York was invigorating. I had two pieces of good fortune when I arrived in New York which helped me. The first was that having stayed at Chicago University's International House, it enabled me to make a booking at Columbia University's I H which meant I again had the benefit of affordable accommodation, meals, etc., while there.

The second was that in the background were the Treibers, long-standing central banking friends of my wife Pat's parents. Bill Treiber had a senior position in New York's Federal Reserve Bank and he and his wife Betty took me under their wings and on one weekend I stayed with them in their late 18th century weekender in the old town of Litchfield NY.

And this is before I was adopted and welcomed by leaders of the legal profession as well as frontline New York legal aid lawyers.

I soon learnt that I had to become more assertive while moving around downtown, particularly when, with so many people always around, as when trying to catch a cab or be served in a deli. I also soon adjusted to the place and by the time I was leaving, realised that it was a fascinating part of the world where I knew I could happily live for a while.

Another lasting impression was that life in Harlem for the black population was light years ahead of those living in the infamous South Side of Chicago. Perhaps it was New York's sophistication that it elevated even the poorest.

An Introduction to the Legal Aid Society of New York

Having arrived in New York, one of my first meetings was a fortuitous one. This was an appointment with Paul De Witt, the executive director of the Association of the Bars of the City of New York who mentioned that the Association was, an hour or so later, holding the annual meeting of the Legal Aid Society of New York. Paul suggested I stay for the meeting, and I could meet the main lawyer power brokers behind the funding of the Society which seemed to be a timely opportunity.

Paul told me about the Association's role and, because of my background with the Law Society's Associate Committee, we discussed what steps the Association took to engage young members with its activities. These activities included the operation and conduct of the Association sponsored legal aid service known as Community Law Offices (CAL) which was a very significant provider of legal services. Paul arranged for me to visit it and meet its director.

The Legal Aid Society meeting was interesting as the Society was a body established and controlled by the New York legal establishment and, after the formalities had been concluded, I was introduced to several Board members including long standing Board Chairman and former President of the ABA, Orison Marden. He was a senior partner in a major law firm and the doyen of New York legal aid. He was a major figure involved in expanding the services of the Society in the 1930s and, besides being a significant fund raiser for the Society, also promoted the concept of pro bono legal services as being a major professional responsibility of lawyers in private practice.

Following the meeting, I talked to Hank Healy, the Society's treasurer and Wall Street lawyer, who was interested in knowing more about what my impressions were of the legal services scene to date.

He took me to the Century Club, an establishment club for artists and lawyers during the latter part of the 19th century, not unlike the London clubs I was later to visit. It was a rather quaint atmosphere, very elegant and dominated by a rather non-traditional, very imposing recent portrait of retiring club president, Francis Plimpton, the founder of leading Wall Street firm Debevoise & Plimpton, the firm in which my host was a partner.

Plimpton, besides being a very eminent lawyer, also served as John Kennedy's Deputy US Representative to the United Nations for four years. He was also a somewhat controversial President of the Bar Association who broke with tradition and spoke out on political issues such as supporting protests against the Vietnam War. According to his *New York Times* obituary, when in an official meeting, he had tried to convince Pope Paul VI of the need for population control.

Dining in the rather old-world club dining room under his portrait was a unique New York experience. After dinner we withdrew to the drawing room for more drinks and this rather bizarre evening took another turn, when my host sat down at the grand piano and demonstrated his skill as a classical pianist. Somewhat later than I expected I caught a bus up Madison Avenue and on the way up to my 125th Street stop I saw the iconic Times Square for the first time.

A few days later I met with Orison Marden at his office who told me a lot about the history and politics of legal aid in New York. Only by talking to others later, did I really appreciate his personal and longstanding commitment to legal services. When I was leaving, he generously gave me a copy of Emery A. Brownell's landmark study entitled *Legal Aid in the United States*, which proved to be a very useful historical resource.

Another senior Board member was Leon Silverman, who also invited me to meet him in his office, where he gave me a personal briefing on his view of the Society's role and the friction caused by the OEO legal services funding policies. He talked of the Society being seen as insufficiently aggressive on behalf of their poor clients. This view led to the establishment of CAL, without the Legal Aid Society being given the opportunity to pitch for funding for a greatly expanded service.

Silverman's view of OEO funded programmes was that they were "on Cloud 9" and out of touch with reality. He told me that the Society had recently been appointed by the City's administration, with funding of $5 million, to provide a public defender service for indigent members of society facing criminal charges. Leon was a mercurial figure, yet one of the lucky ones of his generation. He was born into a poor Jewish immigrant family, raised by his seamstress mother and grandparents. From these humble beginnings, he progressed through the public school system, Brooklyn College, Yale Law School and, ultimately, the London School of Economics.

In 1949 Silverman joined the law firm now known as Fried, Frank, Harris, Shriver & Jacobson and later served as an Assistant Deputy US Attorney General. He was involved in desegregating the schools in Little Rock, Arkansas, after the *Brown v. Board of Education* ruling by the US Supreme Court in 1954.

Back in practice he became a highly successful commercial litigator and turned the firm around from being a rather staid establishment firm into a commercial powerhouse. He had a full, rich and long life and when writing this I was surprised to find that he only passed away in February 2015. My trip was enriched by meeting someone who had devoted considerable energy and skill in promoting equality through the courts.

Legal Aid in Harlem

My next visit was to the offices of the Legal Aid Society, historically the main provider of legal aid in New York. The Society had been in operation since 1876, having been established to assist German immigrants with legal issues. The society's activities were supported by charitable donations, funding from large law firms and a modest allocation from the OEO Legal Services Program. It operated through 27 branch offices staffed by approximately 400 lawyers with a support staff of 300.

Unlike other OEO funded programmes, its traditional role was providing legal aid to the city's poor, although it had an appellate division which provided back up to the branch offices and engaged in taking some matters on appeal to a higher court, as well as some legislative reform activities. Most of the work undertaken would fall into family law, criminal matters, welfare related matters, landlord and tenant and civil matters arising from consumer issues.

Its operation seemed to be very accessible, with initial contact often via a phone call. An appointment would be made and, on arrival, the clients were greeted by an administrative staffer who collected the information about their particular issues before they saw the lawyer assigned to them. The Society offered the lawyers employed there with interesting work, a reasonable salary and a long-term career with promotional opportunities. I was very impressed with the professionalism which was tempered by a relaxed non-intimidating approach to assisting clients.

A few days later I visited the Society's branch office in Harlem not far from where I was staying at Columbia's International House. There I met a very interesting lawyer Shyleur Barrick, a man in his early fifties who managed the branch made up of a team of 25, including 12 lawyers. The branch offices each had advisory boards which met monthly. The boards were made up of people with business, professional and welfare backgrounds who provided useful feedback on issues concerning the largely black local community.

According to Barrick, the branch office allowed for great flexibility of action. Each year about 10,000 people were assisted, all from the Harlem area, where 1.25 million were said to be welfare recipients.

According to Barrick, being in local neighbourhoods helped the branch office break down barriers. However, with a case load of 10,000 cases they were at the limit of their resources.

NEW YORK: POWER AND SOPHISTICATION

After our meeting he suggested we take a walk around his part of Harlem. I remember it looked a lot wealthier than Chicago's black areas and was relatively speaking a lot safer. It was quite an education. There was a new office building partly completed which the New York state administration had been building for five years. It made the time taken to build our then uncompleted Opera House look a little better. Apparently, it had got off to a really bad start when Governor Rockefeller threw the switch on the crane to make the first demolition blow. Unfortunately, he directed it wrongly and he wrecked a perfectly good apartment; red faces rampant. The people in the damaged building got the quickest re-location on record.

Prior to leaving New York I called Pat who told me that Ken Smithers, the Chairman of the Law Foundation, had called to confirm my consultancy with the Foundation and that a formal offer would be soon sent. This was great news as I was really champing at the bit to communicate what I had learnt during my fellowship and to have the opportunity to translate some of the findings into the Law Foundation's initial agenda.

In anticipation of my upcoming role with the Law Foundation, through newly established contacts in New York, I was able, at short notice, to arrange visits to the Russell Sage Foundation and the Ford Foundation, both of which were supporting initiatives in the legal access space and also funding research into various aspects of the legal system's operations. The time and materials given to me by the people I met at both organisations meant that in due course I had several more role models to guide the advice I would, in time, provide to the Law Foundation's Board.

The enthusiasm of the New Yorkers I was lucky enough to meet was truly infectious and I was immensely grateful for the generosity they showed me. However, it was now time to leave the US and head for Canada.

9

CANADIAN LEGAL AID: A BROAD ACCEPTANCE OF REFORM

And so to Canada. A competent legal aid system was already up and running there, so I would be looking at an established, mostly successful scheme. The lawyers were as enthusiastic as their US counterparts but without the background of political turmoil.

Having been aware that the Ontario government had been influenced by the approach to legal aid pioneered in the UK, I was keen to see how well those ideas translated to Canada, a similar society to Australia, not underpinned by welfare state policies as in the UK.

In Canada I would soon miss, however, the seeming unstoppable vibrancy of those lawyers in the US who were directly involved in the delivery of legal services and in the productive impact of improving the lives of large numbers of the country's poor. I would miss the fascinating coalitions that had been formed to keep legal services viable. These coalitions included those amongst members of the US Congress, Bar Associations, influential representatives of large law firms, as well as academics and law students.

On the other hand, after the considerable political turmoil surrounding the legal services programme in the US, it was somewhat of a relief to find that legal aid was more uniformly accepted in Canada by the late 1960s and had become a priority for both the federal and provincial governments. Unlike the situation in the US, by the time of my visit to Canada there appeared to have been a political consensus on the need to improve both civil legal aid and criminal legal aid.

I have no doubt that the willingness of the various Canadian governments to look at their own legal aid services was because of the proximity of what was taking place in the US including the recognition, in the latter part of the 1960s, among young Canadian lawyers that their own legal services needed major improvements, confirmation of which I found during my various meetings in Canada.

During my visit I found that, while legal aid was more uniformly accepted in Canada, there was a lack of uniformity within the provinces with each one developing its own system to suit the needs of their communities.

Ontario had opted for an improved version of the English system whereby the profession represents those unable to afford a lawyer with the legal fees being paid by the government.

Quebec had a scheme not unlike that provided by the Legal Aid Societies in Chicago and New York. It was established, managed and funded by the Montreal Bar with paid staff providing representation. It did receive some funding from the Quebec government, but its services were, at the time, mainly restricted to Montreal where the Legal Aid Bureau operated.

When I visited Montreal, the Quebec government was in the process of legislating for the first time to establish a government funded legal aid scheme with the Bureau continuing to have a major role. The legislation included provision for a neighbourhood law firm programme to be known as Community Legal Centres each with its own corporate management structure with strong local representation at board level. It was proposed that this would be closely modelled on the US Legal Services Program and was the result of lobbying by some young lawyers. Besides this legislation, the Quebec government was threatening to legislate to control the professions which the legal profession was very concerned about and was objecting to such interference.

I was unaware of this threat when I first arrived in Toronto. During my very first formal meeting in Canada, which was with Kenneth Jarvis, the Secretary of the Law Society of Upper Canada, the association of solicitors in Ontario, I was told about the history of the move to establish the Ontario Legal Aid Plan. He commented, rather colourfully, that those attacking the legal profession in Canada were being "supported by Communists".

Marxist Terrorists in Peaceful Canada! Who knew?

It later became clear that he was referring to the attacks on the professions by the Quebec government, with the reference to "Communists" being a reference to the then recent separatist crisis which had erupted some years before in Quebec. This crisis arose during the previous decade when a Marxist paramilitary group known as the Front de libération du Quebec emerged in 1963 and carried out numerous violent acts. They exploded 93 bombs and, in October 1970, the terrorists kidnapped a British diplomat and a Quebec Cabinet minister Pierre Laporte, the latter being subsequently murdered. This led Pierre Trudeau's national government to invoke martial law in Quebec which effectively crushed the Front.

Apparently, it was later established that the Marxist terrorists had Cuban and Russian support and were dedicated to making the province independent through terrorism and propaganda. The attacks were largely directed against English institutions and, clearly, when I visited it was still a matter of great concern in neighbouring Ontario. This crisis dominated politics in Canada for the next decade. I was somewhat surprised how violent the Quebec separatists had been and felt embarrassed that I had not appreciated the extent of the crisis Canada had to deal with over the previous 10 years.

One of the outcomes of all this was the patriation of the Canadian Constitution in 1982 which saw Pierre Trudeau's government negotiating with the UK government to legislate to transfer control of its constitution to the Canadian government. The history behind this move flowed from the Durham Report following the 1837-38 uprising in French speaking Quebec, which was brutally crushed by the British army. The 1840s report outlined a governance structure for the various provinces which today makes up modern Canada.

The changes which eventually occurred in 1867 were seen as a model for other British colonies.

Interesting to note, however, Australians of that era who were starting to press for independence quickly recognised that the Canadian governance structure was not one which met the needs of our colonists and wanted their own Constitution drawn up by Australians for Australians.

The next day I was back on my programme and met with the director of the Ontario Legal Aid Plan, Andrew Lawson, who briefed me on the plan's background. I was then taken to lunch by the senior management team, and I discovered that one of the team had just returned from the US where he apparently had followed me around and had heard a lot about me

The New Ontario Legal Aid Plan

I learned that, in March 1967, the Province of Ontario and the Law Society of Upper Canada established a legal aid scheme known as the Ontario Legal Aid Plan. The plan was to be financed by the Provincial government and administered by the Law Society and was intended to provide both civil and criminal legal aid. The Law Society was required to report annually to the Attorney General, who would then table their report in Parliament. Also, not unreasonably, the Attorney General had an Advisory Committee on Legal Aid which reported separately to the government on the functioning and operation of the Plan.

Under the new plan the legal profession was the work force. Lawyers in private law firms nominated whether they wished to participate in the plan. If they did, they could be placed on a civil or criminal panel or both and agreed to accept only 75% of their normal fees when acting for a person receiving legal aid.

The Duty Counsel system, which applied to criminal matters, was perhaps the most interesting feature of the Ontario Legal Aid Plan. The aim of the scheme was to advise all those in custody following arrest, who were unrepresented, as to their rights in relation to plea, bail and adjournment. The Duty Counsel also advised those who wished to plead not guilty how to apply for legal aid.

My last meeting was with staff at the legal aid plan's head office, and I learnt that the Attorney General's Advisory Committee on Legal Aid had recommended in 1971 that the Law Society should establish a community legal aid centre pilot project. This was intended to provide community counselling, to carry the law to the poor in their own environment and was likely to be a response to critics of the Ontario plan who were advocates of the US neighbourhood law office approach.

I came away from Ontario impressed with how well designed and funded their programme was and in my Churchill Fellowship report I suggested how Australian legal aid could be improved by including a number of the features of the Ontario Legal Aid Plan.

I later visited Ottawa to learn more about the federal government's role in providing legal aid which was under review and later in the year I learnt the federal government was to provide funding.

Canadian Postscript: A Fantastic Parting Gift

While my stay in Canada was limited in both time and geographically, visiting only Ontario, Quebec and Montreal, I admired the level of professionalism, particularly in Ontario, in respect to the provision of legal aid services.

One regret I had was that my visit to Canada was probably in the worst time of their weather cycle which the locals referred to as "the slush". It involved lingering piles of dirty muddy snow which periodically starts melting and then re-freezes with the next cold spell. It is particularly unattractive and dangerous, and it was nothing like the images of Ontario promoting it as a dream summer holiday destination in magazines such as *Popular Mechanics* which I loved reading at the local Burwood library after school.

My final stop over was to be in Montreal to follow up and learn what was happening with the application of computer technology to the legal information being undertaken by the University of Montreal.

This was a topic which some members of the Law Foundation Board of Governors raised with me prior to my departure and, while some interesting applications of computers were being experimented with in various legal services programmes to manage workflow in the US, nobody mentioned *full text retrieval* of case law or legislation.

On my flight to Montreal the plane was a "clapped out" 20 year old Vickers Viscount turboprop which had disappeared from Australian skies quite some years before. I was depressed during the flight, thinking I would never make it to Montreal, and bone weary after three months of constant travel in North America.

Everyone I met showed great interest in what I was doing, where had I been, whom did I meet, what did I learn, and what I thought of both, the experience, and of America. Each day was like giving evidence in court and then being cross-examined. These exchanges were almost always with lawyers, senior officials, academics, programme managers, researchers, Bar leaders, etc. – not an easy audience as many were experienced cross examiners!

A couple of years later I read Paul Theroux's *The Great Railway Bazaar*. I recognised a point in his story where one day he suddenly became tired of all the travelling, but also tired of the constant need to explain oneself in a similar way. This same tiredness occurred at a similar stage in my journey.

Fortuitously, on the flight to Montreal, I found that I was sitting next to a guy called Murray Wilker. Murray asked what I was doing and for the several hundredth time in the past couple of months I explained what I was doing and where I had been. He immediately responded by saying that he had spent the past six months talking to lawyers about computerised legal information retrieval. He worked for the Canadian Justice Ministry and this project was being carried out in conjunction with the Canadian Bar Association.

With some excitement, I immediately expressed interest in knowing more about his work and he offered to brief me on what the project found over a drink at the Montreal airport bar. Apparently, he was heading to New York but had to wait a couple of hours for the connecting flight. He then provided me with a fantastic "gift" by sharing the knowledge he had accumulated about the use of computer technology for the full text retrieval of legal information by searches of statute and case law databases. Murray's offer gave me a second unintended gift, a burst of energy just when I needed it.

Murray was different. He did not want to ask me questions but was keen to tell me about his own personal odyssey over the previous year or so. For the second time on my journey a chance meeting on a plane showed promise of being a transforming encounter. Meeting Tom Carr on the flight from Albuquerque to Chicago had helped open many doors in Washington and greatly enriched my time there. Similarly, Murray's enthusiasm was like a tonic, and he explained to me in considerable detail the objectives and methodology of the project, the report of which, *Operation Compulex*, was soon to be published.

At the end of our meeting, I realised that, for a few days at least, I was the second most informed person in the world about the current status of the complex area of computerised full text legal information retrieval. Murray was extremely generous with his time and expertise – even buying me a drink. He recognised that I was someone who had at least some understanding of the topic and that in my impending role I was likely to have the opportunity to use the knowledge he shared.

Briefly, Murray's project was aimed at identifying the needs of lawyers in order to optimise their information handling capabilities. It involved several parts. The first was a survey of law firms to find out more about these issues. Another was a review of the various types of information accessed or needed by lawyers. A further part was a review of various projects then underway both in Canada and elsewhere, where the solutions to the challenge of creating computer-based systems capable of making full text retrieval of legal information available were under development.

Later, after my return to Australia, I immediately took steps to obtain a copy of the *Operation Compulex* report as well as collecting the other reports recommended by Murray from projects being undertaken in the US, Canada and the UK as well as other publications devoted to this subject. Having these at my disposal put me in a position to contribute to the first steps being taken towards Australia having its own full text legal information system.

10

UK Legal Aid: A Uniquely Benevolent Concept

My visit to the UK was timely because British legal aid, part of the post war "welfare state", was under scrutiny. Unlike the US initiative, the Brits were not looking to save money but to get the scheme to reach more people who needed it.

This reflected on how differently both countries viewed their responsibilities to their poorer citizens. Apart from Roosevelt's New Deal in the 1930s and Johnson's War on Poverty, the US federal government typically left domestic issues and needs to the state, county and city administrations. The other two factors at play were the vast size of the US and the historical reliance on the private sector to provide solutions.

In the UK the inequities created by the industrial revolution, compounded by the impact on the British working class of two World Wars, soon forced the British Parliament to start addressing these inequities assisted by the growing political strength of the Labour Party which led to the introduction of the welfare state concept following the end of the Second World War

My arrival in London, compared to most of the many arrivals at airports over the previous few months, was unexpectedly grand. I was met by an official from the Reserve Bank's London office and his driver. I was then driven to Richmond, where I was to caretake a Reserve Bank apartment for seconded employees and their families. Fortunately for me, the secondment of the family to live in the bank's apartment on Richmond Hill was delayed for several months and the bank was happy for me to stay there while I was in London. This wonderful opportunity was thanks to my wife Pat's connections through her father, a recently retired Senior Advisor at the Reserve Bank of Australia.

My wife Pat and her family were in London for two years in the early 1960s while my father-in-law Jack was Manager of the Reserve Bank London. They lived in nearby Putney in a very nice 1930s complex of townhouses with beautifully laid out grounds – quite innovative for its time.

Later when I discovered the English writer Laurie Lee and read his delightful memoir, including *As I Walked Out One Midsummer Morning*, I realised that there was a reference to those townhouses. Lee notes that before heading off to travel through Spain in the mid-1930s as a 19-year-old country lad, he had worked as a builder's labourer in London. He tells how he worked on the townhouse development which clearly made an impression on him and describes walking up the hill to it from Putney Bridge tube station to get to the site. Literary connections continually bring me joy.

Adapting to English Ways!

However, I was soon to learn a lesson about Londoners and that was their typical English reserve was occasionally combined with a barely concealed sense of *"Oh damn, another bloody visiting colonial wanting to take up my time"*. It was very different from the reception I had been used to in both the US and Canada.

My education in the English way of doing things came when, having settled into my new accommodation, I called the office of the head of the Law Society's Legal Aid Scheme, Seton Pollock. Not only had I written to him several times, both before and during my trip, mentioning when I would be available to meet for a preliminary discussion of how best to proceed with my inquiries, but I had crossed paths in Chicago with his Society's President. When I was put through, I was greeted by: *"Oh you have arrived old chap, I was not expecting you so soon – how about we meet for a spot of lunch next Monday and we can then work out how best we can help you"*.

This took me back completely as it was then only Tuesday and all I could do in light of this response was to agree and, after he told me where to meet, the conversation ended.

I was stunned, being homesick and weary of travelling and talking, I nevertheless wanted to get on with finding out as much as possible about the highly regarded British legal aid scheme.

My feelings of deflation and depression lifted as I idly looked out the apartment's window and saw Richmond's stunning Terrace Gardens across the road with its beautiful, colourful flower beds leading down to the Thames. Also, in the distance on the other side of the river was Twickenham, the home of English Rugby, the spring growth on the trees in the Gardens not yet having appeared to block this wonderful view.

I immediately realised that there was much to see in the UK and the proximity of the Continent created possibilities for a tired researcher. I began to re-think my programme and decided to combine my work schedule with playing tourist on my free days – exploring the country and, as the English say, "going abroad".

In effect, I realised that with six weeks ahead of me there would be time to meet my fellowship obligations as well as expanding my horizons in the legal sphere and catching up with people I knew from home who were also in London. There would be ample time to undertake the programme the Law Society was likely to suggest on the basis that, like Canada, the British legal aid scheme was essentially uniform across the country.

Also, I had already accumulated a good knowledge, enhanced while in the US and Canada, of those involved in the establishment and management of the English Law Society scheme. I had also been given names of many of those in the independent legal centre movement and related pressure groups, including leading academics, foundations and those in the major political parties pushing for reform.

The next day I hit the phone making appointments with several key figures in the then current debate over the proposed reforms to the legal aid scheme. One was Professor Michael Zander from the London School of Economics while another was Susan Marsden-Smedley of the Nuffield Foundation and the Legal Action Group. I met with Susan for lunch the following day and she briefed me on the current reform proposals, gave me some material to read and recommended that I obtain copies of a number of recently published reports on the topic.

As her office was close by Lords Cricket Ground I wandered in and, finding a match underway, sat in the cold while watching English Test player John Edrich complete a century in a county game on this historic ground which I was surprised to find was built on a quite a slope. My diary records that the fielding side was hopeless with the game being played before a couple of dozen spectators.

An Invitation to Socialise with London's Young Lawyers

Later that week I was invited to attend a meeting of the Young Lawyers national committee at the Law Society's Hall in Chancery Lane. The meeting went for several hours and was reminiscent of the meetings of the NSW Law Society's Associate Committee. Followed by drinks in the Law Society's bar and later dinner at a local Italian restaurant, it was a very pleasant evening getting to know a number of young British contemporaries.

The Law Society, I was surprised to learn, besides being the administrative heart of the solicitors' profession and the national legal aid scheme, also operated as a city club for its solicitor members. It was in the heart of the legal precinct and its neighbours were the fabled Inns of Court where the members of the English Bar had their chambers.

Helpfully, the leading legal publishers were also located in this Chancery Lane area or nearby, as was Her Majesty's Stationary Office where you could buy copies of legislation as well as government reports. It was a treasure trove of legal publications and a place of fascination to a young lawyer from "the colonies"! I duly acquired copies of various reports, etc., dealing with the review of the legal aid system.

For my first weekend outing I travelled to Oxford with a law school friend I had met by chance. This trip had its highs and lows due to the heavy rain and the rental car getting a flat tyre. However, I did get to visit some of the famous Oxford colleges and to see the Bodleian Library.

While there was never a possibility that I could have studied at Oxford or Cambridge, I was always fascinated by stories of student life in these so traditionally English establishments. One in particular made an impression. It was written by Ross Campbell, a journalist and humourist with *The Bulletin* magazine and who, probably in the 1960s, wrote a long piece about his student days in Oxford as a Rhodes Scholar in the late 1930s. This was after *The Bulletin* magazine had thrown off its old-fashioned pink cover and large format, and become a modern news magazine which I then regularly read.

Back in London the weather was better, and I spent the Sunday with some kind Reserve Bank people who took me on a tour of historic gardens, such as Hampton Court Palace, where the flowers were all in full bloom, with their dazzling displays of colour. They were unlike any gardens I had ever seen growing up in Sydney. We then drove around Richmond Park before heading back into the city to visit Kensington Palace gardens which again were magnificent. I concluded that the English did "the history stuff" very well, which I later confirmed by visits to St Paul's Cathedral, Westminster Hall and the Tower of London.

Being Welcomed by the Law Society!

After my first weekend in England playing tourist, I finally got to meet with Seton Pollock, the head of the Legal Aid Scheme, at the Law Society's Hall in Chancery Lane. He was a tall balding man probably in his fifties, who was generous with his time, providing me with relevant materials and suggesting other publications which might assist me.

He also took me to lunch in "the club" dining room at the Society's Hall where we discussed the changes which the Law Society was keen to introduce, and which were then in draft legislative form. He was interested in what I had found in North America. However, he had been well briefed on the current situation in the US as Sir William Carter, the President of the Society, whom I had met when in Chicago, had obviously reported back on what he found in the US. Later in the day I had another meeting with Sir William and discussed our mutual experiences regarding the US legal aid scene.

After our pleasant lunch Pollock then introduced me to his deputy Gerald Dougherty who had outlined a suggested itinerary which involved meetings with a range of local area offices both in England and in Scotland. My itinerary involved heading up to Sheffield later in the week to spend a day at the Leeds Area Office, following which I would drive on to Newcastle to meet the manager and staff of that office.

Gerald gave me the names of key people I should meet both within the Law Society and also those who were active participants in the reform debate. He was easy to talk to and we diverted at one stage to a discussion of our respective Irish names. Apparently, his father was born in Ireland but having come to England to further his career had, according to Gerald, a lifelong fear of his children going back to Ireland.

Before I left for the day, I had been granted honorary membership of the Society, which apparently allowed the various officers I met with to talk to me quite openly about the operation of the legal aid scheme. I felt quite honoured!

My prior limited knowledge of this long-established government funded programme with legal aid provided by solicitors and barristers in private practice, with overall management being delegated to the Law Society of England and Wales, was quickly expanded. I learnt the catalyst for the inclusion of legal aid as part of the Britain's welfare state umbrella, was the large scale breakdown of marriages caused by the war which had given rise to major social problems and the very modest existing legal aid services were unable to cope with the demand for divorces.

What interested me was that the new British Labour Government's response was the polar opposite to the government funded legal services in the US, which were effectively limited to those living below the poverty line. They would never be likely to reach most of those struggling to exist just above the poverty line because of the vast numbers of very poor Americans.

The Origins of British Legal Aid

Also, of significance, was the tradition, almost as long as there has been a judicial system in Britain, of concessions enabling the poor to have access to the courts. The first recognisable form of legal assistance, namely, the status of *in forma pauperis*, was established by Statute in 1495.

This, plus the long-standing tradition amongst the legal profession of representing the just causes of the "little man", finally became embodied in a government funded legal aid scheme in Britain in 1950. From the turn of the 20th century, concurrent with the growing social revolution in Britain, the concept of organised legal aid had been finding increased acceptance amongst lawyers and politicians.

In 1944 the government responded by establishing the Rushcliffe Committee to report on legal aid and legal advice in England and Wales. In its report, the committee recommended a scheme whereby legal aid would be available in all courts for people of limited incomes, with the legal profession being mobilised to man the scheme but with the government being responsible for the cost. The profession was to receive adequate remuneration for the work done and the administration of the scheme was to be left to the Law Society.

In an article in the UK Law Society Gazette marking the 70th

anniversary of Rushcliffe Report, the number of people seeking divorces, coupled with a national shortage of solicitors and articled clerks, had created an 'almost intolerable burden' on the so-called Poor Persons Rules scheme. Under this scheme, lawyers on local panels were expected to give free help to clients owning less than £50. This pressure forced the government to act.

In accordance with the Lord Chancellor's request, the Law Society prepared and submitted a detailed scheme along the lines of the Rushcliffe Committee's recommendations so that legal services would be provided by the legal profession. This scheme was accepted and resulted in the *Legal Aid and Advice Act* being enacted in 1949 which was an historic first, formally extending the welfare state to include legal aid.

Because of the stringent economic conditions prevailing at the time, the various provisions of the Act were not immediately implemented but were staggered over a timetable which eventually lasted 20 years. It commenced in 1950 with the scheme beginning with civil legal aid in High Court matters, while the criminal provisions were introduced from 1952. By 1959 all the superior and County Courts were included in the scheme and on 2 March 1959 the legal advice sections were implemented.

These were followed by the claims provisions and some appeals to the House of Lords in 1960. A limited number of proceedings in Magistrates Courts and at Quarter Sessions were included in the scheme in 1961, with further legal aid coverage being extended in 1965 and 1969. In 1970 the last provisions which related to the Lands Tribunal were implemented.

Proposed Reforms of the Legal Aid Scheme

Unlike the destructive turmoil around the American OEO legal service programme, largely orchestrated by the Nixon administration and its allies, the political spotlight which was on the UK legal aid scheme when I arrived in London was far more benevolent. It had become widely recognised in the late 1960s that the scheme was not answering the needs of its initial target group, the British working class and those dependent on supplementary benefits.

In 1972 there were several forms of legal assistance available to those who qualified. One was legal advice, which could be obtained from a solicitor in their normal practice provided the customer could pay 2/6 (two shillings and sixpence, or approximately 25 cents in Australian currency at the time). The impracticality of this form of legal aid meant there was little interest in this facility by either the public or solicitors.

The most common form of legal aid the public wanted was for legal aid for proceedings, which was usually obtained when a person was involved in litigation. This involved an application by the solicitor nominated to conduct the action and obtain all such professional help as was required to pursue or defend the matter. This form of legal aid was available for County Court level proceedings all the way up to hearings before the House of Lords, which in 1972 was the ultimate appeals court.

To qualify for the issue of a certificate, the applicant's financial situation had to be assessed by the Supplementary Benefits Commission, as the government welfare agency was known in 1972. Not only did the Commission decide whether the applicant was eligible financially for legal aid, but it assessed their capacity to make a contribution towards their costs.

The requirement of such a financial contribution was one of the distinctive features of the English system of legal aid. It was adopted by the Ontario Legal Aid Plan and the later scheme conducted by the Law Society of NSW to provide legal aid for civil litigation.

Once the eligibility assessment was made, the Local Aid Committee, made up of volunteer local solicitors, decided whether there were reasonable grounds for taking or defending the action. If the decision was in the applicant's favour, the committee then had to assess what contribution should be payable in light of the projected cost of the action.

It is apparent from a close study of the various English legal journals that until the late 1960s it was assumed, by those concerned with legal aid, that the Scheme was effectively coping with the legal needs of the target section of the population. However, in its 1966/1967 official report, the Lord Chancellor's Advisory Committee on Legal Aid, the government body established to monitor the effectiveness of the scheme, initially voiced concern about the effectiveness of the scheme when it noted that:

> ... the financial limits of the advice scheme are too low, the solicitors giving legal advice were not paid enough, and the schemes give no encouragement to people to go to a solicitor to avert trouble; and the scheme has been mainly confined to helping people in actual litigation. This by-passed the traditional role of the solicitor, which has always been to keep his client out of trouble by timely advice and action to avoid litigation.

The Lord Chancellor's findings also stimulated a wide range of formal responses from various pressure groups including from lawyers associated with the main political parties with them both publishing reports in late 1968.

The Society of Labour Lawyers, in their report *Justice for All*, were concerned that the current cost of matrimonial cases meant that there was an unmet need for other types of civil problems. They also pointed out that remuneration for matters in County Courts was too low and discouraged lawyers from taking on such matters. They were also particularly concerned about the failure of the poor to consult solicitors. In their view, one of the reasons was that there were relatively few lawyers who worked in poor areas of British cities. Perhaps predictably, they saw benefit in the type of neighbourhood law offices through which the US Legal Services programme reached out to the poor.

Another valuable report entitled *Legal Aid as a Social Service* was published by the *Cobden Trust*, the research arm of the National Council on Civil Liberties. Michael Zander, an academic commentator, was another outspoken critic of the Law Society's administration who argued in favour of a neighbourhood law office programme modelled on the US Legal Services Program.

The Society of Conservative Lawyers produced *Rough Justice*, which argued against the introduction of a salaried legal aid service but acknowledged that the current scheme was not reaching those the scheme was intended to assist.

Modernising Legal Aid: The Twenty-five Pound Scheme

Following lengthy consideration of such informed views as these, the British Parliament in July 1972 passed the *Legal Advice and Assistance Act*, the purpose of which was to implement an additional form of legal aid which was commonly referred to at the time, as the "Twenty-five Pound Scheme". There had been considerable debate about the efficacy of this proposal when I visited the UK. At the time the amount was considered to be generous enough to encourage a wider range of solicitors to participate in the new service which was to be widely advertised and promoted. This new service was aimed at enabling someone requiring help from a lawyer to receive the appropriate form of assistance.

Concern continued to be expressed about other aspects of the Legal Aid Scheme, including the unavailability of legal aid before the abundance of administrative tribunals. These affected the rights of many, particularly those people dependent on the welfare state for housing and benefits. Similarly, the absence of it in Coroners' Courts and the inadequacy of it in Small Debts' Courts, gave rise to many complaints.

Hitting the Road!

However, having absorbed most of the competing proposals and arguments it was time to learn more about how the legal aid scheme operated and to visit some regional centres in accordance with Gerald Dougherty's itinerary. I left London on a Wednesday afternoon and was due in Sheffield on the Thursday morning. I decided that, rather than take a train, I would drive north and take advantage of the growing twilight to see some of the country when driving between my meetings in the north. So, I booked a small rental car, thanking Frank O'Grady as I did so, which turned out to be a new Escort, a pleasant surprise, and after collecting my bag in Richmond I headed out of the city eventually joining the A1.

The weather was fine and as I drove north to my destination in Sheffield, I could see a tall building in the distance and checking the map I discovered it was Lincoln Cathedral. When I arrived in Lincoln, I explored this lovely old town. Later in the afternoon I decided to visit the Cathedral and shortly after I stepped inside, the organ suddenly erupted and soon after a choir burst into song. This large building was transformed as the sound reverberated around its stone walls. I stayed sitting in the Cathedral for some time transfixed by the choir's beautiful singing of the various hymns/ It was a wonderfully fortuitous experience, reminding me how choirs singing hymns can stir the emotions.

In a letter home to Pat, I described the experience thus:

> It was in very good condition considering its age although some of the stone is crumbling in parts. One of the great essayists, perhaps Chesterton, when writing about the joys of walking through the English countryside, said that as he was walking along through Lincolnshire and suddenly over the rolling hills the spires of a high church appeared. It is exactly as you see it when you approach Lincoln – it appears just over the trees and it is high above the town on a hill.

After spending the night in a nice village outside Sheffield, I arrived the next day in Leeds at around 11.00 am and spent the rest of the day with the Deputy Area Manager, Jim Stead, and the staff of the Leeds Area Office, learning about the day-to-day operation of the scheme in a provincial area. I took copious notes as the briefing was very thorough and learnt a lot about the legal profession in the various York ridings and their distribution.

I was surprised by the relatively small number of solicitors and barristers, with 29 and eight respectively in a city such as Leeds, the urban area of which in 1972 had a population just under 1.7 million. This confirmed the claims I had heard from critics of the legal aid scheme. With so few solicitors available to service such a large urban area, the economy of which was then suffering due to the slowing down of manufacturing industries, the people who needed legal aid were not getting it.

After leaving Leeds I decided to detour to visit historic York which appeared to be smaller with a population of around 150,000 when I visited. Nevertheless, I soon found my way to the mediaeval part of the town and was pleased by my decision as I noted in a letter to Pat:

> The Minster is being restored at great cost. I was not as impressed as I was with Lincoln ... The town, however, is more interesting with fascinating little streets such as the Shambles with many original Elizabethan buildings swaying all over the place. They slope at the most incredible angles.

On leaving York I drove across the misty moors towards the coast and soon reached Scarborough, the largest holiday resort on the Yorkshire coast. It was an interesting place with a fascinating array of large Victorian buildings dominated by large 19th century hotels lining the cliffs above the beaches separated by a large headland with the ruins of the 12th century Scarborough Castle. I loved that there was a cute little harbour full of colourful fishing boats and fun parlours.

The gardens and public spaces were in impeccable condition. This neatness had impressed me since arriving in England and contrasted with what I had seen in the US. I thought it was a great place and was my first introduction to a famous Victorian holiday town. Such holiday towns arose due to the growing affluence flowing from Britain's industrial revolution with much wealth being created in the relatively close by industrial towns of the midlands.

As I wanted to only have a short drive to Newcastle the next morning for my meeting with the local legal aid area office, I decided to head for Whitby where I had planned to stay the night. However, there was still plenty of twilight left and my next stop was the picturesque Robin Hood's Bay, which I had heard about from Pat and her parents, who said it was a "must see"! It is a small village built in a fissure between two cliffs and somehow over the centuries small sandstone houses and pubs were built seemingly on top of each other in little streets and lanes which wend their way to a small beach and a protected port.

Again, I reluctantly left his extraordinary place and drove on to Whitby, finding a room at the old Royal Hotel above its small harbour. This was where Captain Cook came from and where he learned his shipping skills on colliers that carried coal to other parts of Britain. These colliers did the same job as the steam driven colliers I had seen during my early life in Cabarita also bringing coal from "our" Newcastle.

Newcastle: Test Bed for TV Promoting Legal Aid

I had several reasons for visiting Newcastle, one was that it was highly recommended by the Law Society because it was a busy area for legal aid. A further reason was that it was the centre for the first attempt anywhere to promote legal aid by combining television advertising with newspaper advertisements with coupons. These were supplemented with pamphlets and specially designed stickers to be placed on the windows of high street solicitors' offices.

It was apparent from my visit to the Newcastle legal aid local area office that there was a lot of enthusiasm in the office due to its key role in the Law Society's new initiative. The commercial was shown at 'prime' viewing time on Tyne-Tees television and appeared 19 times over a four-week period.

I was also able to follow up on a range of practical issues associated with the provision and management of the services. I learnt of its coordination with the local office of the Supplementary Benefits Commission which assessed the applicant's eligibility.

Over lunch with the Area Manager, I told him of my plan to spend the weekend travelling west to the Lakes District and he urged me to travel along the ancient Military Road which ran parallel to Hadrian's Wall. He told me it started not far from Newcastle. I am so glad I followed the advice of a local because it became another highlight of my trip. I was able to visit Roman ruins and museums and eventually went for quite a long walk along the Wall reaching a fort with a hundred feet drop on the northern side. The weather was closing in and I soon found myself in rain and fog. I thought how unpleasant it must have been for those manning the Wall almost 2,000 years earlier.

The next day I headed west to the far coast of Wales before finally on the Sunday driving back to London. As I was about to drive off, looking at the map and trying to decide which would be the more interesting route back to London when an elderly man stopped and asked me if I needed any help. I explained what I was planning to do, and he offered some local knowledge which solved my problem. Noting my accent, he said that he was very unhappy about what the government was doing to stop Australians coming to the UK, as the government was then planning to join the European Union. He then offered a personal apology in light of all the help we Australians gave the British during the War. The genuineness of his sentiments was really very poignant.

In the UK so much is packed into a comparatively small island. With a modern road system, it was a relatively easy journey with the odd detour to take in places like the Cotswolds made even easier by the advice I had received.

On my return to London, my first appointment was with the venerable Sir Thomas Lund, former secretary of the Law Society. In this role he was heavily involved in establishing the new legal aid programme in the post war years. When I met him, he had retired from the Law Society and had roles with the International Bar Association and an international organisation seeking to promote legal aid.

After a discussion in his office, he suggested we have lunch and took me to his club, The Athenaeum. He told me that the membership of the club in its early days was made up mainly of writers and bishops. Its magnificent library contained many historic first editions as writer members were expected to donate copies of all their publications.

My recollection is that initially we had a pre-lunch drink in the bar before ascending by the most extraordinary lift I had seen since my days working for Burns Philp. This lift was quite small and barely one per person wide but about two metres long. My host explained that it was used to bring deceased members' coffins down from the upper floors where members could stay and over the years many an old bishop had passed away. I am still not sure if my host was joking!

After a pleasant lunch during which I told my host about my North American adventures, we retired to the library for a port or two! Meeting Sir Thomas and my visit to The Athenaeum was another memorable highlight of my visit to London.

Management and Provision of Legal Aid

Back in London I met with the Area Director for West London, Alistair Panton. I spent several days there getting to understand how the legal aid scheme was managed. I was thoroughly briefed on the procedures and also had the opportunity to observe the processes gone through by the Local Area Committee made up of experienced solicitors.

The committee members were volunteers and usually experienced litigation lawyers nominated by their local Law Societies. This office had a full roster of 100 solicitors and 20 barristers who each attended once every six weeks. The quorum for a committee meeting was three and having a barrister was a requirement. One of the meetings I attended processed 62 applications. Some of the meetings were convened to review appeals from the refusal by a committee to make a grant and these were dealt with once a week on Tuesdays.

Before a formal grant was made the applicant's financial and asset circumstances, as noted elsewhere, needed to be assessed by the Supplementary Benefits Commission, a somewhat complex process which was explained to me.

The Subtle Differences of Scottish Legal Aid

The next visit Gerald Dougherty had arranged for me was to go to Scotland to see how the legal aid system operated there, taking into account its unique continental style Civil Law legal system established long before the union with England. It is referred to as a hybrid legal system.

I decided to start and finish my visit in Edinburgh and to use the weekend to drive from Edinburgh and traverse the Scottish Highlands, visiting the odd loch, such as Loch Awe. This trip also coincided with spring arriving and new leaves and flowers were in abundance. I also managed, after a day being briefed on the operation of Scottish legal aid in Glasgow, to play a round of golf at the end of the day in the long twilight with a kind fellow lawyer from the legal aid office.

The next morning, I spent an hour or so driving back to Edinburgh where I spent a long day visiting the Scottish courts and learning how the Duty Solicitor Scheme operated. This was a unique feature of the Scottish system and historically not offered as part of the English legal aid system. I was so impressed with the scheme, having seen the cost effective good it offered there and in Ontario, where a similar scheme operated, that I included its adoption as one of the major recommendations in my Churchill Fellowship report. It was later very pleasing to see a duty solicitor programme introduced into NSW Local Courts as part of the upgrade of the NSW legal aid scheme which came following the election of the Wran government in NSW.

I liked the Scots I met very much. Their easy manner, sense of humour and pragmatism were refreshing and like a tonic to a weary traveller. I wondered if those traits were contributions by Scottish settlers to the Australian ethos.

During my time in London, while I had the privilege of being looked after by the people at the Reserve Bank who were happy to invite me for the odd meal, I also made contact with a number of other Australians. Amongst these were Michael Sexton, who was in London in his then role as associate to High Court justice, Sir Edward McTiernan, who was sitting as member of the Judicial Committee of the Privy Council hearing appeals from various Commonwealth countries. This connection enabled me to spend some time sitting in on an appeal case being heard by this august body.

This anachronistic and very expensive process was finally brought to an end by the *Australia Acts* initiated by the Hawke government, with similar acts passed by the Australian and British Parliaments in 1986 abolishing the right to appeal from an Australian state court decision to a British court.

Weekend Visits to the Continent

While in Britain Pat was keen for me to spend a weekend with a French friend from university, Jacqueline, who had returned to France on finishing her degree. So having returned from Scotland I caught the boat train to France and on arrival in Paris I was met by Jacqui and we were later joined by her lawyer husband, Jean. We then drove to Crespiers, the village where they lived some 20 miles out of Paris. They were very welcoming and I had a great weekend with so much to see in Paris, while thinking I would probably never get back to France again. It was also my first introduction to Citroens and eventually, after many years, I acquired my own much loved C5 wagon.

Back in London, another unexpected highlight was to be invited to a cocktail party being hosted by the then NSW Agent General. The role was an historic hangover from the colonial era and came to an end in 1992. At the time I was there, it was still an important and prestigious role. The hosts were Sir Jock and Lady Pagan, and the party was a regular event to which those on official visits to London were invited. Fortunately for me, the Attorney General Mr McCaw had kindly notified the Agent General's staff that I would be visiting London.

The event was held in the Pagans' home which was one of those classic white colonnaded Georgian row houses in the West End. My arrival was duly announced loudly by the butler. This took me by surprise and, much to my embarrassment, everyone turned around to see who was being introduced. However, with my first glass of bubbles consumed, I relaxed and had a most delightful evening meeting the other guests who included Sir Kenneth Manning, a former senior NSW judge and at the time Chairman of the NSW Law Reform Commission, who invited me to meet with him before I left for home.

I also met the Pagans' children, in their late teens and early twenties, who were very welcoming. Later I was introduced to Australian racing royalty, Tommy Smith and his wife and their young daughter Gai, whose own career has almost eclipsed her father's.

On a later weekend, Michael Sexton and I visited a brother of a Sydney friend who lived in Utrecht, staying with his family which gave us a brief taste of Dutch life, and they were kind enough to lend us their small DAF sedan, a vehicle unique to Holland which had no gear box but operated with a simple lever which you moved to go either forward or backwards. Its simplicity could only work in a country as flat at Holland, but it did allow us to explore the local area and also to visit Amsterdam. Later, on the last day of our short visit, we went on an excursion to Rotterdam before flying back to London.

After doing further study in the US, Michael's career ultimately led to the Bar and in due course he was appointed the NSW Solicitor General. He has also become a successful writer responsible for a number of well received books.

My last few weeks in the UK passed very quickly but I managed to spend productive time having meetings with a range of senior Law Society officials. One of these was John Warren. He was responsible for implementing the Ormrod Committee's recommendations regarding providing practical legal training for the growing number of law graduates. This was at a time when the traditional system of articled clerks was a failing to meet the demand and was also a major concern back in NSW.

Some New Legal Centres

Towards the end of my stay in the UK I also visited several local law centres, one being the recently opened Fulham Road Legal Advice Centre in Fulham which had opened a few months earlier in March 1972. It was operated with six volunteer lawyers attending two nights a week and was primarily an advice and referral centre operating from a shop front and funded by a council grant. The legal problems were largely (90%) a mix of family law and landlord and tenant issues. It was an interesting experiment and was to become one of a large number of similar legal advice and referral centres.

I also met on a number of occasions with Simon Hillyard, a young lawyer with the Society, who had an experimental role which involved him liaising with social agencies operating in Brixton, then a poor part of London, attempting to ensure that they were aware of how the legal aid scheme could be used more effectively – an interesting "bottom up" approach.

I later visited the North Kensington Neighbourhood Law Centre with Simon. It was then the only Centre of its type and, founded by local lawyer Peter Kandler, had been operating since July 1970. When I met with him, he explained that centre was started with financial support from a group of Labour lawyers following a conference at Oxford in 1968.

The Centre opened with the permission of the Law Society and, similar to what happened when the Redfern legal advice centre opened, it was given permission to advertise the service. The Centre also received favourable coverage in the Law Society's Gazette and from local community organisations.

Another important meeting was with Gerald Sanctuary, the Law Society's secretary responsible for public relations and architect of the Legal Plan's Tyne-Tees TV advertising strategy. A year or so later, Gerald visited Australia at the invitation of the Foundation as, amongst his responsibilities, was developing legal studies teaching resources for a programme he had initiated with secondary schools. His advocacy for such a programme as helping young people to get a better understanding of the role of law in society impressed the Board of the Foundation and led directly to the establishment of the Foundation's highly successful High School Education Law Project.

The last few days were spent having final meetings, including one with Seton Pollock, the head of the English Legal Aid Scheme. He was keen to learn from me what I had found and seemed genuinely keen to get my impressions about their scheme. He was also keen to find out the views of the wide range of experts and commentators I had met with.

Time to Go Home.

While trying to make the most of my last few days in England, a momentous event was taking place in Sydney with my pregnant wife Pat having been admitted to Mater Hospital because of health concerns. However, I later learned that my younger brother, Denis, then a policeman, played surrogate father and spent many hours keeping Pat company while entertaining the staff and other patients with his endless stories. Finally, my very proud father-in-law, Jack, called me to tell me that Pat had given birth to John safely and both were well.

The final social highlight of my visit to England before heading for home the next day to see Pat and to meet my son John, was the privilege of attending the historic Trooping of the Colour. I had a prime seat at the historic event held in Horse Guards Parade to mark the official birthday of the sovereign in early June.

This opportunity came via my friend Michael Sexton who had

received a ticket to the event but, having other plans for the weekend, he passed his ticket onto me – another lucky break.

The event that year was particularly special in that it was also in part a memorial service for the Duke of Windsor who had died earlier in the year and a special musical lament was played during the Queen's inspection. It was quite moving, with the military and the Queen all wearing black arm bands.

So, my odyssey lasting four months came to an end on a particularly Royal note. I was now heading home to pick up the reins as a husband and father and to take the first tentative steps towards a possible new career path via the Law Foundation.

I returned home in time to call into the Mater Hospital where Pat and John, our third child and first son, were waiting for me to take them home and to catch up with lots of cuddles from Anne and Jane. John, to this day, regularly reminds me of my absence at the birth of my first son!

However, settling back into a "normal" routine was a challenge, having regard to the extraordinary events and people I had been exposed to, or encountered, on a daily basis during the previous four months. It had been a very tense time to be in the US, with its people torn apart by the Vietnam War as well as the increasing impact of Nixon's war on the Office of Economic Opportunity's legal services programme.

On reflection, after leaving North America, I had moved into much calmer waters, almost like a different era. The people I met with in the UK were calm, measured, orderly and yet very determined to ensure that their citizens had access to legal services which was accepted as a part of good governance.

But if I am honest, by comparison to the Americans I had met and dealt with, and who were part of a genuine legal revolution, the contrast could not have been greater. Fortunately for the citizens of Canada and the UK, no major legal services revolution was needed but only some fine tuning.

Nevertheless, both experiences emphasised what a political and international backwater I had returned to. Ordinary Australians faced a lack of access to legal aid services and legal rights. This access and those rights enjoyed by citizens in the US, Canada and the UK were not even on the political radar as far as I could tell. But the radar was ramping up as we were headed to a federal election later in the year with a Labor Party under Gough Whitlam's leadership promising change and national revitalisation on their agenda.

11

THE LAW FOUNDATION AND ME

In November 1972 the Foundation Board met to consider my plans for implementing the Foundation's charter which I had developed during my consultancy for them after my return from my Churchill Fellowship. The Board not only readily adopted the initiatives I had recommended, but also appointed me as the Foundation's first Executive Director.

Looking back at this, for me, momentous meeting, the outcome seemed to flow from a strong dose of serendipity and the willingness of the Board to take a punt on a young solicitor brimming with ideas acquired during his travels.

The Lead Up to the Law Foundation?

The Law Foundation of New South Wales was another early legislative initiative of the relatively new Askin government and was established by the *Legal Practitioners (Amendment) Act* passed in March 1967. The cornerstone of the legislation was the creation of a Statutory Interest Account, a new statutory process whereby the funds held in solicitors' trust accounts would be used to generate income for broadly beneficial purposes.

Solicitors' trust accounts were used to hold clients' money, such as proceeds of sale of property, deposits held by the solicitor pending completion of a sale of a property, or court awarded damages. In banking terms such accounts were classified as trading bank accounts which did not pay interest. The banks had the money effectively for free and this new statutory mechanism was a way for some income to be earned on those accounts not for the benefit of the solicitors who owned the accounts but for public purposes. While much of the English legal system was followed in Australia, the English tradition whereby solicitors received interest earned on such trust accounts was not.

The need for this rather radical initiative was largely driven by concerns within the NSW Law Society and its solicitor members about the need to properly fund a new Solicitors' Fidelity Guarantee Fund. Such a fund was needed to compensate clients who lost funds stolen from solicitors' trust accounts.

The second proposed beneficiary of the new income stream established by the legislation was the Law Foundation. It was a statutory fund established to foster legal education, legal research, law reform and the establishment, operation and maintenance of law libraries.

Additionally, the Attorney General saw the need to extend legal aid to those who did not qualify for legal aid for civil actions and so enable them to have legal representation in such cases.

The new Act imposed an obligation on solicitors to deposit a small proportion of the funds held for clients in their trust accounts into this new statutory account to be managed by the Law Society. The funds deposited were to be invested and the income earned would go towards funding the above initiatives.

This innovative funding mechanism had been pioneered by the Victorian government and the Law Institute of Victoria in 1964 for the sole purpose of establishing a fidelity fund, although it was later extended to support legal aid and to create a law foundation.

In NSW, this initiative had been first proposed by former President of the Law Society, Barry McDonald, and had caused considerable division amongst solicitors. This resulted in one of the largest ever gatherings of solicitors when 700 attended a meeting to consider the proposals. It was held in the Sydney Town Hall on 18 February 1965.

Those vigorously opposing the proposals included solicitors representing the banks, which hated the idea of being required to pay interest on solicitors' trading bank accounts. The banks' lawyers prevailed on the day and the proposal was defeated by a narrow margin on a show of hands. This led to a poll of members being called for and the meeting was adjourned until 11 March 1965 to enable the poll to be held. However, when the poll was eventually held it was inconclusive and the matter was referred to the Council of the Society for further consideration.

According to the Society's 1965 Annual Report:

> ... the Council with great care and deep consideration examined every aspect of the question and by a large majority resolved to re-submit the proposals to members of the Society in a modified form.

The new proposal required a lesser amount to be deposited by solicitors into the proposed Statutory Interest Account, with the income in turn being required to be used to establish the new Solicitors' Fidelity Guarantee Fund with a capital of $500,000 which would be used for the purpose of paying higher amounts to clients whose funds had been misappropriated by their solicitors.

The second object was to fund the establishment of a Law Society Foundation Fund with a capital of $500,000 which would only be funded once the Fidelity Fund's capital target had been met, and its purposes were recorded as being funding for legal education, legal research, law reform and law libraries.

In the further poll of members following the Society's Annual General Meeting, the members narrowly authorised the Society's Council to formally request the Attorney General to initiate legislation to give formal legal authority to use clients' funds in this way. It was reported in the editorial of the March 1966 edition of the *Law Society Journal* that McCaw was disappointed that the proposal did not include funding for the provision of legal aid as well.

By the time the Bill proposing the amendments to the *Legal Practitioners Act* was tabled in Parliament on 15 March 1967, Attorney General McCaw had got his way and a third recipient of the funding had been included. It was the proposed new legal aid scheme to be conducted by the Law Society. This much needed initiative was intended to complement the existing services of the Public Solicitor's Office established by the McKell Labor government in 1941.

The new legal aid scheme was modelled on the British legal aid model and was to provide funding for civil litigation by members of the community who normally could not afford to sue for breach of contract or damages for injury or loss suffered because of the actions of others. The scheme was later absorbed into the new Legal Services Commission along with the Public Solicitor's Office by the Wran government in 1979.

In response to the introduction of this legislation the shadow Justice Minister, Jack Mannix, while supporting the creation of the Statutory Interest Account, was reported in Hansard in relation to the proposal to establish the Law Foundation as presciently saying:

> The Opposition supports in principle the establishment of the Law Foundation. Those of us in the legal profession and, indeed, people in any other profession appreciate the valuable work that a foundation can do in the interests of the public, centred on certain aims and objectives that the foundation can set itself in the field of research, law reform, and scholarships for persons pursuing their law studies.
>
> One could probably think of a long list of items of valuable work that could be done by the Law Foundation. The legal profession would no doubt say that it is running last in this field. Scientists, engineers, medical practitioners, dentists, and others have, quite rightly, had so much public money applied through the universities and various institutes and foundations to first-class research in their professions that one can well appreciate the tremendous field that can be covered by a similar foundation in the legal profession.

The legislation was largely adopted as proposed with the support of the Opposition and the Law Society quickly created the Statutory Interest Account and the Fidelity Guarantee Fund.

The members of the new Foundation's Board were a distinguished group: Kenneth Smithers CBE (Chairman), the Hon K M

McCaw MLA, QC, (Attorney General), J K Bowen CBE, N R McDowell, J R Broadbent CBE, Bishop F O Hulme-Moir and Dr John Ellard. The Attorney General was an ex officio member, while Bishop Hulme-Moir and Dr Ellard occupied positions for non-lawyers, as the legislation required, and were appointed respectively by the Attorney General and the Minister for Justice. The four other members were appointed by the Council of the Law Society which also nominated one of its members as Chairman.

Working with the Board

For its part, the Board was taking a very large "punt" on someone brought to their notice by my fellowship award about whom they knew very little other than me being something of an innovator but whose legal pedigree and academic qualifications were modest at best.

However, I was very fortunate, as was the Foundation itself, in having former Law Society President, Ken Smithers CBE, as the initial Chairman of the Board. Besides being very bright and politically astute, he was a very able mentor and, in time, a good friend to me. Fortunately, a similar role was played by the very eminent psychiatrist Dr John Ellard, a lay member nominated by his friend the Minister for Justice, John Maddison. Soon after my appointment, Ken Smithers was appointed to be the first NSW Ombudsman, but thankfully neither the Attorney General nor the Minister for Justice saw any reason for Ken not to continue as Chairman of the Foundation.

I cannot overstate the importance of the influence those two had on me and on the Foundation in its early years, with Ken being Chairman until the Foundation was separately incorporated by legislation in 1979 during the tenure of Attorney General Frank Walker. John Ellard was appointed the newly independent Foundation's first Chairman. During my first 10 years at the Foundation, John was a constant source of good advice and he and Ken both protected the early Foundation from changes in the Law Society's leadership and its periodic negative attitudes to the way the Foundation applied its funding.

The other person, who would play a significant part in the Foundation being made independent of the Law Society by removing its control of the Board and the annual allocation of funds, was Trevor Haines of the Attorney General's Department. From the very earliest days of the Foundation, Trevor saw its long-term potential and the need for it to be free from control by the Law Society. The Law Foundation's significant contributions to reform of the law and the legal system, as well as its focus on increasing the community's access to legal information and legal services, was a direct result of the visionary approach of these three leaders whose view of the Foundation was later strongly endorsed by Terry Sheahan when he became Attorney General.

However, had I not had the experience of visiting the US in 1972 via my Churchill Fellowship, I would not have had the capacity to help mould the Foundation into the body, which, in the ensuing 20 years or so, became such a significant contributor to Australia's golden era of reform.

In early July 1972 it was time to undertake the responsibilities allocated to me by the Board of the Law Foundation. I soon learned of the Law Society's plans to replace articles of clerkship with a six month full-time Practical Legal Training programme for all law graduates or their equivalents to be offered by a new institution, the College of Law. This path had been pioneered by the Law Society of Upper Canada in Ontario. Norman McDowell, who had stepped down from the Law Society Council, was now the first director of the College of Law and charged with its establishment.

The profession's leadership had recognised that the traditional method of providing practical skills training, namely articles of clerkship inherited from the English legal profession along with the British legal system, was inadequate and an unnecessary barrier to the many baby boomers flooding into law schools who wanted to join the legal profession.

I also learned that the Law Society saw the Foundation as the conduit for funding the establishment of the College of Law. These decisions, though welcome, meant that as the Law Society largely controlled the Statutory Interest Account, the Law Foundation's Board was expected to "rubber stamp" the establishment of the College as a priority. I quickly realised that it might be years before funding would be available for the Foundation's own projects.

Nevertheless, I was keen to formulate an operational strategy which would provide a basis for the Foundation's Board to carve out a role which would not compete with existing legal agencies. For the most part these agencies had very limited capacity to undertake reform or innovation. I was keen to map out a plan which would see the Foundation undertaking activities which would complement and support their various roles and commence the process of implementing the Foundation's statutory objectives. I also attended Board meetings, prepared the minutes and generally acted as the Foundation's administrator.

From time to time, I assisted Norman McDowell with some of the conundrums he faced in not only mapping out the new College's curriculum, but also in finding a suitable site from which to operate the new College. The rest of my time was spent reviewing both my written accounts of my meetings while on my fellowship, and the extensive amount of source material I had collected and been sent back home for me. This in turn was a vital part of the process of completing my report for the Churchill Fellowship Trust which I hoped would allow a wide audience of policy makers and academics to have a better understanding of the reforms needed to improve the community's access to the law and legal services.

The two tasks of proposing initiatives to the Foundation's Board to be discussed at its meeting on 24 November 1972 and finalising my Churchill Fellowship report, which recommended what needed to be done to significantly improve our legal aid services, were in a sense complementary. I was keen to ensure that my recommendations to the Board were soundly based. I wanted to take into account much of what I had learned during my visits to various research centres and foundations as well as meetings with those involved with formulating policy in relation to the delivery of better legal aid services with a strong public interest element.

Completing the task of writing an informative and useful account of my meetings, analysing and interpreting the material gathered and then formulating a set of conclusions and recommendations as to how I thought legal aid in Australia could be upgraded, proved quite a challenge. This was more so because the content of a law degree at that time was more practically oriented. While there were harder, more theoretical subjects, students were not expected to write long essays, unlike today's undergraduate courses.

However, both tasks were eventually completed. My Churchill report when finalised was almost 300 pages, including extensive case studies, and reached the Churchill Fellowship Trust a few months later than originally planned.

Early Proposals to the Board

Initiatives to be put to the Board on 24 November 1972 included the proposal nearest to my heart. Having seen what was possible in the US through bodies such as the American Bar Foundation, I proposed that socio-legal research be seen as a priority and this was readily adopted by the Board which endorsed the need for, funds permitting, a permanent research unit within the Foundation. In addition to this general resolution, the Board also agreed that I should investigate the feasibility of mounting a survey of the legal profession and to report back to it on cost and modus operandi. The Board recognised that as the legal profession was moving into a new era, the policy makers needed much better information to assist major decision making.

Another proposal was in line with an interest which had been raised with me by the Foundation's Board members when I first met them almost 12 months previously. This was the need for the Foundation to take the lead in investigating the application of computers to law libraries, the use of computers as a legal research tool and the projected costs of such steps. The good fortune of meeting Murray Wilker in Canada and being briefed on his recommendations to the Canadian Bar Association and the Justice Department, and my subsequent investigations, provided an excellent foundation for this proposal.

In addition to fully endorsing this project, the Board resolved to request the Chairman to write to the Commonwealth Attorney General, Senator Ivor Greenwood QC, seeking to have me appointed to his Consultative Committee on Computers and the Law. The Board also wanted the Foundation to undertake a development role in respect to continuing legal education (CLE), an issue I was personally interested in because of the paucity of programmes when I was an employed lawyer.

Also having seen something of the steps taken by the US Legal Services Program to provide ongoing education for the lawyers working on the front line, I was very happy to be asked to undertake a research project aimed at implementing a professionally run and high-quality process of delivering continuing legal education to the profession.

The Law Society representatives on the Board were keen to see continuing legal education as a priority for the new College of Law, with it to be a second education stream focused on providing high quality continuing education for the profession. To enable this to happen I was requested to carry out an information gathering exercise in the US and Canada which I undertook by visiting a number of leading CLE programmes.

The Board of the Foundation also made two other significant decisions at the November 1972 meeting. The first was to fund the building of the College of Law's new premises on a site adjacent to St Leonards Station.

The other significant decision was to appoint me as the

Foundation's first Executive Director. This latter decision meant that I now had an unprecedented opportunity to steer the Foundation along a path of innovation, research and reform. The Board also endorsed the need for the Foundation to establish its own identity separate from the Law Society and to acquire its own premises from which the Foundation could operate and in which the Board could meet.

With the Board taking these steps and continuing to endorse its widening range of activities over the next few years, the support of Ken McCaw, Ken Smithers, John Bowen and John Ellard was particularly crucial. In time, it resulted in the Foundation establishing a reputation as a unique contributor in the fields of socio-legal research, legal education, promoting the development of computerised legal information, and law reform.

On reflection, I have no recollection of any Board member, at the meeting held on 24 November 1972, commenting on the forthcoming federal election, due in little more than a week, or showing any concern that the Liberal-Country Party government, which had been in government for 23 years, might be swept out of power and be replaced by Gough Whitlam's Labor Party.

In the previous year or so during which I had got to know the Board members quite well, there was no secret that most of the solicitor members had strong historic connections to the Liberal Party, many joining as young lawyers on returning from war service. I was not sure if it was "head in the sand" or traditional reserve re all things political.

Kicking an Early Goal! Getting Federal Funding for the New College of Law

Very soon after the November 1972 Board Meeting, the Law Foundation received a significant allocation from the Statutory Interest Account to fund the purchase of the land at St Leonards and the construction of the College building. With the election of the Whitlam government and the implementation of its key election promise of making tertiary education free to those who qualified to attend university, steps were being taken to have the College qualify for federal funding as a tertiary institution.

Based on my investigations during a 1973 study tour of professionally run continuing legal education programmes for legal practitioners in the US and Canada, I duly advised the Board of my findings and recommended that the Foundation make funds available to the College of Law to recruit suitable staff. Russell Stewart, a well-qualified, and very experienced solicitor, was appointed to head the establishment of the College of Law's new continuing education department and he quickly developed a programme which attracted immediate interest from the profession for its content and the educational standards it set.

As time passed, I soon became concerned that the priority being given to funding the College initiative meant that the implementation of the various projects approved by the Board at its November 1972 meeting was uncertain, without any guarantee of funding in the medium term.

By the latter part of 1973 the College of Law was a serious drain on available funds, leaving limited resources available for other Foundation projects. I also learned that the College's director, Norman McDowell, had applied for federal funding on the basis that the College was a tertiary institution and ought to be eligible for funding under the Whitlam government's policy to fund tertiary education, but this application had been rejected.

Concerned about the long-term effects of this decision on the Foundation's future, I decided to take it on myself to see if the federal funding response could be changed. With the Whitlam government now in office, I made inquiries amongst some friends in the Labor Party and it was suggested that I approach the Minister for Posts and Telegraphs, Lionel Bowen MP, who prior to his political career had been a solicitor in private practice.

He readily agreed to see me and I explained the Foundation's role and that of the new College of Law. I outlined the funding issues, including the failure to obtain federal funding under the new government's Tertiary Funding Program. Lionel expressed considerable interest in this alternative to articles, as his own experiences of being an articled clerk and, later, a master solicitor supervising articled clerks, were both unhappy. He readily recognised the great opportunities such a broad ranging practical skills training programme would have for law graduates and the legal profession generally. He said he would look into it and get back to me.

Several months later, after the Whitlam government was returned following the 1974 double dissolution, Lionel got back in touch. He was now acting Minister for Education and called to say that he would like to meet with the College's Board. He invited me to come to his office beforehand so we could drive over to the newly completed College of Law building, giving him time to explain the funding strategy.

Although I had discussed it privately with Ken Smithers and John Ellard, this intervention on my part took the College's leadership by surprise.

On arriving at the College, I introduced Lionel to the College's Chairman, John Bowen, and its Director Norman McDowell, who took Lionel on a tour of inspection of the College's facilities before returning to meet the other College and Foundation Board members. Lionel then proceeded to advise them of the path to qualifying for federal funding. He proposed that the College affiliate with the nearby Ku-ring-gai College of Advanced Education, which was located at Lindfield, and that the Practical Legal Training programme be treated as part of the undergraduate education of law students.

There was little hesitation on the part of the Law Society or the College Board to accept this proposal. I was elated by this amazing outcome and knew that the Law Foundation's future had been secured!

John Ellard appreciated my innovative approach to this and a range of other issues and soon became one of my strongest supporters on the Board and a long-term friend.

12

LIFT OFF FOR THE LAW FOUNDATION

Between the Foundation Board meeting appointing me Executive Director in late November 1972 and my starting work in this new role in early January 1973, an almost revolutionary change hit Australia with the Whitlam government's election on 2 December 1972. Australia suddenly went from being one of the most backwards thinking Western nations to one at the forefront of change with initiatives, such as the recognition of China.

This was an amazing new era to be taking up such an exciting new role with my new responsibilities suddenly being in a context where reform and change in the public arena, rather than being anathema, was a living thing under exciting new leadership at the national level.

Undertaking my new role in the context of the new government, determined to transform Australia, gave legitimacy and hope that change and reform could also be brought about within the Foundation's frame of reference.

A Busy Start

This soon began on several fronts, including my appointment to the Computerisation of Legal Data Committee established by the new federal Attorney General, Senator Lionel Murphy QC, in early 1973. The Board's approach to the previous Attorney General, to have me appointed as a member of the federal Attorney General's committee investigating this topic, was delayed by the election of the new Labor government. In time, the Chairman's letter seeking such an appointment surfaced in Canberra and it resulted in my being appointed to Senator Murphy's committee on the Computerisation of Legal Data. This appointment also meant frequent trips to Canberra over the next few months.

This was in addition to my being given the responsibility of establishing the College of Law's new additional role of providing a Continuing Education Program for the state's solicitors. Also high on my agenda was planning the Foundation's establishment of a research programme applying social science research techniques to examining the state's legal system, the latter soon attracting the interest of various legal agencies.

Another Board priority was taking initial steps towards developing a community education programme via the teaching of legal studies. This initiative was soon attracting the interest of teachers, the NSW Education Department and the federal government's new Curriculum Development Centre (CDC).

Against this extraordinary backdrop, my new professional life started with a series of meetings arranged by the Chairman Ken Smithers to introduce me to the leaders of the profession, the judiciary, the Law Reform Commission and the Attorney General's Department. The aim was, in part, to get the word around quickly that the Law Foundation was now a reality and a new player with its own resources, role and an agenda unlike any other legal institution.

In these early days at the Foundation there were not enough hours in the day. But it was exciting, and I was an enthusiastic participant.

At that same time, I was desperately trying to finish my report to the Churchill Fellowship Trust. When completed, and with the Board's blessing, multiple copies were published and circulated both in Australia to policy makers and also to various institutions in the US, Canada and Britain which had provided me with great assistance and keen to receive copies.

The Board, from the outset, wanted to establish a separate identity for the Foundation from its "parents", the Law Society and the Attorney General and his department. This meant that I had to find suitable office space. Fortunately, I readily found premises in Frederick Jordan Chambers in Macquarie Street, opposite the old Mint building, which had ready access to the Law Society's facilities

Contemporaneously, I was planning a North American study tour following the Board's adoption of continuing legal education as an early priority for the Foundation, which required me to work out which were the leading continuing legal education providers in the US and Canada, and then obtain their co-operation and prepare an itinerary.

I also had to start planning a programme for the visit by Gerald Sanctuary, the English Law Society's head of public relations, as both the Law Society and the Board were keen to invite him to Sydney later in the year. The Board was particularly interested in his role in legal studies taught to secondary school students in the UK and his visit was the catalyst for the Board soon deciding that the Foundation should initiate a similar project.

However, I was also occupied with the ongoing tasks of administering the Foundation, organising and recording Board meeting decisions and then implementing those various decisions, as well as setting up and furnishing the Foundation's new office.

In August 1973, I embarked on the study tour to investigate American approaches to providing high quality continuing legal education. Fortuitously, this trip coincided with a study tour being undertaken by other members of the Computerisation of Legal Data Committee and planned before I was appointed to it, which meant that I was able to participate in a number of high-level meetings with them in Washington. The trip was particularly productive and enabled me on my return to, not only establish a highly professional new Continuing Education Department within the College of Law but also greatly added to current knowledge of progress being made in the US with the computerisation of legal data.

This recent experience meant that on my return, there were more regular meetings in Canberra as the committee started to formulate its conclusions and recommendations. By the year's end I could, with some satisfaction, point to significant progress in advancing the Foundation's profile as well as accumulating the knowledge and the direction to take with the application of computers to legal information retrieval.

In addition, significant steps had been taken towards seeking to introduce legal studies into the secondary school curriculum via the Gerald Sanctuary's visit, learning from the UK experience in developing teaching materials and working with educators.

Meanwhile, the Foundation's finances were still under a cloud. This meant that little progress could be made with implementing the Board's other key objective of establishing a social science research unit to shed light on the operation of the law and the legal system and whether they met society's needs.

Taking this step came closer, following the Commonwealth government's decision to accept the College of Law as being eligible for funding as a tertiary institution in the latter part of 1974. This meant that the Board of the Foundation could look forward to a higher level of both the continuity and the amount of funding from the Statutory Interest Account.

Establishing the Foundation's Research Unit

With the College of Law new building completed in 1974, the Board of the Foundation obtained approval from the College Board to enable it, and its staff, to occupy some of the College's as yet unneeded offices as the College was not expected to achieve full capacity for several years.

The move to the College of Law building enabled the Foundation to establish a social science research unit and to recruit research and project staff. The Board was keen to see the Foundation fully operational and able to implement another of its goals.

In undertaking this task of establishing the first such research unit in Australia I was able to draw on the experience gained from the time I spent with the American Bar Foundation situated on the University of Chicago campus. They had generously provided a base for me during the three weeks I spent in Chicago while on my Churchill Fellowship. In Chicago I met with and observed the varied work being undertaken by that Foundation's extremely well qualified and resourced research staff. That exposure proved immensely valuable in both setting a research agenda for the Foundation and with recruiting appropriately qualified research staff.

Also, while in New York, there were meetings with the Russell Sage Foundation and the Ford Foundation which were relevant as both were allocating funds to research the operation of the legal system and happily shared something of their experiences with me.

All this meant that over the next 18 months or so a research team of Ian Campbell, Roman Tomasic, David Mills and later Jacklyn Robinson, all young lawyers with an interest in research, were recruited and worked on a number of groundbreaking research projects and initiatives. Their growing expertise and reputation were soon attracting requests for assistance to undertake research papers from various government agencies and soon being sought after as conferences presenters.

Underpinning the Foundation's later contributions to other legal agencies were various pioneering surveys of the profession and later of the community by Foundation research staff.

One example was an Australian first community survey undertaken by the Foundation in 1975 whose purpose was to provide policy makers and administrators concerned about the delivery of legal services with relevant and current information. A survey was planned and supervised by Roman Tomasic and his later analysis was published by Allen & Unwin and the Foundation under the title *Law, Lawyers and the Community*. Allen & Unwin venturing into the Australian market led to a number of the Foundation's research reports reaching wider audience through their marketing and distribution capabilities.

Soon the Foundation staff started to receive requests to assist various government agencies and inquiries. Ian Campbell prepared a research report on law schools for the NSW government's Inquiry into Legal Education comparing standards for admission to Law School both here and in the US where the so-called LSAT dominates entry to law. Ian also undertook a study at the joint request of the NSW government and the Law Society into overseas experience with small business assistance programmes and published his findings as *Perspectives on Small Business Assistance* which was of interest to small business agencies and commerce and business educators.

Another major initiative was an extensive survey of NSW solicitors and barristers which sought to provide the first comprehensive and balanced account of the work patterns of the legal profession and its capacity to absorb newly qualified lawyers. This *Profile of the Profession* study was also undertaken by Ian Campbell and was intended to assist the Inquiry into the Legal Education and the NSW LRC's Inquiry into the Legal Profession.

Following a request from the government-sponsored Inquiry into Legal Education, another study of the training and use of paraprofessionals in NSW was undertaken by staff researcher Jacklyn Robinson, which involved a review of selected law firms and educational institutions.

Research assistance was given by Roman Tomasic to the Royal Commission into NSW Prisons. Roman had undertaken research on bail and pre-trial release, deterrence and the drink driver, and the Foundation later published reports on these issues. Much of this work was in response to the Board's desire to work collaboratively with the NSW Law Reform Commission and to carry out research into innovations being pioneered in the US in the Criminal Justice area which resulted in the various reports prepared by Roman.

Roman later assisted the Australian Law Reform Commission with respect to a reference on the ACT Breathalyser Law and he also gave extensive evidence before the Senate Select Committee on Social Welfare on the issue of the non-medical use of drugs.

The Foundation was also instrumental in planning and funding the first National Conference on Legal Education which was held at the College of Law during 1976. The Conference drew academics and members of the legal profession as well as representatives of educational institutions from all states and territories and a number of overseas countries. The conference provided a broad review of the problems facing administrators, policy makers, educators, students and members of the profession in light of the rapid growth in numbers of school leavers wanting to study law.

The High School Education Law Project

The improvement of the Foundation's finances allowed the Board to proceed with establishing a project to see legal studies become part of the junior secondary curriculum, thus enabling students to learn more about the law and the legal system

As noted previously, Gerald Sanctuary's visit started the Foundation on a journey which was to last until Legal Studies would be included as an elective in the Higher School Certificate curriculum in around 1986. This was a fantastic result which started with a modest investment via an outlay on Gerald's travel expenses and resulted in those students who were interested in knowing more about the law for personal or career reasons to have the opportunity to do so.

This long journey was an example of the unique advantage a Foundation has when it believes an issue or programme would require long-term support, particularly when partnering a government department or agency.

It began in 1974 with some research being carried out amongst teenagers by Tjerk Dusseldorp and Susan Churchman, then mature age law students at the UNSW Law School. This research revealed that there was a real interest amongst many school age students in knowing more about their legal rights.

While the Board were interested in this idea, it was agreed as a matter of policy that any Foundation supported initiative would need to be carried out with the co-operation of the Education

Department. The Foundation's focus was on students in the junior secondary area. This was seen as ensuring that there was a real prospect that all secondary level students would learn about the law before many, as was the case then, would leave school after completing the School Certificate in year 10.

Tjerk and Susan were employed by the Foundation while they were still law students and worked initially part time for the Foundation on this project which soon became known as the High School Education Law Project (HELP). Their initial focus, based on inquiries with teachers' groups such as the commerce teachers, was the need for teaching materials to which students in years eight and nine could relate.

This resulted in the HELP team developing a teaching resource in the form of a tabloid newspaper called *Legal Eagle*, which soon created widespread interest and over 300 schools soon requested and received multiple class sets. Perhaps many 1970s and early 1980s school kids would remember it well. The project also received national recognition when it was awarded a significant two-year grant in 1976 from the federal Curriculum Development Centre, an independent statutory body that was established by the Whitlam government to develop school curricula and educational materials. With this Commonwealth support, the materials produced by the team were distributed to schools Australia-wide and the CDC became a continuing supporter of the project, along with major funding and other support from the Foundation.

In the Foundation's 1977 Annual Report it was noted that the Project's reception by junior secondary teachers, pupils and the Education Department continued with the trialling of a full-scale legal studies course. This confirmed growing interest in legal studies units in the curriculum. Over 500 NSW and Victorian high schools subscribed to its teaching materials.

The HELP team also developed programmes aimed at assisting teachers to gain the confidence and requisite knowledge to be effective legal studies teachers, with the 1980 Annual Report noting that:

> Literally thousands of teachers have attended HELP in-service courses to be introduced to the materials and to learn how to incorporate them into their teaching programmes.

A major distribution and resources breakthrough came in 1978 when a publishing and distribution arrangement was made with the Australian arm of the international tax law publisher CCH, which was keen to broaden its publication list and saw HELP as a great way to enter the secondary school market.

This resulted in the development by the HELP team, with the financial support of the CDC, of the *Eaglebook* series with four separate titles: *Jobs, The Environment, Consumer Protection* and *The Family*. Like the other titles, *The Family*, published in 1979, had a Foreword by a leading legal figure and, in it, Justice Elizabeth Evatt, then the Chief Judge of the Family Court, wrote:

> The purpose of this book is to introduce to young people some of the basic concepts of the legal system. They will learn some of the ways in which the legal system affects family relationships and what the law has to say about the rights and obligations of members of the family towards each other.

She concluded her Foreword saying:

> If as result of studying this book young people are better able to understand and to question with confidence the social values implicit in our legal system, then it will serve a worthwhile purpose.

In the Foundation's 1980 Annual Report, it was noted that the *Eaglebook* series, which was sold in multiple copy class kits with an accompanying teacher's manual, had sold over 1,000 in 1979 with another 450 kits having been distributed in the first half of 1980. *Legal Eagle* was also still very popular and was published three times a year, but in a revised format, moving away from the newspaper format and allowing for more pages. Once a term, it brought articles on topical events involving law and accounts of interesting law cases relevant to the subjects they studied.

One such case referred to involved the mining of beaches in Queensland to extract rare metals, such as rutile, which somehow reached the notice of the company involved and resulted in an angry letter and calls demanding a retraction. I recall calling the company and having to explain the context of the reference to the case and eventually they recognised that more harm than good would come out of taking it further. Thankfully *Legal Eagle* and the Foundation did not become involved in litigation.

Recognition of the acceptance and need for law-related education in schools came from such influential figures as the Governor General, the Chairman of the Australian Law Reform Commission, the NSW Law Society, the Parents and Citizens Association, the CDC and Film Australia, which made a series of six films based on the *Eaglebook* series,

Also, bodies such as the Australian Institute of Criminology, the Australian Legal Education Council, the NSW Education's State Development Committee were all actively interested in the impact of legal studies on secondary students.

Probably the most important indicator of how well the idea of law-related education had been accepted was that the 1979 NSW Draft New Commerce Syllabus had law as one of its seven areas of study, while the 1980 NSW Home Science Syllabus highlighted the importance of Family Law and Consumer Law.

In addition to publishing and training work, the HELP team saw a need for a different type of experience for students and, during 1979, it started a Mock Trial Competition among schools which subscribed to *Legal Eagle*, still a much sought-after resource. Over 50 high schools, each represented by a team of six students, participated. Each school was assisted by local solicitors nominated by the Regional Law Societies who coached the students in the basic principles of evidence. The final was held in the Banco Court on Law Day, held during Children's Week in October. The Law Society liked the idea of the Mock Trial Competition so much they agreed to take over its organisation and management and it is still, over 40 years later, an important part of high school for many senior students.

Another significant step for the project was the establishment of a Law Related Education Working Party by the Department of Education with the Foundation's project staff participating. Progress was also made with the Catholic Education Office with the Foundation co-funding the appointment there of a Legal Studies Adviser. The project also had a highly influential advisory committee representing a wide range of legal and educational figures.

After Tjerk Dusseldorp and Susan Churchman moved on, the new project leader, Lyn Tan, soon continued their good work. The 1982 Annual Report noted the major achievement of official recognition from the NSW Department of Education of the value of adding law-related education approach to the school curriculum. An outcome of this move forward was the joint appointment by the Foundation and the Department of Ms Tan as a Curriculum Consultant in the Directorate of Studies. Meanwhile the publishing activities continued to be self-supporting.

The fact that legal studies is part of the HSC and with law-related elements integrated into the early years of high school flows from the effort put into creating HELP by Tjerk Dusseldorp and Susan Churchman and from the faith various Boards of the Foundation had in them and their team. The later efforts of Lyn Tan were also very important, as was that of Margaret White who worked for many years ensuring *Legal Eagle* continued to be published, later also under the auspices of the Law Society. This was a great project and again like so many others would not have seen the light of day without there being a Law Foundation of New South Wales.

Looking back on what had been achieved in the few short years remaining of the Askin era, it is clear that the Foundation and its staff had more than exceeded the initial expectations of the Board when taking the first tentative step towards implementing the Foundation's charter in late 1972.

These early achievements went a long way to fulfilling the role foreshadowed by the shadow minister Jack Mannix when in 1967 he spoke in support of the Foundation's creation in Parliament, during the second reading speech on the *Legal Practitioners (Amendment) Act 1967*, about the need for such a body:

> Those of us in the legal profession and, indeed, people in any other profession appreciate the valuable work that a foundation can do in the interests of the public, centred on certain aims and objectives that the foundation can set itself in the field of research, law reform, and scholarships for persons pursuing their law studies. One could probably think of a long list of items of valuable work that could be done by the Law Foundation.

I hope Mr Mannix watched with keen interest the Foundation's development and approved of its emerging role. However, none of this would have been possible without the vision and foresight of both Attorney General Ken McCaw and the leadership of the Law Society, particularly Barry McDonald, the Law Society President responsible for getting the backing of the members of the Society.

Finally, the other great parliamentary supporter from that era was former Attorney General and Minister for Justice John Maddison who, upon his retirement, was appointed as a consultant to the Foundation on the recommendation of his successor Frank Walker. John was a classic liberal reformer in a government which too rarely shared his zeal for reform, but with his vast experience and liberal attitude, he enjoyed working with and advising those involved in a large number of Foundation projects and he was sorely missed by many, not the least by me, when he sadly fell ill and passed away prematurely.

13

THE ASKIN GOVERNMENT AND ITS UNLIKELY REFORMERS

The Askin government left bad memories with many baby boomers coming of age during the 10 years it was in office. Later allegations of Askin's corruption consigned it to being falsely labelled as an era of bad government. However, that was far from the truth, as it included a group of ministers who truly deserve the acknowledgement of being Australia's first responders to the desperate need for legislative reform on many fronts.

This chapter tells the story of these wide-ranging reforms including modernising the NSW court system, establishing Australia's first Law Reform Commission, introducing key prison reforms, and innovations such as the Ombudsman, the Privacy Committee and establishing the Law Foundation of New South Wales. The environmental protection reforms led the way in Australia with strongly enforced pollution controls which removed industry from our waterways, while NSW also led Australia with road safety reforms and many consumer protection innovations. It is a notable record that needs to be recognised and recorded.

For many of the baby boomer generation the Askin era is best remembered for police brutality against young protesters and for NSW Premier Robert Askin's purported direction to "run the bastards over". Askin was referring to anti-war protesters when, during the 1966 visit of US President Lyndon Johnson, Askin and Prime Minister Harold Holt were travelling in the Presidential cavalcade through Sydney while jointly hosting Johnson's visit to Australia. Johnson had come seeking more support for the US efforts in Vietnam.

To later generations, Askin is remembered, if at all, as being infamous because of his government's sacking of Joern Utzon from the Opera House project and, later still, because of corruption allegations made following his death.

Despite such headlines, the Askin government's 10 years in office were largely successful. Askin's political skills enabled him to maintain a long-term stable leadership team and, once in office, a ministry with few changes. This all contributed to him winning a then unprecedented four consecutive elections. This was during a tumultuous period at the federal level where there were five prime ministers, including the colourful and dramatic tenure of the Whitlam Labor government.

The previous state Labor government had been in office since the McKell Labor government took office in 1941 and was able to introduce a number of wide-ranging social reforms. This was despite having to operate under severe wartime restrictions and controls introduced by a Commonwealth government which, by December 1941, was actively engaged in defending Australia from threatened invasion by the Japanese. Once the war was over, the NSW Labor government was confronted by a wide range of social and economic pressures, challenges brought about by the return to civilian life of ex-servicemen, post-war growth and a massive influx of migrants from war-torn Europe. This presented it with a significant challenge in just maintaining basic services and ensuring there were adequate housing, schools, hospitals, transport and new roads to service the booming outer suburbs.

By the time of the May 1965 state election, there was growing pressure for reform due to rising community expectations. Many, perhaps unfairly, saw the incumbent government, which had been in office for a record breaking 24 years, as being incapable of addressing these issues. With its roots dating back to the Second World War and a whole new generation voting for the first time, the mood of the electorate had moved on and the Labor government was finally defeated by an Askin led rejuvenated Liberal Country Party coalition.

According to Murray Goot's biography of Askin in the *Australian Dictionary of Biography,* on attaining the party leadership Askin took the then highly unusual step for the times of selling his business and devoting himself full-time to the role of Opposition Leader. He declared "last and always, I am a politician – a professional politician", a pioneering practice followed by later aspiring Opposition leaders.

Eventually, when the coalition attained office on 1 May 1965, it contained a core in the ministry who, after years in opposition and facing a tired and aging Labor government, recognised that there was a great need to modernise legislation and legislate to improve the lives of the people of NSW.

However, the new government's capacity to pursue such goals was limited by the need to complete the Sydney Opera House, a massive project initiated by the previous Labor Premier Joe Cahill in 1955. The government held an international competition inviting designs from the world's leading architects which resulted in the adoption of Danish architect Jørn Utzon's radical design in 1957.

By the time the new government was elected considerable progress had been made with building the Opera House and most of the design and engineering issues were well advanced, but the project was far from completion and running substantially over budget. Utzon fell out with the new Minister for Public Works, Davis Hughes, and soon resigned, departing for his home in Europe. The government retained brilliant young Australian architect Peter Hall to supervise the completion of the project which was eventually opened to international approbation by Her Majesty Queen Elizabeth II on 20 October 1973.

There is little doubt that the cost of completing the Opera House impacted the NSW budget but, despite this, much needed legislation was soon being initiated.

A review of the legislative record of the Askin government's 11 years in office shows that the Askin ministry included an unexpected group of successful reformers. This group was made up of Attorney General Ken McCaw, Minister for Justice John Maddison, Minister for Water Conservation Jack Beale, Minister for Transport Milton Morris and Eric Willis, Minister for Education and later Premier, who, once elected and appointed to the ministry, all hit the ground running. This can be seen by the list of reformist legislation submitted to the Parliament during the new government's first five years particularly, and reveals a remarkable record of reform.

Modernising the Legal System: Ken McCaw MLA and John Maddison MLA

Looking back over the period of nearly 25 years, during which time I worked in reasonably close proximity to each succeeding NSW Attorneys General, and, from time to time, with Commonwealth Attorneys General, I have been surprised and impressed that so much important, cutting-edge legislation relating to the law and the NSW court system was given priority in the early days of the Askin government.

Part of the reason was, I believe, the influence that a number of the Law Society leaders at the time had with the new government. It was not surprising as the incoming Attorney General, Ken McCaw, who had been admitted to practice in 1934, had long been associated with the Law Society prior to his time in politics, and by the time of the election of the Askin government had been in Parliament for almost 20 years on the Opposition benches.

John Maddison, the incoming Minister for Justice, had long been interested in reform. It was believed his ministerial career suffered because of his progressive views, yet despite this he was responsible for a number of key reforms within his portfolio.

The legislative reforms of the legal and justice system introduced by the two law ministers were clearly facilitated through their close working relationship with, not only the Law Society leadership, but also with the leaders of the state's judiciary.

Once in office, McCaw was quick off the mark and one of the first targets for reform was to deal with the Supreme Court's backlog of appeals. This was to be achieved by creating a separate Appellate Division of the NSW Supreme Court which did away with trial judges doubling up and acting as members of the Full Court to hear appeals from their colleagues.

The new NSW Court of Appeal was a long overdue reform and clearly influenced by such courts in the UK and US. For the first time, the new appellate court would be presided over by a President who was not the Chief Justice and six other permanent members, all of whom would have extensive appellate court experience.

When McCaw introduced this Bill on 30 September 1965, he said that the purpose was to establish a division of the Supreme Court to be called the Court of Appeal, as the lack of a specialist appeals court diminished the efficiency of the Supreme Court. The Court of Appeal would be a division of the Supreme Court with the Chief Justice still having overall responsibility for the court.

He also referred to the importance of a recent announcement by the Minister for Justice that agreement had been reached with the federal government for the construction of a modern new court building in King Street to house the Supreme Court and Commonwealth courts.

Another important early reform, with significant long-term economic advantages, was the introduction on 21 February 1967 of the Real Property (Conversion of Title) Bill. This was a much-needed reform that would benefit a significant proportion of property owners as it was intended to bring to an end the inherited Old System Title regime which was still the method of proving ownership of land by demonstrating title back to the original land grant.

The NSW government had introduced the South Australian Torrens Title system in 1863, based on a certificate of title with the ownership recorded on a government register confirming ownership of land by the holder of the certificate.

However, NSW being the oldest settled state had a large amount of land granted to settlers and purchasers prior to 1863. This meant that current owners of such land, much of it in the old inner-city suburbs or around country settlements, held their land under what was referred to as Old System Title. Their proof of ownership rested on being able to establish a documentary chain of ownership back to the first land grant via deeds and other documents providing evidence of each transfer of ownership down through the years. Having regard to the changes in land use and industrial development which had taken place in NSW since 1863, this system was a severe brake on the speed with which governments could open up new urban land for housing and other uses.

The proposed legislation made it simpler for those owning Old System Title to upgrade their title to the Torrens Title system. Until then, those selling and buying such land had faced substantially greater legal costs and were often open to disputes compared to those buying and selling land under the Torrens Title system. It was another much-needed reform of the legal system.

Attorney General McCaw, when introducing the Bill, said:

> Though the unconverted land is so small a percentage (5%) of the total area the fact is that the conveyancing costs and the expenses of dealing with it are estimated to exceed by $2,000,000 per annum the costs that would be involved if the land were under the Torrens system.

While I was still a part-time law student in 1966, my father retired and decided to use some of his very modest superannuation money to purchase a block of land on a newly sub-divided headland in Kiama near where we had taken family camping holidays for many years. He did so in the hope that the family might build a holiday home there. However, that dream never came to pass and in the early 1970s he decided to sell the land and asked me to handle the sale for him, the land having increased in value by 10% per year since he purchased it, again another sign of the changing times in NSW.

While I had studied conveyancing during my law course, I had very limited practical experience with it, being a solicitor engaged in insurance litigation, and so approached the task with some trepidation. I then discovered when my father gave me a pile of legal documents evidencing the title back to the original 19th century grant that it was Old System Title land. By that time handling such land transfers was becoming a costly specialist legal task.

However, with advice from legal colleagues and friends, I was able to satisfy the purchaser's solicitor that my father indeed had a "good root of title" back to the original land grant and the sale went through. Nevertheless, it demonstrated first-hand how dealing with such land was slow, unnecessarily costly and the process was in desperate need of this much-needed reform.

In many ways one of the jewels in the crown of our governance system has been the Torrens Title system of land registration and its integrity is one of the foundations of Australia's system of governance and economic stability.

In a country where home ownership on a quarter acre block has been the dream of most Australians for the past 150 years or so, it has been important to know that the title to the property was as safe as the British Crown Jewels because of the early adoption of the Torrens Title land registry system.

In early 1967, the government introduced the *Criminal Injuries Compensation Act 1967*. The Attorney General, Ken McCaw, explained in Parliament on 8 March 1967 during his second reading introduction that it was much-needed legislation to provide compensation for injuries suffered by victims of crime, a first for Australia.

This was an issue that both the government and the Opposition agreed on, but it had not previously been dealt with because of a potential problem for victims receiving social security benefits. In other words, the challenge of introducing such a scheme in Australia was complicated by possible overlap with the Commonwealth social security scheme. The solution was for the new scheme to be referred to as providing compensation for victims of crimes of violence and, provided the trial judge ordered compensation to be paid to a victim, it did not affect their pension rights.

The *Costs in Criminal Cases Act 1967* was introduced by the Minister for Justice, John Maddison, on 8 March 1967, and provided an extension of legal aid to members of the public who did not qualify for assistance under the *Legal Assistance Act*. It was intended to mitigate, if not entirely remove, the expense burden to which people on trial for a serious criminal offence, but acquitted or found not guilty, were exposed to in the course of legal proceedings.

Under this legislation, a judge would have the discretion, in appropriate cases, to authorise the award of costs to a defendant acquitted of a serious offence where it would not have been reasonable on the available evidence to institute such proceedings in the first place.

When it was passed in late 1967 the *Workers Compensation (Amendment) Act* was of professional interest to me as a solicitor who spent most days in the Workers Compensation Commission settling workers' claims. The Act was noteworthy for improving workers' entitlements and most of the those who worked in the jurisdiction saw it as an attempt to increase the government's standing amongst workers. The legislative changes significantly improved benefits payable under the Act while including a new right enabling workers to receive compensation both by weekly payment and a lump sum where they had suffered a significant permanent injury such as a loss of use of a limb, hearing, an eye, etc. If a worker had, for example, lost use of a limb prior to 1967 and had decided to take a one-off lump sum compensation payment, they could not then receive a weekly payment to compensate them for the loss arising from their injury.

This workers compensation reform was to provide a bonus for my uncle Mick, who like my father spent his working life at the Gas Works and who, through a permanent injury suffered late in his working life, received a weekly compensation payment reflecting his reduced working capacity. He had elected not to receive a one-off lump sum, but to receive a weekly payment for life which he was still receiving following his retirement some years before the legislation was amended.

A short time after the compensation benefits were improved and, while I was still working as a litigation solicitor, Mick received a letter from his insurance company requiring him to submit to a medical examination which they were entitled to do. Their motivation was to put pressure on him to end his weekly entitlement by offering him a lump sum to get him off their books.

Dad then asked me to speak to Mick about his rights. After reading the insurer's letter, I was considering the best way to respond on his behalf when I remembered that because of the way the new legislation was drafted, Mick still retained his eligibility to claim a lump sum for his disability without putting his weekly payment at risk. I then advised Mick to ignore the insurer and advised him that I would apply for him to be granted a statutory lump sum by the Workers Compensation Commission calculated on the percentage loss of the use of his arm which he was now entitled to do without jeopardising his weekly payment.

I arranged for him to be medically assessed by one of the orthopaedic specialists my firm used as an independent expert. The medical assessment duly confirmed that he had lost about half the use of his arm. This report resulted in Mick receiving a lump sum of several thousand dollars – manna from heaven to an elderly pensioner. While I became an instant family hero, I thought about the thousands of other older workers in Mick's position and the probable failure of their former unions to draw to their attention the availability of this potential windfall.

With the passing of the legislation establishing the NSW Law Reform Commission in 1967, the Askin government finally settled the long and vexed history of formal law reform bodies in NSW. This history dated back to the 1870s when the state's first formal body, chaired by the then Chief Justice, was set up. It apparently met with limited success. There were various later failed attempts to establish law reform committees during the first half of the 20th century.

The government's first attempt in 1966 to legislate on the issue failed as, in the view of the Opposition, the Commission should not be allowed to put forward legislative initiatives. Such initiatives it believed should arise from requests or references from the Parliament through the Attorney General of the day.

The legislation finally overcame most of the reservations of the Opposition and the new body was established with the requirement that the Commission be chaired by an experienced Supreme Court judge or retired Supreme Court judge with three other commissioners who were senior experienced lawyers drawn from the profession and the Law School. Their role was to review and make recommendations to the government on repealing or replacing out of date laws – many inherited from the UK in the earliest days of the colony of NSW. It was also expected to consult widely with the community, a process with which the Law Foundation was later to provide great assistance.

Further major legal reforms followed including the *Public Defenders Act 1969*. This act continued to make provision for representation of poor persons facing serious criminal charges by experienced barristers. However, instead of these barristers being employed by the Public Service Board and therefore part of the executive government, they would from now on be appointed under this legislation and put on the same footing as Crown Prosecutors. They would be officers of the court and no longer public servants employed by the government.

On 12 March 1970, the Supreme Court Bill, one of the largest

Bills ever tabled in the NSW Parliament at 460 pages, which had been prepared by the NSW Law Reform Commission over several years, was introduced.

In real terms, this Bill introduced much needed reforms. It meant NSW was finally catching up with UK reforms via adoption of the 19th century *Judicature Act* whose reforms had been quickly implemented in Queensland and South Australia but not in NSW. One 1880 report cited by McCaw in the Parliament said litigants in Queensland were able to obtain speedy settlement of their respective suits as a small cost compared with the extensive delays and high costs faced by litigants in NSW.

When tabling the Bill, according to Hansard, the Attorney General said:

> It is not proposed that the bill should be operative overnight. Obviously, the profession in particular has to become familiar with it and with its operation. It is proposed to retain the rule-making authority in the bill so that the rule-making committee can start functioning upon the proposed draft rules, and perhaps twelve months after assent has been given to it the legislation can come into full operation.

The new Act codified court rules and modernised the operation of the court case handling procedure and allowed the fusion of common law and equity. This finally overcame the need for the same parties involving the same complex civil dispute needing to start separate cases when both damages and restraining orders were required. Previously they could only be obtained via separate hearings in the common law and the equity divisions. The new system gave the trial judge power to make orders for both and this significantly reduced hearing costs and produced speedier results.

The *Supreme Court Act* was eventually passed on 12 August 1970 after many long parliamentary sessions dealing with the myriad provisions contained in its monumental 460 pages. The sheer detail and complexity of this new omnibus Bill was largely the responsibility of McCaw as Attorney General. He faced a monumental task as the Bill was debated in the House over the many sessions with him on his feet most of the time, yet such was his deep knowledge of this incredibly important piece of legislation, he did so despite being handicapped by very serious sight impairment.

As a young newly admitted solicitor, this new legislation meant forgetting all that I had learnt during my law course and learning about the new rules and procedures for matters being commenced in the Supreme Court. It was a steep learning curve and I recall attending a number of lectures at the Law School trying to quickly come to grips with the new requirements of Supreme Court matters.

Similar root and branch changes were later introduced to the District Court by the *District Court Act 1973* intended to modernise court procedures to bring it into line with the Supreme Court practice.

Earlier In 1970, the *Court of Petty Sessions (Civil Claims) Act* extended the jurisdiction of that court to deal with civil claims whereas previously the role of such courts had been limited to the role of police courts.

These significant legal reforms introduced by the Askin government were directed at modernising and improving the case handling efficiency of the court system at all levels. Steps were also taken to allocate funds to improve court facilities for all three levels of courts.

Another noteworthy justice reform was the *Periodic Detention of Prisoners Act* introduced on 17 November 1970 by Justice Minister John Maddison.

In introducing this legislation Hansard recorded the minister as saying:

> The purpose of the measure is to introduce a system under which certain classes of persons convicted of offences may be ordered by the court to serve periods of imprisonment at weekends rather than as full-time detention.

He added by way of explanation:

> The intention is that when a court would otherwise impose a term of imprisonment it may now, if it is considered that the offender is a suitable person to be absorbed in a weekend detention programme, still impose a term of imprisonment but order that the imprisonment be served at weekends only.

The minister explained that a system of periodic detention recognised the principle that an offender should be made aware that he has done wrong while at the same time also recognised the importance of maintaining the family unit. When a person is gainfully employed and needs to sustain and support a family, the periodic detention system allows the courts the opportunity of committing certain classes of offenders to a weekend sentence.

The legislation was welcomed by the shadow minister who, according to Hansard, said:

> The Minister has my full sympathy and whole-hearted support in bringing legislation of this type before Parliament.

However, this legislation was in sharp contrast to the grant of dubious additional powers to police under summary offences legislation introduced into Parliament on the same day to deal with victimless crimes such as vagrancy, and public disorder caused by demonstrators and social activists.

This highlighted the differences within the Askin Cabinet between Maddison, a progressive reformer on social issues, and the Premier, who controlled the Police portfolio, who was more socially conservative and accused of "pandering" to the tabloid press.

With so much major legislation bringing in much needed reforms to both the law itself and the legal system generally being introduced by the Askin government in its first five years, it is not surprising that there were fewer "big ticket" items introduced by the law ministers during the latter half of its term. The previous momentum for reform tended to dissipate.

Nevertheless, several significant reform steps were taken towards the end of the government's time in office and not long before Askin retired. One of these was to legislate for the purposes of creating the position of Ombudsman, while another was to establish a legislative base for the Privacy Committee. These were both initiatives of Attorney General and Justice Minister John Maddison.

Maddison had long been a supporter of adopting the European Ombudsman model, having apparently raised it in Parliament as early as 1964.

The Ombudsman Bill was first introduced into the Parliament on 27 August 1974 and it met with stiff resistance from the Opposition. This was mainly because of the government's failure to accept all three recommendations of the Law Reform Commission. Nevertheless, despite strong concerns of the Opposition the *Ombudsman Act* was passed.

Maddison also introduced the Privacy Committee Bill on 19 February 1975. In response, Frank Walker speaking for the Opposition said that there was a growing trend of invasion of privacy which he saw as getting worse as more personal records were being stored on computers. He argued that the proposal seemed to be less than half a measure, but the Opposition would look at the Bill and, if what it contained was worthwhile, would support it.

After a long and, at times, heated debate, the *Privacy Committee Act* was passed with the Opposition highly critical of the limited power of the committee and with little confidence in it being a strong safeguard of the privacy of individual citizens.

The achievements of Attorney General McCaw cannot be underestimated. He was not a flamboyant personality, but he somehow overcame the extraordinary disability of being virtually blind and managed to steer such monumental pieces of legislation as the *Supreme Court Act* safely through the Parliament. He also made excellent use of the new NSW Law Reform Commission with this and other legislation, which gave new Bills significant technical credibility when being considered by the Parliament. He and his colleague, Minister for

Justice John Maddison, were unsung reform heroes of that era who earned the respect of their counterparts in the Opposition.

Major Environmental Protection and Planning Reforms: Jack Beale MLA

The Askin government also introduced legislation in respect to environmental protection, road safety and consumer protection which, for the times, was cutting edge legislation.

Modern environmental protection legislation began way back in 1970 with a number of important pieces of new legislation being introduced. *The Clean Waters Act 1970*, the *State Pollution Control Commission Act 1970*, the *Waste Disposal Act 1970*, the *Clean Air (Amendment) Act 1972*, the *Clean Air (Further Amendment) Act 1972*, the *NSW Planning and Environment Commission Act 1974* and the *Noise Control Act 1975* were all introduced during this period.

The minister responsible for these acts was Jack Beale, a qualified engineer who, at the age of 25, was elected to the NSW Parliament in 1942 as an independent member on the death of his father, the sitting member.

In this capacity, he represented the seat of South Coast for 22 years until he was invited by the incoming Premier Askin, who had been impressed with Beale's ability, to join his Cabinet.

Beale is reputed to have rejected Askin's offer to be Minister for Public Works, electing to take on the more junior portfolio of Conservation. He apparently wanted to be responsible for the state's water, soil and forests which interested him particularly. The state at the time was in the first major drought for over 20 years.

According to a later minister, Andrew Constance:

> He embarked on a programme to develop the state's water resources, initiating comprehensive river valley surveys and an infrastructure programme constructing new dams and weirs.

This experience meant that in 1970 he was ready to deal with long ignored environmental issues and tabled the *Clean Waters Act*, the first such legislation in Australia, which was followed by an Act creating the State Pollution Control Commission, an agency given wide powers to enforce the new environmental controls, and the *Waste Management Act*.

I had personal experience of the effect of the *Clean Waters Act*. As noted earlier, I had spent my formative years living in Cabarita which, in effect, was on a peninsula surrounded on three sides by Hen and Chicken Bay, the Parramatta River and Kendall's Bay. Fortunately, in the 19th century, partly because that stretch of the Parramatta River was used as the main Sydney course for international rowing regattas and Cabarita Park provided the grandstand for the finish of such events, it had remained remarkably pristine. The park had been promulgated early in the life of Concord Council. As a bonus, for the suburb's children particularly, Concord Council in the 1930s built one of the first swimming pool complexes in Australia.

As a result, along with my brothers and sisters as well as the other neighbourhood kids, I spent weekends at the pool or fishing from the old wharf or playing on several sandy beaches in the park. While it was a kid's paradise initially, by the late 1950s and early 1960s the sandy beaches and the fishing disappeared due to the heavy pollution. This came from upstream industry – oil refineries at Clyde, toxic industries on the edge of Homebush Bay along the Rhodes peninsula and, of course, the outflows from the Gas Works on the other side of Kendall's Bay, as well from the BALM paints factory adjacent to the park, and other factories lining Hen and Chicken Bay. It was an environmental disaster.

However, thanks to the measures introduced by Jack Beale, by the mid-1970s the river soon began to recover and by the late 1970s the sandy beaches reappeared. This was because of two things. The first was the pollution was stopped by government action while the second was the amazing capacity of nature through the river's tidal flows to rid itself of the pollutants in the little shoreline beaches. This is an indicator as to how forward-thinking Jack Beale was and shows the importance of making an early start to limit noxious and toxic inflows into the Parramatta River. Another positive outcome was the impact of good environment laws and regulations complemented by planning controls.

These laws and regulations accelerated the movement away from the riverside of dozens of polluting industries which had been forced to shut down, remediate their sites and move their operations to more suitable and planned locations such as Wetherill Park.

Much of the credit for this vital and rapidly implemented transformation is almost certainly due to Jack Beale. The support his state Pollution Control Commission was given in terms of the powers the Commission had and the substantial penalties which could be levied on industries which breached the new anti-pollution standards made all the difference.

During the time I was writing this I was discussing Beale's role with a friend who was at one stage of his career a ready mixed concrete plant manager in both the metropolitan and country areas in the 1980s. While he had never heard of Beale, he was fully aware of the powers of the Commission at the time. He told me that it was the only government authority, in his experience, which could intimidate senior head office managers. They recognised the threat to their businesses of allowing breaches of the Commission's regulatory standards, such as by water pollution.

It was a tribute to the Askin government that it wisely supported Beale's foresight as the environments we all live in today are significantly improved by his various legislative interventions.

In 1971 Beale's portfolio was re-named and he became Australia's first Minister for Environmental Control with several *Clean Air Amendment Acts* introduced. The original *Clean Air Act* to curb industrial pollution had been introduced in 1960 by my good friend Terry Sheahan's father, Billy Sheahan QC, when he was the relevant minister. The first amending Act introduced by Beale sought to ban open air fires, while the second was the requirement that anti-pollution devices be fitted to cars.

By the end of his term as minister in late 1973, Beale's final legacy was the legislation to establish the NSW Planning and Environment Commission, which was passed and assented to in April 1974.

Road Safety: Milton Morris MLA

Road safety in NSW owes much to Milton Morris, the Newcastle-based Askin government Minister for Transport for 10 years. When he was appointed minister, per capita the road toll in the state was one of the highest in the world and he immediately put in place several reforms to try and stem the toll.

His first moves were to introduce a provisional licence scheme and stricter driving tests for new drivers. He increased numbers of traffic police. Initially the death toll fell but within a year it had risen. Morris then introduced other measures including rest periods for long distance drivers and alcohol breath testing. Breath testing was a highly controversial move but evidence from other jurisdictions showed it resulted in a significant drop in alcohol related accidents. Morris was spurred on to take this step because evidence showed that half of the drivers in road accidents had been drinking.

Perhaps Morris's most innovative steps was to establish Australia's first permanent traffic accident research unit. He also was responsible for the compulsory use of seat belts. Morris's road safety initiatives were an important legacy of the Askin government.

While these ministers came to prominence via the introduction of groundbreaking legislation, Eric Willis made his reputation as an administrator while responsible for the Education portfolio as he presided over a substantial expansion of the school system and later, when Premier, by establishing the Nagle Royal Commission to inquire into the prison system.

Important Consumer Reforms

There was also a steady flow of reforming legislation which was aimed at increasing the rights of consumers. Some of these Acts were aimed at modernising various institutions and services. They ranged from establishing a process for licensing builders via a Building Licensing Board in 1971 and imposing minimum qualification requirements for those contracting to do such work. It established the always much-loved state emergency service via the *State Emergency Services and Civil Defence Act 1972* and in the same year modernised legislation underpinning the Ambulance Service which had been reliant on its 1919 legislation.

The government also passed the *Consumer Protection Act 1969* which set up a Consumer Affairs Bureau and later established a Consumer Claims Tribunal to provide a low-cost way of dealing with consumers' complaints. It also passed the *Door to Door Sales Act* granting consumers a five day "cooling off" period and improved workers compensation entitlements.

Legislation also offered consumers faster and cheaper conveyancing, protection via the *Therapeutic Goods and Cosmetics Act* and warnings of the dangers of smoking via cigarette packet labelling. Consumers also benefited by the modernising of the Registry of Births, Deaths and Marriages. They codified the law regarding registration of births, deaths and marriages as well as still births and adoptions. They also allowed for the recording of legitimisation, a matter of concern to many people.

This short review of the Askin government's reforms demonstrates why they needed to be included in the study of Australia's golden era of reform. While some critics insist many of its reforms had limitations, they represented a generational change in thinking and enabled NSW to move forward on so many fronts. They provided a platform upon which later governments were able to build, while setting a cracking pace on the first leg of the reform relay.

14

THE WHITLAM ERA: COLOUR AND LIGHT

For most young Australians, particularly the baby boomer generation, Whitlam's election win meant dramatic and yet long overdue changes on many fronts. These included the ending of conscription, withdrawing Australian forces from the Vietnam War, lowering the voting age to 18 and promising free university education to all. These and many other administrative and legislative decisions were greeted with almost constant obstruction by members of the former government now in opposition. For many older Australians the pace of change was threatening, largely due to the way the new government's programme was being implemented. But Whitlam was determined to leave behind a society which was demonstrably different from the one Labor inherited. The price his government, and the country, paid for its lack of discipline was extremely high and exposed the limitations of long held assumptions and conventions about the relationship between an elected government, the Queen's representative and leaders of the High Court.

Much has been written about Whitlam's term as Prime Minister from all political points of view, about what it achieved and its failures, about the Governor General's unprecedented step, and about the subsequent overwhelming defeat of the Labor Party at the election held on 13 December 1975. However, my focus is on highlighting the broad scope and content of legislative and administrative reforms introduced by the Whitlam government during its terms in office and their lasting impact.

This impact on Australia was comprehensively reviewed by 93 members of the federal Parliament who spoke in Parliament in an extended condolence motion following the announcement of Gough Whitlam's death at the great age of 98 on 21 October 2014. These speeches were re-published, along with those made at his State Memorial Service held on 5 November 2014 at the Sydney Town Hall, in a book edited by Wendy Guest and Garry Gray under the title *Not Just for This Life – Gough Whitlam Remembered*, Newsouth Publishing, 2016.

Laurie Oakes, political journalist, in his contribution to the book quotes Whitlam's statement to an ALP National Executive meeting:

> When faced with concern about what one party official termed 'the confusion of the incessant decision making' in his early months as prime minister, he responded 'I am not going to leave behind a society which is not demonstrably different from the one we inherited'.

It is clear, from the contributions by members from all parties in the Australian Parliament during the condolences on Whitlam's death that the Whitlam government's reforms were genuinely recognised as having dramatically improved the lives, opportunities and aspirations of the great majority of Australians, including those of the members who spoke. The Whitlam era's nationwide impact was undeniably the formal start of the nation's golden era of reform and provided the solid foundations which underpin modern Australia.

The election of the Whitlam government on 2 December 1972 brought an end to 23 years of Liberal-Country Party Coalition government, the only federal government most of the baby boomer generation knew. Young Australians were particularly excited by the prospect of a Whitlam Labor government which promised to deal with the myriad problems and issues which they felt had been too long ignored by its conservative predecessors.

A quick review of the legislation it passed is very revealing: how it changed Australia for the better. Initially the new government had operated as the interim Whitlam/Barnard government or "duumvirate", a term which seemed to appeal to Whitlam, although in his book *The Whitlam Government 1972-1975*, Penguin Books, 1985, he said that he preferred the term "triumvirate" because this short-term unusual government had three participants as the Governor General Sir Paul Hasluck was a vital third member, or as Whitlam notes, the first member.

This course was taken as there were key administrative decisions the new government wished to make immediately, and the finalisation of the election count was at least two weeks off. Also, the Labor caucus could not meet to finalise the full Whitlam ministry until then. This meant that the new ministry could not be sworn in until Tuesday 19 December 1972 to become the first Labor Cabinet in 23 years.

This unusual outcome followed negotiations between Whitlam and the Governor General Sir Paul Hasluck and resulted in an agreement to have Whitlam sworn in as Prime Minister and the minister responsible for 12 portfolios. His deputy, Lance Barnard, would be minister responsible for the remaining 14 portfolios. The short-lived Whitlam/Barnard government made around 40 important decisions via federal Executive Council with the Governor General participating. According to reports at the time, Lionel Murphy QC, soon to be Senate leader and Attorney General, was unhappy not to be part of this interim government.

Whitlam had a clear agenda and a mandate as leader and was keen for the new Whitlam/Barnard government to exercise its new ministerial authority by immediately implementing a number of election promises which did not require legislation. These included the ending of conscription and freeing young men held in gaol for objecting to being conscripted, the withdrawal of Australian forces from Vietnam and the intention to formally recognise the Peoples Republic of China led by Mao Tse Tung. It also barred racially discriminatory sports teams from Australia and instructed the Australian delegation at the United Nations to support sanctions on apartheid in South Africa and Rhodesia.

On the domestic front, it removed sales tax on contraceptive pills, announced major grants for the arts, appointed an interim schools' commission and re-opened the equal pay case pending before the Commonwealth Conciliation and Arbitration Commission while appointing barrister, Elizabeth Evatt, a member of the commission.

Whitlam was signalling that the Labor government would be very different from its predecessors and, for young voters like myself, it was an incredibly exciting time with the promise of modernising Australia and re-positioning it on the world stage.

Following the completion of the counting of seats, the second Whitlam ministry was announced in early 1973.

Review of Legislative Changes

Work commenced on a wide range of legislative initiatives and, once Parliament resumed, Acts passed included lowering the voting and marriage ages to 18. Another Act removed restrictions preventing Aboriginal people travelling overseas through amendment to the *Migration Act*. The need for this initiative in the early 1970s clearly demonstrated how out of date the previous national government had been. It had apparently learned little from the almost universal support given by Australians to the 1967 referendum on the status of our Indigenous people as seen by its failure to remove such racially discriminatory restrictions.

The death penalty under the laws of the Commonwealth was removed, and self-government was granted by the *Papua New Guinea Act*. This Act removed Australia from the embarrassing position of being aligned with the small group of remaining colonial powers.

Other early initiatives taken by the Whitlam government which were of particular interest to me included the passing of an Act to establish Australian Law Reform Commission. This in turn was complemented by the announcement in July 1973 by the Attorney General Lionel Murphy QC of the decision to establish the Australian Legal Aid Office as an administrative body through a budget allocation. According to Murphy's biographer Jenny Hocking, in *Lionel Murphy: A Political Biography*, Cambridge University Press, 1997, p. 174:

> Murphy viewed the ALAO as being at the very heart of the government's law reform package, through it equity in access to the law would become a reality, without it all other legal reforms would come to nothing.

I recall hearing Murphy speaking on the radio as I was driving to a meeting, when he announced that the Commonwealth would fund legal aid via its own legal aid structure and he was quoting from my Churchill Fellowship Report's recommendations, which Murphy's office had access to. To say I was over the moon was an understatement. Later, this decision sent shock waves through the conservative legal profession, many of whom who saw the decision as the first step towards nationalising the profession.

Such a reaction was in part because there was very little dialogue between my conservative profession and this "radical" new government which passed over 200 pieces of legislation in 1973 alone, the majority bringing in some very significant policy, social and legal changes.

However, many Australians who were younger and politically unaligned, but desperate to see Australia dragged out of its 20 plus years of torpor, welcomed decisions to bring back the young, conscripted troops from Vietnam, introduce free tertiary education, increase subsidies for secondary schools and significantly increase social security and veterans' pensions.

Other major policy innovations included legislation providing for Australia's first universal health coverage system via Medibank, a Prices Justification Tribunal, a Film and Television School, the allocation of major funding for the arts generally and an Aboriginal Affairs Department, to name just a small number of the early reforms.

The Big Picture

While many of the initiatives already referred to might be seen as righting policy wrongs, there was a range of other bigger picture issues viewed by Whitlam and his team as of fundamental national importance. These have been the focus of a recent academic review of the major changes initiated by the Whitlam government which were seen as intending to make the lives of ordinary Australians better and which had not previously been seen as matters of importance to the national government, except perhaps during the Second World War. Entitled *Making Modern Australia – the Whitlam Government's 21st Century Agenda*, edited by Jenny Hocking, Monash University Publishing, 2018, its various writers remind us of how groundbreaking, and highly significant many of the policy priorities examined were.

The first essay by Michelle Arrow reminds us of the benefit which flowed from the Royal Commission on Human Relationships which was a bi-partisan response to dealing with "a fractious parliamentary debate over abortion" which had been raised in 1973. The Royal Commission, headed by newly appointed federal Judge Elizabeth Evatt, journalist Anne Deveson and progressive Anglican Bishop of Brisbane, Felix Arnott, became a way to resolve the issue to neither party's disadvantage. This initiative clearly enabled many issues flowing from human relations to be given a very public airing, and meant that governments from then on needed to start addressing the legal issues flowing from such issues. My own subsequent involvement with the Victimless Crime Seminar held early in 1977 probably only became possible because of the Royal Commission which was then being finalised.

David Lee reminds us in *Buying Back the Farm* of steps taken by the Whitlam government to "get greater control of mining" which was largely foreign controlled. Under Rex Connor's leadership new foreign investment rules were introduced requiring local ownership of 50% in all resources projects. This was complemented by the requirement that overseas owned mining companies and oil explorers needed to deposit 25% of the capital with the Reserve Bank.

Export controls established by Connor and Whitlam were adopted by the government for most minerals and it is noteworthy that this policy remained unchanged by the Fraser government.

Lyndon Megarrity sheds light on a topic of great personal interest to Whitlam who, while in Parliament, lived in western Sydney with its serious shortcomings in terms of services, health, education, sewerage, transport, in environments with a rapidly growing population.

Whitlam had grown up in the newly developed Canberra which offered unprecedented urban facilities and opportunities to those lucky enough to live there. This experience led him to form the view that local and regional authorities could play a larger part in improving social amenities and infrastructure in their communities.

His goal as recorded by Megarrity was to:

> ... enliven and invigorate people's lives, to make sure that the rewards and satisfaction of the arts, and decent opportunities for sport and recreation and holidays, are shared by as many people as possible ... It's surprising how much can be done with small sums applied carefully for local purposes. It's not necessarily a matter of building vast stadiums ... mainly it's helping local groups and authorities improve existing facilities – a new changeroom, an extra tennis court, floodlighting for an oval.

The Australian Assistance Plan (AAP) arose because Whitlam was frustrated that he had to find a way around Section 96 of the Constitution to avoid states' rights issues. He even initiated a referendum held in conjunction with the double dissolution election but was rebuffed largely because the change was not supported by the Opposition.

The AAP attracted both endorsement and criticism. This approach was influenced by western democracies moving towards an evidence-based approach to policy reforms together with community engagement and consultation. The creation of the Department of Regional Development in December 1972, with similar policy and ideological origins to the AAP, was seen as being a major Commonwealth response to the groundswell of grassroots activism in areas such as planning, urban amenities, ethnic affairs, heritage protection and citizen participation.

Whitlam's goal for these strategies represented a new approach to public administration with AAP having some support within Liberal ranks, particularly from Don Chipp, but history was not on Whitlam's side as he moved into 1975.

For a peacetime federal government, the Whitlam government took unprecedented steps to allocate more Commonwealth funds to state governments enabling them to introduce sewerage systems to outlying suburbs, provide more welfare housing and funds for much needed flood mitigation.

While these were widely welcomed and changed Australia forever, the politically active conservative elements in society were unimpressed and started to use their political power. The Opposition rejected key legislative proposals, including a threat to employ the radical tactic of using their Senate majority to reject supply bills, the normal funding for government.

Double Dissolution

After barely 12 months in government, Whitlam faced continuous obstruction by the Opposition. The Coalition controlled Senate refused to pass Bills which were key parts of the new government's mandate when it won office. Whitlam put his faith in the Australian people and called a double dissolution election in order to pass legislation he felt Australia desperately needed. This meant the first half of their second year in office was overshadowed by the April 1974 election and the last half of its third year in office was severely disrupted by the Senate's refusal of supply.

When the government refused to buckle, the Opposition led by Malcolm Fraser negotiated with the Governor General Sir John Kerr who, contrary to convention, did not consult the Prime Minister but dismissed the Whitlam government without notice on 11 November 1975 at the urging of the Opposition and aided and abetted by the Chief Justice of the High Court, former Liberal Sir Garfield Barwick.

It is interesting to note that cornered conservative politicians both here and in the US Congress resort to "throwing out the rule book" when confronted with duly elected governments with mandates to implement policies not to their liking. This practice has been seen in recent years when Tea Party Republicans resorted to this tactic regularly during the term of President Obama and more recently with the Trump-backing Republican members of Congress seeking to undermine the progressive policies of the Biden administration.

However, many in Australia believe that the conservative opposition parties in the Australian Parliament resorted to such undemocratic practices 40 years earlier than their US counterparts, leading to the unprecedented removal of an elected Australian government in late 1975. The later demonising of the Gillard government and attempts at obstructing its legislative programme was another recent example.

Nevertheless, the rejection of Whitlam's voting equity and Medibank proposals were the catalysts for a double dissolution of the Parliament and, having won office the second time at the ballot box, these important legislative initiatives of the Whitlam government were passed and helped shape the Australia we have today.

Before the dismissal on 11 November 1975, despite substantial political opposition, the Whitlam government continued to implement its legislative agenda by codifying aged health care via the *National Health Act*, protecting the environment via the *National Parks and Wildlife Conservation Act* and establishing the Australian Film Commission via its own Act, an initiative which Cate Blanchett spoke so passionately about at the Memorial Service for Gough Whitlam. She said it gave birth to the Australian film industry which has been so successful since.

From a legal and symbolic perspective, the *Privy Council (Appeals from the High Court) Act* made the High Court the last court of appeal for actions under Commonwealth law, while appeals to the Privy Council from state courts would eventually be curtailed by the 1986 *Australia Acts*. Also in 1975, the *Racial Discrimination Act* was passed, as was the *Family Law Act* which introduced no fault divorce and made divorce possible for ordinary Australians.

Other noteworthy Acts were those creating separate bodies, Australia Post and Telecom, to manage Australia's postal and telecommunications services, establishing the Australian Heritage Commission, the Australian Bureau of Statistics, the National Gallery, the Great Barrier Reef Marine Park, the Administrative Appeals Tribunal to review administrative decisions, the *Defence Force Reorganisation Act* to establish a single Defence Department, and, one of the last Acts passed, the *Aboriginal and Torres Islands (Queensland Discrimination Laws) Act* to overrule discriminatory Queensland legislation.

While the ultimate demise of the Whitlam government was due in part to a lack of internal discipline, it nevertheless left an extraordinary legacy, much of which survived despite the Fraser government's promise to wind it back.

The Impact of the Dismissal on My Generation

The dismissal of the Whitlam government, while welcomed by some, left many younger Australians devastated. I and my fellow colleagues at the Foundation felt as though there had been a coup and found it difficult to comprehend how the Constitution and the long-standing parliamentary conventions could be so abused by the Queen's representative.

We felt angry and wanted to take some type of stand. However, it was such an unprecedented occurrence we had no idea what we could do. We were rendered powerless and despaired about the future of Australian democracy. Our confidence had already been badly dented by the actions of the Opposition senators to deny supply to the Whitlam government. Adding to this, in the same year, conservative state premiers Lewis and Bjelke-Petersen ignored the long-standing convention of replacing a retiring senator with a member of the same party by nominating an independent instead, thus reducing Labor's numbers in the Senate.

It seemed that the framework of our democracy was very fragile and open to being willingly abused and manipulated by the country's conservative political class who trampled over a government which had earned the right to govern at two recent elections. We were all shattered by the callous manipulation of power by the judicial and vice regal conspirators prepared to provide a veneer of legitimacy to Fraser and his colleagues.

It was not long before young political aspirants amongst the Labor ranks such as Gareth Evans and others were taking the lead via the organisation of the National Conference for a Democratic Constitution at Melbourne's historic Exhibition Building, the scene of the formal opening of the new Australian Parliament on 9 May 1901. The organisers had invited Whitlam, Ellicott and others who were major players in Whitlam's dismissal. Terry Sheahan, by then a Labor member of the NSW Legislative Assembly, suggested that we ought to go down to Melbourne for the three day event which was held over the weekend of 24 and 25 September 1977. In hindsight, holding a major event like that over the weekend of the VFL grand final seemed to be a curious decision and probably reflected Gareth's disinterest in such frivolous Melbourne traditions, but it made it hard for interstate visitors to find accommodation.

It was a vibrant and important event with colourful contributions from prominent speakers from most of the political spectrums which resulted in the creation of a new grassroots organisation, the Campaign for Constitutional Change. I came away determined to find a way in which I and the Law Foundation could make a contribution to heal some of the wounds the Australian body politic had suffered following that fateful decision by the Governor General.

Gareth Evans, I am sure, was speaking for most young people

interested in Labor politics who experienced the trauma of the dismissal, when he says in his 2017 autobiography, *Incorrigible Optimist*, Melbourne University Press, 2017:

> It was one of those handful of situations, like the Kennedy assassination in 1963, and 9/11 in 2001 where you remember exactly what you were doing when the news broke.

He was attending a Futurology Conference in Melbourne and according to his account:

> … someone had just begun painting a scenario of 'Australia as an authoritarian society'! 'Stop the presses', we said: 'It's just arrived'.

He recounts that they rushed to the City Square, to start building barricades for the revolution which never quite took off.

At the time of the 1977 event, Gareth had just been admitted to the Melbourne Bar having realised, as he says in *Incorrigible Optimist*, that as he aspired to be Commonwealth Attorney General, he had been advised to demonstrate that he was a successful and capable advocate at the Bar. However, this part of his career was cut short by being elected to the Senate in 1978.

I must say that I came away from my visit to Melbourne envious of the vibrancy of the left political scene. Despite the Wran government being in power, NSW machine politics never seemed to generate the vibrancy I had been exposed to in Melbourne.

However, it was not too long before Gareth re-appeared in my life seeking the Foundation's support for his idea of generating a publication about the Constitution for the lay community.

15

The Whitlam Era: Inside the Reform Tornado

The timing of my commencing a new role, coinciding as it did with the Whitlam government getting off to a flying start and making big changes, meant innovation and reform were the buzz words. My recently acquired awareness of the potential application of computer technology to legal information resulted in an invitation to become part of its reform agenda via my appointment to the Commonwealth Attorney General's Computerisation of Legal Data Committee. This meant that I was rubbing shoulders with the leaders of the Attorney General's Department and being a valuable contributor to the final report. Later, the Foundation's HELP initiative and its research team won recognition from other Whitlam era reform agencies.

One of my first priorities after returning to Australia from my Churchill Fellowship had been to take steps to obtain a copy of the Canadian government's *Operation Compulex* report. I also collected the other reports and publications of projects using computers to search and store legal information being undertaken in the US, Canada and the UK.

These information sources meant that I was able to brief the Law Foundation Board in late November 1972 on the progress being made overseas with computer based legal information retrieval. They needed little convincing as to the role the Foundation could play in working with both the Commonwealth and NSW governments under the auspices of the Foundation's statutory object relating to the support of law libraries.

Accordingly, one of a number of priorities the Board set for me as their new director was to undertake wide consultations to assist with a study and investigation of:

a) the ways in which computerised systems, as an adjunct to libraries, could assist lawyers;

b) the feasibility of adapting computers for use as a legal research tool;

c) the preliminary steps and investigations necessary before computers can be so implemented; and

d) the projected cost of implementation of computers as lawyers' tools.

By this stage, the new Attorney General, Senator Lionel Murphy QC, had taken the initiative and established two committees dealing with computer technology, one to investigate computerisation of criminal data, with the second looking into the computerisation of legal data.

These were relatively low-key enquiries, compared with higher profile issues such as environmental law, family law, human rights, trade practices and legal aid, to name others on Murphy's long held reform agenda.

My First Government Committee

Eventually, I was invited to meet Senator Murphy in his Sydney office to discuss the work of the Committee on Computerisation of Legal Data which had been appointed several months prior. Before meeting with Senator Murphy, I decided to meet the committee chairperson Jean Mullin, at the time a senior editor of the Law Book Company.

However, while she seemed to have little detailed knowledge of the move towards the computerisation of legal data, she was a prominent woman lawyer who had a distinguished career as a legal editor and was an appropriate choice as an independent chair of the committee.

When I met with the Attorney General, I took the collection of reports I had acquired and explained the Foundation's interest in the topic and, having seen the make-up of the committee, expressed reservations about being involved.

I also learned that the committee was planning an exploratory trip overseas which they were relying on to gather the type of knowledge and information I had already acquired. Considering my comments, Murphy was kind enough to express the view that the committee definitely needed me as a member and, in light of his frankness, I responded by saying that I would be honoured to be appointed to the committee.

By the time I joined the committee in May 1973, plans were well underway for a delegation from the committee to undertake this study tour, with no suggestion that I should participate. I was not particularly concerned as I had my own travel plans to go to the US for the Foundation. I then arranged to join the committee for a number of meetings in Washington and New York.

Fortunately for me the one member of the committee I knew was Frank Mahoney, as only a few years earlier he had been my boss at the Deputy Crown Solicitor's in Sydney and some of his sons had also played tennis with the Roseville group. He was probably a bit taken aback by my appointment to the committee but went out of his way to ensure that I was brought up to speed with its work.

In turn, I ended up being the main committee member involved in a drafting team of several departmental officers charged with producing the committee's report. This happened because when the time came to write up the committee's conclusions, the senior representatives of the Attorney General's Department were frantically pursuing Murphy's reform agenda on a large number of fronts against the backdrop of the looming double dissolution election.

From my observation, the Departmental personnel I engaged with through the work of the committee seemed to be enthusiastic about Murphy's reform agenda. Ross McMullin, in his 1991 history of the ALP, *The Light on the Hill*, OUP Australia and New Zealand, 1991, commented:

> Many public servants welcomed the election of the Whitlam government. However, there were inevitably tensions between the incoming ministers and some of the senior public servants who were not used to such a cracking pace.

It was an extraordinary opportunity to observe and be part of the "tornado" of activity created by this activist Attorney General whose reform agenda, capacity and vision were unprecedented in the usually staid legal arena.

Being able to meet regularly with departmental members of the committee, Deputy Secretary Frank Mahoney, Bronte Quayle QC Parliamentary Counsel and Jim Carnsew, the Department's IT director and, from time to time, Sir Clarrie Harders, the Department's Secretary, I observed at firsthand what McMullin was referring to with the term "such a cracking pace". This was more so with the Attorney General's Department because with so much legislation being put before the Parliament by the new government, virtually all of it needed to be formulated with input from Murphy's department.

On its return, the committee met regularly over the next six months reviewing the large amount of overseas material gathered as well as mastering arcane matters such as the growing use of magnetic tape for storing data and its use in the printing industry, the emerging technology of optical character recognition and sorting through the growing number of programmes being developed in different parts of the world. Equally relevant was deciding on the material to be held in a computer database and setting priorities for providing access to such materials.

In turn, a report was commenced, and I was directly involved in this process over the next four or five months. I have vivid memories of working late into the night on a number of occasions in the, by then largely deserted, dimly lit, cavernous (and somewhat creepy)

Administrative Building in Canberra, working on drafts with departmental staff appointed to assist the committee.

The committee's report was finalised in March 1974 and presented to the Attorney General.

Ultimately, the committee concluded that the project should move forward according to a plan set out in the report with the first stage starting with an interim phase, largely because there were still too many unknowns. There was a dual purpose to this phase, as it was intended to provide a service to users and to give guidance to those responsible for developing the second stage. The initial phase was intended, when operational, to be for the use of the Department and the Office of Parliamentary Counsel.

The first database was to consist of the Constitution and the 1901-1973 consolidation of Acts of the Australian Parliament, to be accessed via magnetic tapes produced as a by-product of the printing process, supplemented by legislation passed from 1974 onwards stored on service bureau computers using IBM's STAIRS full text retrieval software. In the committee's view, this approach meant that the learning curve could be accelerated rather than waiting for other programmes to be adapted or developed.

The committee had been aware of STAIRS, which IBM developed in the US as a way of storing and accessing vast amounts of information it needed, because of an anti-trust case brought against the company by the US government in the mid-1960s. It was the programme a number of members of my Board had seen demonstrated prior to my involvement with the Foundation.

The report provided extensive detail on the later stages of this project. In due course the Department moved ahead with the development of the project but eventually decided against the recommended interim approach, opting for British software STATUS, which in turn led to the AUSTLII system currently providing online full text retrieval of both statute and case law from all Australian jurisdictions.

Being a member of a ministerial committee intimately involved in the formulation of the committee's conclusions and then drafting the final report was a unique experience, particularly working alongside such exceptionally gifted senior government lawyers.

A later appointee to the committee was John Traill QC, a nominee of the Law Council of Australia, and later a close friend. After the work of the committee was completed John and I continued to be members of the Attorney General's Consultative Committee on Computers and the Law which enabled us to monitor the department's move towards developing the new retrieval system. Regrettably, following the dismissal of the Whitlam government, the incoming coalition Attorney General seemed not to share Senator Murphy's commitment to the new technology.

Foundation Takes the Baton

With the committee's report completed, it provided me with a much clearer understanding of what was involved in establishing a workable full text legal retrieval system. I also saw that working with IBM might be a way forward, even if Murphy's initiative was getting lost in the back wash of the "tornado" in the department which came to an abrupt halt with Murphy's appointment to the High Court in February 1975.

With the backing of the Board, it was decided to develop a pilot programme following the path suggested in the committee's report by co-opting contacts I had made within IBM Australia Ltd. to provide access to STAIRS and computer time to initiate a database focusing on the new legal area, trade practices law. IBM was happy to assist so I then spoke to Jane Levine, an American law lecturer at UNSW teaching Trade Practices Law, whom I first met in New York in 1972 with her husband Jim Beattie. I knew Jim from when he was a young lawyer with US firm Baker & McKenzie in the same Bridge Street building as me.

Subsequently I had visited a number of major US law publishers monitoring their progress with implementing full text retrieval systems and West Publishing Co of St Paul Minnesota, publisher of the

US Statutes, provided me with machine readable tapes of a selection of relevant US anti-trust case law which Jane had suggested would complement the growing body of Australian case law and which she was familiar with having gained her legal qualifications in the US.

This project was an excellent demonstration vehicle and established the utility to lawyers of such databases.

While participation in the work of the Computerisation of Legal Data Committee was the first engagement the Foundation had with the Whitlam government, later the Foundation's HELP initiative came to the notice of the Curriculum Development Centre. Recognising the value of the work being done by HELP, the Centre made a substantial two-year funding allocation to the project which enabled it to develop further resources and gave the project some financial independence from the Foundation.

Similarly, it was not long before the Foundation's research staff was being sought out by Justice Michael Kirby, Chairman of the Whitlam government-established Australian Law Reform Commission. As a result, various research projects were undertaken over the next 10 years or so to assist with various Commission references, with the work done by Foundation staff researchers Roman Tomasic initially and later by Peter Cashman and Concetta Rizzo.

Looking back, while the Foundation's involvement with the Whitlam government was interesting, my personal experience of being on a ministerial committee alongside a number of senior public servants and one of the academic leaders in computer science, was invaluable at various levels.

Also, the quality of the work being undertaken by HELP and the Foundation's research team soon gained serious recognition from new Commonwealth government agencies created by the Whitlam government.

The experience with the Whitlam government facilitated a long-term relationships with successive federal governments and its pace of reform energised me and the Foundation's Board to forge ahead with its reform agenda.

16

WRAN'S SURPRISE ELECTION RESULT AND HIS REFORM INITIATIVE

Less than five months after the fallout from the Whitlam dismissal and a massive swing against federal Labor, Neville Wran defied the odds and the press to win office for Labor in NSW. His policy was to act cautiously and win public acceptance.

This is an account of Wran's major achievements during his term as Premier and I follow up with accounts of the enormous amount the Law Foundation was able to achieve during this reform era with the co-operation of his government and its successor, the Unsworth government. The Wran/Unsworth governments both, in my view, are justified as being considered significant contributors to Australia's golden era of reform.

The double dissolution election imposed by Governor General Kerr as a condition of his dismissal of the Whitlam government held on 13 December 1975 decimated the federal Labor Party, leading many to think that the Labor brand had been tarnished beyond repair. This was the view held by then NSW Premier Sir Eric Willis.

In late 1974 Premier Askin announced his retirement and unexpectedly and secretly supported Minister for Lands Tom Lewis as his replacement instead of his long-term Deputy and heir apparent Eric Willis. However, the somewhat erratic Lewis quickly lost the support of his party and was dumped in late January 1976 and was replaced by Willis. By this time the government was into its last year of the current term and Willis was faced with the need to hold a by-election for the seat of Monaro. As the polling was negative, rather than see out the full term he opted for a 1 May election.

However, he was facing a revitalised Labor Party under the

leadership of the charismatic Neville Wran QC, who had been Leader of the Opposition since 1973 following the defeat of Pat Hills by Askin in his record fourth successive election win. Neville Wran brought to his role as leader the smooth sophistication of a successful QC beneath which were the experiences of having grown up during the depression in the then rough and tumble suburb of Balmain. However, being a bright child, Wran won a place at the fabled Fort Street Boys High School.

Willis, no doubt hopeful that some of the antipathy shown to the federal Labor Party in the very recent federal election following the dismissal of the Whitlam government would transfer to the state election, rolled the dice and called an election

From Labor's point of view, as Antony Green put it in *The Wranslides and Electoral Politics*, his contribution to *The Wran Era*, edited by Troy Bramston, Federation Press, 2006:

> Running against a tired and divided Coalition government, Wran would have won easily. However, Labor was also running against the memory of the Whitlam government, and a front-page editorial in the *Sydney Morning Herald* on polling day described Wran as 'simply Mr Whitlam writ small'.

Green noted the difficulty a popular Don Dunstan in South Australia had in holding onto office the previous year and the recent swing to the sitting Hamer Liberal government in March 1976, both of which would have encouraged Willis. Green also pointed out that "Labor had to overcome the rural bias in the electoral system."

Wran ultimately won by a margin of one seat despite gaining almost 50% of the popular vote. The government's primary vote was 46.3% which, according to Green, was attributable to Labor's campaigning heavily on public transport issues which enabled it to win the key commuter seats of Gosford, Blue Mountains and Hurstville by small margins.

Once in office Wran's approach to governing was relatively

cautious, and according to Steketee and Cockburn's *Wran, an Unauthorised Biography*, Allen & Unwin, 1986:

> From the outset Wran made it clear his government would act cautiously and deliberately in implementing its election policies. 'There will be no mad rush to introduce all of our policies overnight – this is government not a sprint,' he said, in one of his first interviews as Premier ... 'Moderation', 'caution' and 'stability' were to become bywords of Wran's government.

Wran's campaign, according to Steketee and Cockburn, gave hope to many people including conservationists, feminists, migrants, Aborigines and law reformers. They also noted that from the outset Wran made it clear his government would act cautiously and deliberately in implementing its election policies.

However, despite Wran's much publicised "softly, softly" approach to reform, several months after the new government's 1976 election word came through to me from the Attorney General's Department that the new young reformist Attorney General Frank Walker was keen to explore the electorate's tolerance to the reform of so-called victimless crimes.

This was the Foundation's first engagement with the new Wran government and followed a request from Walker for assistance from the Foundation with the funding, organisation and management of a proposed public forum on Victimless Crimes. The Foundation's Board readily agreed to assist this groundbreaking public seminar and I joined a planning committee made up of senior public servants with various responsibilities within the NSW justice system.

Victimless Crimes Seminar 24-27 February 1977

The intention was to hold the event early in the New Year which meant that over the next few months the committee had to settle a programme, select speakers including a number of overseas experts, find a suitably large venue and publicise the event. What follows is the story of this remarkably brave attempt at public consultation about so-called victimless crimes.

Trevor Haines, Under Secretary of the Attorney General's Department, chaired the planning group responsible for organising this unprecedented public seminar. The intention was to focus specifically on the offences of drunkenness and vagrancy, suicide, homosexuality, prostitution and drug abuse, and to elucidate the public's view of reforms in respect to such issues. The venue selected was the York Theatre in the University of Sydney's Seymour Centre, which had seating for around 800. It was to have a formal opening on the evening of Thursday, 24 February 1977, with the final session being held on the morning of Sunday, 27 February 1977.

The Premier, Neville Wran QC, formally opened the event with an address which heralded a new approach to managing reform and outlined his government's determination to be a reformist government, while distancing itself from the Whitlam government's relatively undisciplined reform approach.

At the start of his address, Wran asked the question, "Why hold a seminar?" He noted that it had not been the usual course for governments in this country to hold seminars to assist in the preparation of laws. The tradition was that new laws were usually formulated in great secrecy. He also commented that rarely did the public get the opportunity to take part in the initial stages of law making. He added that he had long been convinced that it was time to move on from the old-fashioned way of doing the business of government.

The event, he said, was in the nature of an experiment. If it succeeded his government would use:

> ... machinery such as this often to ventilate ideas in the public way to secure expert and public comment upon which we can fashion legislation appropriate to the State.

These sentiments no doubt reflected the genuinely held view of an incoming reformist government.

On this Thursday evening in February 1977, when Wran and Walker had been in government for a little over six months, Wran noted in his opening address:

The Government had been elected on a platform of reform and it intends to reform the laws relating to victimless crimes. Already we have begun the process of modernising the State's criminal law with a special division being created in the Attorney General's Department to perform this review on a regular ongoing basis.

He mentioned in passing that a review of the law and procedure relating to bail and the crime of rape were already underway.

Wran then adopted a somewhat philosophical approach, indicating the seminar would focus on the question "What are the proper boundaries of the criminal law?", an issue he noted that had been explored by Norval Morris and Gordon Hawkins in their powerful tract *The Honest Politician's Guide to Crime Control*, University of Chicago Press, 1970. Wran went on to quote from this seminal work by two prominent criminologists with strong links to Australia:

> The prime function of the criminal law is to protect our persons and property. These purposes are now engulfed in a mass of other distracting, inefficiently performed legislative duties. When the criminal law invades the spheres of private morality and social welfare, it exceeds its proper limits at the cost of neglecting its primary tasks. This unwarranted extension is expensive, ineffective and criminogenic.

Continuing this theme, Wran commented that this was not a new debate and had been ongoing since the early part of the previous century with strong competing viewpoints. But he said:

> In the past it has all too often been a debate in which we Australians have been mere spectators. We have left it to others to articulate the issues, the consequences being that nothing much has been done. The law has remained substantially un-reformed. Daily injustices to the lives of our fellow citizens are the result, and the time has come to change this and the Government is determined to see proper, orderly reform that will reflect the international debate on these issues.

He went on to say:

> What we really have to do as a society is to take a fresh look at the purpose of our criminal law, given the scarce resources which are made available, the expertise of the manpower used and the other practical problems that mostly arise from the present situation. We have to ask ourselves – how would our law enforcement agencies be best used to their maximum utility?

He then returned to Morris and Hawkins, noting with approval that they had just published for incoming President Jimmy Carter's benefit a *Letter to the President on Crime Control,* University of Chicago Press, 1977, that "It might just as well have been written to any Australian politician coming into office."

Wran complemented this view by quoting from their new work:

> The need to rethink and restructure criminal law is important and urgent. It is for these reasons that authoritative support for decriminalisation proposals has come from many responsible organisations.

The Premier then referred to the support given to these ideas by Sir Robert Mark of the Metropolitan London Police and to the growing support for these ideas within the Council of Europe.

The problem Wran foresaw was that:

> In the case of many of the offences under our criminal law, it is clear that the law is being used in an attempt to regulate the private moral conduct of citizens and to coerce them into what is regarded as virtue at the time the law was drawn up ... But who can doubt that some of the virtues of the Victorian age, when our *Crimes Act* was first drafted, are no longer accepted as virtues today.

He then went further, saying:

> In the case of some laws regarding sexual conduct, the law constitutes an unwarranted intrusion into privacy. It acts in an arbitrary and haphazard fashion. In regard to private consensual sexual conduct between adults, intrusion of the

criminal law is just a public nuisance. Certainly, it is proper that the law should protect children and punish force and violence or conduct which openly affronts public decency.

But he added:

When it goes beyond that and seeks in this area to impose a private morality, does not the criminal law exceed its proper function?

While some would later say that the government was too slow to bring about reforms in some of these areas, Wran made it very clear, and put on the public record, his own personal view and support for this unique experiment in seeking public input into the reform debate.

Yet this conclusion is not one shared by his biographers Steketee and Cockburn who, in their summation of Wran in the last chapter, entitled *The Wran Decade*, said:

Wran's starting point in politics was always winning, not changing society. The Wran story is not that of a young political activist who carried his political zeal into Parliament.

Having observed Wran deliver a similarly insightful speech to a totally different audience a couple of years later, I have no doubt his comments on both occasions were genuinely felt but, as noted earlier, in an interview following his resignation in 1976, in which he effectively distanced himself from the Whitlam approach to reform, he said:

… we tried to keep pace with community opinion. When the community didn't have an opinion, we'd endeavour to create an environment whereby the community would accept it as if they'd thought of it themselves.

The Victimless Crimes seminar reflected both parts of this approach, in that the event was clearly intended to create the appropriate environment for change. On the other hand, it was also clear that as the seminar progressed and some of the more strident advocates and critics attracted headlines in the press, Wran's attitude was that such changes needed to have wide community support which, at that time, was not there. As leader he had to balance support for much needed reforms with the reality of a one seat majority.

Having concluded his opening remarks, Wran then introduced the first of two overseas experts, Professor John Kaplan from Stanford University, a prominent American criminal law expert and author who delivered the first keynote address which focused on his wide knowledge of so-called non-victim crime. The other international expert was Professor Stanley Cohen from the University of Essex who spoke at length about the UK experience. The Law Foundation sponsored both international visitors.

The Bureau of Crime Statistics and Research within the Attorney General's Department produced background papers on each topic and bound copies were distributed to those attending the seminar.

The next morning the first session opened with the drunkenness and vagrancy topic, with addresses made by Police Inspector Bob Redhead, academic social worker Dr Margaret Sargent, social scientist, and foundation director of the Bureau of Crime Statistics and Research and prominent academic and reformer, Professor Tony Vinson, and Tony Restuccia, a Sydney lawyer representing the St Vincent de Paul Society. My recollection is that little by the way of controversy was generated from this issue with a consensus that it was time for the law dealing with these issues to change. It was the calm before the storm.

This was followed by a session with a presentation on the law relating to suicide by Law Foundation researcher Roman Tomasic, who had undertaken research on this issue prior to joining the Foundation's staff. Again, it was largely uncontroversial until a rather spectacular interruption. A middle-aged woman rushed towards the stage screaming and as she got to the stage pulled out from a bag a very large crucifix. It seemed at the time that she was intending to beat Roman over the head with it but thankfully she was stopped and escorted from the building before she could do Roman any harm.

Needless to say, that put an end to the session and Roman was somewhat shaken by the experience. As an academic he did not usually get this strong a response!

The Saturday morning session on homosexuality, not unexpectedly, generated the most heat. The speakers were the Anglican Dean of Sydney the Reverend Lance Shilton, Michael Clohessy representing the Homosexual Rights Coalition, prominent consultant psychologist Ronald Conway and Lex Watson from the Department of Government, University of Sydney, a prominent gay rights commentator.

The York Theatre was full and the audience was organised so that the reformists filled up the left tier of seats, those opposing reform were in the right tier of seats and those who supported neither group were in the middle. The session was chaired by Attorney General Frank Walker and, while the speakers were subject to some interruptions, that part of the session proceeded without major incident.

During the general discussion Fred Nile's Festival of Light members were vociferous and objected loudly, attacking contributions from the pro-reformers and making unfounded assertions, such as people going into schools to teach young children about homosexuality. Later a Catholic priest attacked Frank Walker for bias in allowing such a topic to be included on the programme.

At one stage, in a context where the speakers for the gay cause were being balanced and putting forward reasonable arguments, one unidentified man who described himself as a homosexual made a series of outrageous assertions from the audience about continuing:

> ... to engage in sex with other men in public toilets ... I will continue to fuck with minors, regardless to the laws preventing children having sex. I think it is necessary to say all of this because you cannot control me and you will not control me.

This created an immediate uproar, with those from the Festival of Light demanding that the police come and arrest the contributor. Everyone was in a state of shock, none more so than those of us who had organised the event.

Frank Walker's experience thankfully kicked in and after he had called for calm, he said:

> All I can say, sir, to that, is that I deplore this – you are doing damage to your cause and your group.

This session regrettably showed that there was still a long way to go to gain wide community support to change the laws penalising homosexuals. As Frank Walker noted in his essay in the book *The Wran Era*, Wran was attacked by gay groups for failing to act on reform proposals. He had so many conservative Catholics in his Cabinet and public opinion was not ready. As a result, it was only late in his premiership that Wran, no doubt recognising that public opinion now was more positive towards reform, piloted a Bill decriminalising homosexual conduct through Parliament, on the basis of a conscience vote, with the relevant legislation becoming law.

The remaining session that day was on prostitution and it featured Detective Sergeant Brian Rope, the Reverend Fred Nile, Anne Deveson of the Royal Commission on Human Relationships and barrister Helen Coonan representing the Women's Electoral Lobby. Helen was later Chair of the Law Foundation, a Liberal Party Senator and federal Communications Minister in the Howard government.

I had the dubious honour of chairing this session and approached it with some trepidation after the previous homosexuality session. However, I am pleased to say that the papers were objective and balanced and general discussion went comparatively smoothly with a consensus supporting decriminalisation. This was comparatively easier to achieve than the homosexuality reforms. With the passing in 1979 of the *Prostitution Act* and associated amendments to the *Summary Offences Act* prostitution became legal and regulated.

The final day opened with the issue of Drug Abuse which saw contributions by Detective Sergeant Ken Astill, the Reverend Ted Noffs from the Wayside Chapel, and Neal Blewett, the Professor of Sociology, Flinders University and later federal Member of Parliament and Minister for Health in the Hawke government.

Again, this session, while enlightening to many in the audience, did not evoke much heat. It also allowed the government to gauge the level of public support which might exist for appropriate reforms. However, at the time of writing, little real progress seems to have been made with decriminalisation of drug use other than the Carr government's experiment with injecting rooms.

A Brave Pioneering Step

The Seminar was an amazing experiment which probably achieved less than those of us responsible for organising it would have wanted. Nevertheless, it was a brave pioneering step taken by a new reformist government with a small majority and would have added significantly to its credibility in the eyes of many.

However, Wran handled the fallout from the seminar adroitly and it is interesting, when later reflecting on Wran's campaign, commentators Steketee and Cockburn said Wran's election win and approach gave hope to many people including conservationists, feminists, migrants, Aborigines and law reformers.

Nevertheless, they also noted that from the outset Wran made it clear his government would act cautiously and deliberately in implementing its election policies, which probably explains why the reform process would not involve public consultation which had been experimented with in victimless crimes! The NSW Law Reform Commission later took on the role of assessing community attitudes to particular law reform issues with funding from the Law Foundation.

In another interview, a year after the election, Wran said:

> Our greatest achievement is that we have gained public acceptance. After the tumult of the Whitlam Government everyone expected we would be the same. Well we haven't.

The proof of this statement can be seen in his government's legislative record during its first term.

Wran was certainly consistent on these themes, as the day after announcing his resignation on 7 June 1986 at the NSW ALP Annual Conference he said:

> Whereas some Labor governments in the past rushed in and tried to do everything at once, we tried to keep pace with community opinion. When the community didn't have an opinion, we'd endeavour to create an environment whereby the community would accept it as if they'd thought of it themselves.

This approach can be readily seen during the first term of the Wran government. When one reviews the legislation it introduced into the Parliament in that period, while there may have been policy changes brought about by amendments to the existing legislation, the only new legislation passed in 1976 which could be considered reformist or innovative was the establishment of an Ethnic Affairs Commission and a Land Commission.

Other Acts made changes to the Ombudsman's Office by extending its responsibilities to include local government authorities, removed the legal disabilities of ex-nuptial children and extended the jurisdiction of the consumer tribunals.

The following year, 1977, saw a similar pattern with the passing of the *Anti-Discrimination Act*, the creation of the Elizabeth Bay House Trust (later to be revoked and the property transferred to an Historic Houses Trust), the passing of the *Heritage Act* to conserve the heritage of the state and legislating to establish the NSW Film Corporation. A new *Jury Act* was also passed to modernise jury selection and eligibility. An amendment to the relevant legislation allowing women prisoners to be eligible for periodic detention was the only other notable reform. However, having gained the confidence of the community, Wran was ready to seek a mandate for his growing reform agenda via an early election in 1978.

17

WRAN'S 1978 BIG WIN: THE GREEN LIGHT FOR REFORM

In the lead up to the 1978 election and because Wran only had a small majority, his reform agenda was limited but did include a referendum to be held in conjunction with the state's election to amend the state's Constitution by adopting the popular election of Upper House members and to ensure the adoption of "one vote, one value". The community backed his judgment and over 80% of voters endorsed his referendum proposal.

The success of Wran's "softly, softly" approach during the first term was rewarded by massive swings to the government in the 1978 and 1981 "Wranslide" elections. As a result, the government's majority increased from 28 seats after the 1978 election to a massive majority of 39 in the poll held late in October 1981. The Liberals and Nationals ended up with only 14 seats each. As I recall, the only seat held by the Coalition between Sydney Harbour and the Victorian border was the seat of Vaucluse held by Rosemary Foot MP.

With the 1978 election out of the way, the government in 1979 passed the *Public Service Act* which, according to Frank Walker in *The Wran Era*, was Wran's response to the instability the Whitlam Ministry faced due to the inability to control heads of departments, a situation also reflected in NSW. Wran took several major steps to deal with this problem. He made the Premier's Department dominant over the NSW bureaucracy. To achieve this, he needed to deal with the NSW Public Service Board which effectively controlled the public service.

Wran appointed Peter Wilenski, Gough Whitlam's former principal private secretary and later federal department head, to carry out a review of the public service. Following the review's announcement, the Foundation's research team were interested in knowing about how far reaching this review was to be. With the help of the Attorney General's Department, several of us were granted a brief meeting, fitted somewhat reluctantly into Wilenski's tight schedule. We were keen to know if his terms of reference extended to reviewing the quality of any particular government services as we thought that the Foundation might assist by undertaking comparable research about the legal system.

Wilenski promptly told us that such in-depth inquiries were not in the scope of his terms of reference, and added by way of an analogy that he only wanted to know if the suburban rail network had trains and not if they ran on time or went to the right places. This brought an end to our meeting. It was an interesting lesson in how sharply focused the government's goals were and in realpolitik.

Wilenski was to draft a new *Public Service Act* which transferred power over the public service to the government and, in turn, to the Premier's Department, and put an end to the dominance of the Public Service Board. Other Wilenski-recommended reforms improved the rights and work conditions of public servants, as well as the adoption of affirmative action policies all of which were needed reforms.

The government also passed a diverse range of reform legislation that year, including the *Environmental Planning & Assessment Act* to institute a system of environment planning and assessment. In turn, it was complemented by the establishment of a Land & Environment Court, a superior court of record to deal with a wide range of land usage and environmental issues with both judicial members and assessors to provide assistance to the court.

The government also responded to the emergence of the futures market by providing a legislative framework under which such markets would operate. An act to establish a Science and Technology

Council to provide advice to the government in these emerging areas was also passed.

Passing the Law Foundation Act

Within the legal sphere, and from my personal perspective, a great step forward was the Parliament passing the *Law Foundation Act* which commenced on 14 May 1979. This comprehensive Act elevated the Foundation by making it a statutory corporation and significantly broadening its charter and removed the Foundation from the control of the Law Society. It was the first piece of legislation to which I personally made a contribution. I had been asked by Trevor Haines, by then the Secretary of the Attorney General's Department and a strong supporter of the Foundation, to submit a draft of a revised set of statutory objectives for the Law Foundation.

When I saw the legislation as passed by the Parliament I was extremely pleased, as it provided legitimacy for the direction the Foundation had been moving in during the previous five years or so. The objects of the "new" Foundation, as set out in the new Act, were radically broadened in comparison with the original 1967 version, most of which were retained but expanded.

There was now much more focus on promoting greater community access to both legal information and legal services and on educating the community about the law and the legal system, with a particular emphasis on promoting the rights of the socially and economically disadvantaged – a new era!

The new Act also enlarged the Board by increasing the community representation to five, while reducing the Law Society's representation to two members but adding a representative of the Bar Association. These were complemented by parliamentary members from both the government and Opposition, which was a novel and very useful innovation. Finally, the Foundation's director also became an ex officio member of the Board. These changes, which carried the endorsement of both Attorney General Frank Walker and Trevor Haines, were personally very pleasing, as was the key change of ensuring that the Foundation would receive a fixed and larger share of the Statutory Interest Account income.

The government also established the Legal Aid Commission to take responsibility for the provision of legal aid from the Public Solicitor's Office while increasing funding for an expanded range of legal aid services to be provided by the Commission.

Community Justice Centres and Other Reforms

The next year, 1980, saw the government undertake a series of major law reform initiatives including legislation to establish a unique pilot project to test a new concept of access to justice via the *Community Justice Centres (Pilot Project) Act*. This Act provided a way of testing the concept of mediation being used to solve local or neighbourhood disputes outside the formal court system. Significantly, as noted later in more detail, the Law Foundation was appointed the statutory evaluator of the pilot scheme which was further recognition at the highest political level of the value of the groundbreaking research which had been carried out by the Foundation's researchers over the previous five years.

It also meant that the Foundation had a continuing role through the contribution of the evaluation team headed by staff researcher John Schwartzkoff, a heavy responsibility but one we were confident would be carried out to the highest standards of objectivity.

On another more commercial level of dispute resolution, the government introduced the *Contracts Review Act* to provide judicial review of certain contracts and offering relief from harsh or unconscionable contracts. As part of the government's attempt to modernise the public service, it passed the *Government and Related Employees Appeal Tribunal Act*, the purpose of which was to codify rights of appeal for public servants from decisions relating to promotions or discipline.

In 1980 it passed the *Historic Houses Act* to provide for the control and management of certain houses of historic importance including Elizabeth Bay House, its Act being repealed by this new Act.

Graham Freudenberg, the preeminent Australian political speech writer who worked closely with Wran for many years, refers in his own memoir, *A Figure of Speech: A Political Memoir,* Wiley, 2005, to the *Historic Houses Act* as another part of Wran's legacy:

> The approaching Bicentenary gave a focus for Wran's vision of a Sydney transformed. At the heart of his vision was the idea of giving the city back to the people, or, at the very least, encouraging them to share his own zest for their heritage, from which he drew a sense of obligation to add to it ... the Wran Government restored the Hyde Park Barracks and the Mint, created the notable precinct of St James, built the Entertainment Centre, the Parramatta Stadium, established both the Powerhouse Museum and the Wharf Theatre, and revitalised the Rocks and Haymarket areas, effectively creating whole new areas of the city for the use and enjoyment of the citizens, when before they had been neglected and decayed ... and a range of Bicentenary projects around the state and above all the great Darling Harbour project.

In June 1981 the government broke new ground by passing Australia's first *Election Funding Act* to make provision for public funding of parliamentary election campaigns, while it also passed the *Consumer Credit Act* to regulate the provision of consumer credit.

With the Wran government's 1981 re-election, the government moved ahead with a broadening reform agenda. Other constitutional reforms pursued over the next couple of years included the introduction of optional preferential voting, the adoption of a four-year term, and of a register of members' pecuniary interests, all of which became law.

In 1982 the government passed the *Aboriginal Land Rights Act* for the purpose of establishing Aboriginal Land Councils and allocating funds to such councils to acquire land.

An ambitious *Community Welfare Act* was also passed. Its purpose was to promote, develop, maintain and improve the well-being of the people of NSW; to promote the welfare of the family as the basis of community welfare; and to ensure the provision of support services to disadvantaged persons.

The intent and scope of this Act can be seen by the wide range of other acts which were amended to ensure the aims of the Act were achieved. To me this appeared to be a new approach to legislation in which the principles behind it were incorporated in the Act to ensure those providing services under it had a clear idea of the goals to be achieved.

Some Major Reforms

A similar approach was taken with the passing of the *Mental Health Act* in 1983. This legislation flowed from the report prepared by David Richmond, who had previously carried out an inquiry for the government into the handling of those suffering mental health issues. This was a much-anticipated report and resulted in a wide debate in the press and in a range of other forums before its recommendations were incorporated in this legislation.

The title page calls it "an act to make provision with respect to the care, treatment and control of persons who are mentally ill". This was immediately followed by a rare statutory preamble, no doubt to highlight the importance of matters covered by the Act:

Preamble:

WHEREAS it is recognised:-

(a) that the provision of services in respect of persons with mental illness requires both community care facilities and hospital facilities;

(b) that hospital care should be provided on an informal and voluntary basis where appropriate and, in a limited number of situations, on an involuntary basis; and

(c) that the civil rights of persons should be protected and, at the same time, that opportunity should be given for persons with mental illness to have access to appropriate care.

In his contribution to *The Wran Era*, Laurie Brereton, Minister for Health at the time of this reform, recorded the appalling institutional circumstances in which people with mental illness or intellectual disabilities were being cared for up to that point in time. As Brereton said:

> They were just put behind the walls of these vast edifices and forgotten. But they were human beings. We had to improve their treatment and lifestyle.

Brereton adds:

> The main aim was relatively simple: to stop people being locked away in these vast mental institutions unless they were 'a danger to themselves or to others'. This was largely achieved, as our new legislation ensured that before anybody could be locked away the decision had to be certified by at least two doctors.

Regrettably, rather than this turning into a success story, according to Brereton, it was a great disappointment. He felt the alternative care arrangements were never adequately funded.

Another great reform was the *Occupational Health and Safety Act*. The objects of these much-needed reforms were stated as being:

(a) to secure the health, safety and welfare of persons at work;

(b) to protect persons at a place of work (other than persons at work) against risks to health or safety arising out of the activities of persons at work;

(c) to promote an occupational environment for persons at work which is adapted to their physiological and psychological needs; and

(d) to provide the means whereby the associated occupational health and safety legislation may be progressively replaced by comprehensive provisions made by or under this Act.

Michael Easson, former secretary of the Labor Council of NSW, in his essay in *The Wran Era* says about this legislation that its intention was to place greater occupational health and safety obligations on employers and employees while focusing upon injury prevention strategies, employee involvement in occupational health and safety matters and new penalties for breaches of the legislation.

During my time as a solicitor engaged in workers compensation and dealing with work-related common law injury claims in the late 1960s and early 1970s, I periodically visited work sites in factories where workers had been injured. Having worked in local manufacturing plants during summer holidays as a teenager, I used to be appalled at the lack of supervision or proper instruction in working with dangerous machinery. One holiday job I had taken to get some money was at the Arnott's biscuit factory in Homebush, where I worked on the Jatz Cracker line loading compressed dough onto a conveyor which fed it through a series of ovens. After being there for a week or so, I was warned by a fellow worker of the risk of serious injury with one part of the process. No-one had warned me about this danger despite a previous employee having been seriously injured by the machine – it was my last day on the job!

Returning to such plants 10 or so years later as a lawyer, nothing had changed and each year thousands of workers were needlessly injured and sometimes killed in preventable work accidents. I hoped that this legislation would lead to a greater focus on workplace safety.

Easson also mentioned several other important pieces of industrial relations legislation passed by the Wran government, which included:

- making discrimination in employment illegal;
- reforms to the *Industrial Arbitration Act* to cover independent transport contractors, later extended to couriers and taxi drivers;
- establishing the right for women to 12 months unpaid maternity leave;
- establishing redundancy entitlements via the *Employment Protection Act*; and
- increases to long service leave entitlements.

Another noteworthy Act passed during 1983 was the *Probation and Parole Act*, which modernised this process following a review by the Parole Review Committee, of which I was a member, and the establishment of a Treasury Corporation to undertake a central borrowing authority for the NSW government, a further reform to the way government operated.

Having done so much to modernise the public sector, the last couple of years of Wran's period as Premier seemed quiet by comparison. However, the *Darling Harbour Casino Act 1986* was passed which was probably the last element of Wran's major bicentennial initiative, the Darling Harbour re-development.

This more limited legislative programme was possibly a reflection of the distractions which Wran was dealing with caused by a number of momentous occurrences in those past couple of years. These included the Street Royal Commission, the premature death of his younger protégé Paul Landa and the retirement of his long-term deputy and close ally, Jack Ferguson.

The derailing of Wran's federal parliamentary leadership ambitions by Bob Hawke's coup in replacing Bill Hayden in the lead up to the 1983 federal election, followed by the so-called "Age Tapes" scandal used as a basis of attacking Wran himself and his close friend Justice Lionel Murphy, also tarnished his public standing. In Terry Sheahan's view, expressed in *The True Believers*, Wran never recovered from this series of cruel blows and simply lost the drive to continue as Premier.

The Unsworth Government's Notable Legislation

Barrie Unsworth came to power following Wran's shock retirement announcement in June 1986, at the NSW ALP annual conference in the Sydney Town Hall. I was attending the annual conference as an observer and witnessed Wran's final speech as Premier. Like many Labor supporters, I remembered quite vividly the enormous morale boosting impact of his election in 1976, so soon after the appalling ending of Gough Whitlam's reign as Prime Minister.

Pat and I, together with a local friend Don Birkett, had watched the 1976 election count and could hardly believe the pollsters prediction of a Wran victory. Later I was present on a number of occasions when Wran spoke at the opening of several Foundation supported events soon after his election and was hugely impressed by his ability to relate to different audiences.

Like many at the Labor Party conference I had mixed emotions about this unexpected announcement. Nevertheless, I felt both fortunate and honoured to be present at the end of a very important and unprecedented era, particularly for NSW working class families.

Once the 1986 NSW Labor Party conference had come to order following Neville and Jill Wran's departure, his announcement having taken everyone in the packed Town Hall by surprise, the character of the meeting changed instantly. For an interested observer like me, it was fascinating to see the meeting fall into comparative disarray as key delegates started to discuss Wran's likely successor, with three names quickly being mentioned, Barrie Unsworth, Peter Anderson and Laurie Brereton, any of whom would have been a worthy successor to Wran.

However, with the likely support of the major unions, then Upper House member Unsworth soon emerged as the front runner. It was a memorable event to be present at with my old friend Terry

Sheahan, then a senior minister in the midst of the negotiations. It was one of those rare occasions when what was happening on the floor of the Town Hall resembled a US political party Presidential convention.

I remember sitting with Michael Easson shortly before the organisers got the conference moving again. At the time, he was Assistant Secretary of the NSW Labor Council and very much a party insider. He was discussing the pros and cons of the various likely contenders and it was a great day for someone interested in Labor politics to be on the conference floor watching the changing of the guard which resulted in former Labor Council leader Barrie Unsworth being appointed as the new Premier.

No sooner had Unsworth been formally installed as Premier than the government was confronted with serious questions about the integrity of several judicial officers. This led in the latter part of 1986 to the *Judicial Officers Act* being passed by the NSW Parliament, only the second piece of legislation in which I had personally played a role in it becoming law.

The Judicial Officers legislation was directly linked to my longstanding interest in judicial accountability which flowed from my experience of being in court virtually every day for six years in the Workers Compensation Commission, the District Court and the Supreme Court. While the great majority of judges I observed carrying out their duties were beyond reproach, there were periodic instances of what I thought was unacceptable judicial behaviour. I was able to provide a solution to this extremely vexed issue at a later date.

Other important legislation passed during the relatively short term of the Unsworth government included the *Director of Public Prosecutions Act 1986* which created the office of Director of Public Prosecutions which removed the decision to prosecute from the possibility of political intervention. Another interesting decision was the passing of the *Uranium Mining and Nuclear Facilities*

(Prohibition) Act 1986 which prohibited mining for uranium and the establishment of nuclear facilities in NSW. One of the last legislative reforms passed by this government was the *Victims Compensation Act 1987* with respect to compensation for victims of violence via an award by a Victims Compensation Tribunal.

While the Wran/Unsworth governments were in office for over 12 years, a much longer period than the Whitlam government, the pacing of its reform agenda ensured that, by and large, it was a government with a proud legislative record addressing many of challenges facing modern society. My review of the legislation passed during its years in office is very much a personal selection but one which I believe is an accurate reflection of changes which were welcomed by the public as much needed reforms.

There were many other changes in policy and significant improvements in the delivery of health, educational and welfare services which all improved local conditions through better funding, better management systems and improved industrial relations. The government also used the forthcoming bicentennial celebrations as a catalyst for undertaking big ticket infrastructure items such Darling Harbour, the Entertainment Centre and the Conference Centre, as well as finalising the network of new roads giving access to the city from the western approaches.

My friend Terry Sheahan who, as President of the NSW Labor Party in the mid-1990s, awarded Wran his life membership of the Party, commented "… without Wran there would have been no Hawke government, nor any Cain, Bannon or Burke governments."

Wran had made Labor electable again so soon after the Whitlam debacle and created the role of the modern, media savvy leader with excellent communication skills which the other Labor leaders of that generation adopted, with all enjoying long-term success.

Wran's record of long-term reform not only transformed the Sydney CBD into a modern commercial hub as well as tourist destination, but also significantly improved the lives of his constituents.

This was particularly so for those in the outer suburbs where major improvement in health, education, transport, industrial relations and infrastructure were his great legacy. It made his and the Unsworth governments worthy successors to the reform work started by Gough Whitlam, as they made a similarly significant contribution to our golden era of reform.

18

Law Foundation's Contributions to Wran's Reforms

With the Wran government re-elected with a substantially increased majority in 1978 much needed reforms started to appear in the form of Bills introduced in the Parliament. Once passed, departments were often expected to implement the new policies, in some instances without the necessary skills or resources to do so.

As mentioned earlier, the Law Foundation was one of the beneficiaries of the Wran government's re-election. Legislation was passed to make the Foundation an independent statutory corporation with a broader charter and a guaranteed source of income.

It was now well placed to assist the Attorney General's Department and its related agencies. In the ensuing years the Foundation worked closely, often in partnership, with it and a range of other NSW government agencies and the courts. This provided many opportunities for the Foundation to support reform, innovation and improvements within the state's legal infrastructure, increasing the quality of legal services and, in many instances, the public's access to legal information. The following are high profile examples of such contributions.

Parole Review Committee

In late November 1978 I was called by Trevor Haines, in his new role as the Secretary of the Attorney General's Department, saying that Attorney General Frank Walker wanted me to be a member of a committee being appointed to review the 1966 NSW *Parole of Prisoners Act*. This act had come under some criticism from the Nagle Royal Commission into NSW Prisons. The committee was to review the Act and to make firm recommendations to the government for amendment. The government required the report by 31 January 1979, an extraordinarily short time for such a significant review.

Despite this unreasonably short time frame, throwing the committee members' various summer holiday plans into disarray, the report was completed on time. I was a bit bemused by the invitation as, while Foundation staff had undertaken research on topics related to the criminal law such as bail and pre-trial release, deterrence and drink driving and aspects of sentencing (as in the case of social security prosecutions for the Australian Law Reform Commission's sentencing reference), I personally had no direct relevant experience other than that gained from setting research agendas, overseeing researchers and reviewing and commenting on their reports.

The other members were very senior figures in the justice area. The Chairman, Judge Alec Muir, was a senior District Court judge with many years' experience of presiding over very serious criminal trials. The other member with judicial experience was Clarrie Briese, a senior magistrate and later Chief Magistrate. The non-judicial members, other than myself, were L K Downs, representing the Department of Corrections and formerly Secretary of the Attorney General's Department, Ken Lukacs, Director, Probation and Parole Service, John Moroney, respected former head of Corrections and now representing the Parole Board, Ros Wood from the Bureau of Crime Statistics Research and Barry Cross from the Department of the Attorney General and of Justice.

Considering the very limited timetable and the time of the year, the committee resolved immediately to invite written submissions by 18 December 1978 from persons, organisations and public authorities interested in the committee's terms of reference.

This was done by inserting advertisements in the metropolitan press; writing to various organisations noted in the report of the Nagle Royal Commission; contacting the Chief Justice, the Chief Judge of the District Court and the Chairman of the Bench of Stipendiary Magistrates; and inviting written submissions from members of their courts. We also invited, by way of a circular issued by the Department of Corrections, written submissions from prison officers and prisoners. We invited parolees, through the Regional Directors of the Probation and Parole Service, to make written submissions. In light of the shortage of time available to the committee it was decided oral submissions could not be received.

Despite the short notice, a total of 92 submissions were received and the committee's report contains, in an appendix, a summary of the major issues raised. It noted that responses from prisoners fell into three areas of dissatisfaction.

The first was the uncertainty the vast majority felt, as one prisoner put it, with an initial reference to the situation before the Act was introduced in 1966:

> ... a crim came to gaol and knew the day he would get out. Nobody could take that off him unless he did something bad and lost his remission. (Now) crims get minimums but do not get out on them. They don't know why.

The second area raised was the lack of incentive under the present system, with some prisoners expressing the view that:

> ... the system worked against good behaviour – that someone who had behaved badly but who had improved was more likely to be granted parole than someone who had behaved well all along.

The third area of dissatisfaction concerned rehabilitation and counselling, with prisoner respondents saying that this needed improvement both within gaol and outside it. Several prisoners also identified the need for special counselling for drug offenders.

Twenty-three prisoner respondents expressed dissatisfaction with the Parole Board, with most calling for adequate reasons for decisions, the right of personal appearance and/or the right of appeal.

The second category of respondents was from those working in the criminal justice and prison systems. Some of their concerns mirrored those of the prisoners. They referred to uncertainty, validity of assessments, confusion over rationale, and reconciliation of punishment and deterrence, with rehabilitation, in practice. These issues impacted on the running of the correctional system as well as placing an enormous workload on the Parole Board and under-resourced Parole Officers. This group endorsed the recommendation of Nagle Royal Commission for automatic parole for sentences under four years.

A small number of submissions were received from retired judges expressing varying views on sentencing and from a sitting magistrate also commenting on the uncertainty and apparent unfairness of parole.

Probably the most significant submission was from the Probation and Parole Service which strongly supported the abandonment of parole in favour of a system of determinate sentencing. The committee, with some hesitation, interpreted the terms of reference as being wide enough to allow consideration of the issue of some alternative system of parole. However, it concluded that the short time of the review and the limited data did not allow in depth consideration of the issue.

In light of this, Ken Lukacs, the representative from the Probation and Parole Service, produced a minority report. This report supported the determinate sentencing approach promoted by those employed by the service.

A key recommendation of the committee was that a future research programme be conducted to facilitate a more critical assessment of the operation of the parole system.

However, the committee also recommended sentencing guidelines to assist judges, and a number of changes to the operation of the Parole system including a process for reviewing decisions by the Board to refuse or defer release on parole. We also proposed amendments to ensure that the resources of the parole system were applied to areas where more impact could be made.

The committee also identified areas of the Act in need of amendment, and which could lead to significant improvements.

From a personal point of view, being on this committee was a very positive experience. It was not unlike the one I had with the Computerisation of Legal Data Committee in Canberra. Noticeable similarities were the ages and experience of most of the committee members when compared to me, and their willingness to ensure that my limitations with the subject matter were considered during discussions and, of course, another short time frame – in this case a totally unrealistic timetable. However, my education in the strengths and weaknesses of our correctional system was considerably broadened.

Judge Muir arranged for me to visit Long Bay Prison with him so that we could interview prisoners given life sentences, as one of the issues the committee was interested in was whether such prisoners should eventually, subject to a range of criteria, be considered for parole. While we interviewed several such prisoners, one was particularly memorable. He was a very smooth and highly articulate prisoner in his late thirties who apparently was a contract killer. I am not sure if he was likely to be a candidate for such a reform if it was to be introduced.

The second experience was the opportunity to sit in on several meetings of the Parole Board and to have the opportunity to follow their agenda through being provided with a copy of the applications before them. I came away from these meetings more aware of the process and of the issues the prisoner respondents had complained of. I was also left with the distinct impression that the prisons were full of young men aged between 17 and 29 with a small minority of older prisoners making up the rest of the prison population.

It appears that, by the time they were 30 years old, many of this cohort reached some level of maturity which convinced them to stop offending, maybe through the support of families and partners. From what I could determine the great majority seemed to have learnt from their destructive experiences, got on with making something of their lives and rarely re-offended. Whether that conclusion is still valid today is problematic.

However, in retrospect, the urgency seemed to be unwarranted as the amending legislation was not introduced into Parliament until late November 1983, a few days short of five years after the committee's appointment. I have my own ideas as to the reasons for the government's delay in acting on the recommendations, but these were not clear at the time. One reason could have been that the implementation of recommendations of the Nagle Royal Commission into the prison system was being undertaken at the same time. Another might have been that the initial urgency imposed on the committee flowed from industrial relations issues between the Parole Officers union and the government.

When finally introducing a reform Bill and associated legislation on 24 November 1983, the then relevant minister Peter Anderson said:

> The bills are the results of several years' careful and detailed deliberation by members of the Government, the judiciary, the Corrective Services Commission and the general community. That this proposed legislation has taken a number of years to come to fruition is indicative of the sensitive issues involved in the question of releasing prisoners into the community on conditional liberty.
>
> The Government was unwilling to hasten through legislation without ensuring, so far as possible, that the new provisions met with the wishes of all concerned in the judicial and custodial processes.

The introduction of the legislation and its quick passing through the Parliament, followed by its proclamation on the highly unusual and low news time of New Year's Eve, may have been influenced by the conduct of the incumbent minister responsible for the parole service, Rex Jackson, who was later charged and gaoled for corruption for taking bribes connected to the release of prisoners.

Tellingly, the new legislation removed ministers from having any role in parole matters, with Anderson saying:

> In a nutshell, these bills will eliminate any provision for the exercising of ministerial or individual discretion to affect a prisoner's release. Rather, they will put into place a system whereby a prisoner's release from gaol will only result either from the termination of his court imposed sentence, or following the majority decision of an independent body that a prisoner should be granted conditional freedom.

The lesson which flows from this experience is that, had the government acted promptly on the recommendations of the Parole Review Committee and introduced the amendments in line with its recommendations, in all likelihood the embarrassment caused and the impact on the government's image and momentum would never have arisen. The loophole Jackson manipulated would not have been there.

The government recognised that it needed a reformer with a fresh mind to implement reforms of the prison system recommended by the Nagle Royal Commission.

Professor Tony Vinson was then appointed head of the NSW Department of Corrective Services in 1979 and, not long after taking on the role, he approached the Foundation for funds to purchase a major computer so that he could develop a comprehensive prisoner record and management system. As the Department's budget had no provision for such capital items at short notice, Tony contacted me and a proposal was put to the Board which, because of the need to move ahead with the Nagle reforms, readily agreed to the request and the sum of $29,340 was allocated for the purpose.

I remember having discussions with Tony about the choice of computer and visiting the Department when it was installed and operational. I seem to recall that, in such relatively early days, adapting commercially oriented software to the public sector management requirements was a challenge.

Community Justice Centres Pilot Project

The website of the Community Justice Centres (CJC) succinctly explains the history of the Centres thus:

> CJC has provided a mediation and conflict management service for the people of NSW since 1980. CJC was first established as a pilot programme by the Community Justice Centres (Pilot Project) Act 1980 (NSW). The NSW Law Foundation reviewed the pilot programme positively in 1982. CJC became a permanent service in 1983, with the passing of the *Community Justice Centres Act 1983* (NSW). When established, CJC was heralded as 'the most promising step taken this century to provide a system for the settlement of a class of dispute which the adversary processes of our courts have never been able to resolve satisfactorily.

When introducing the Community Justice Centres (Pilot Project) Bill on 19 November 1980, the Attorney General Frank Walker said:

> The bill now before the House is of such significance that I should be less than frank if I failed to express both delight and personal satisfaction in its inception and concept. It is true pioneering legislation. The introduction of community justice centres is the most promising step taken this century to provide a system for the settlement of a class of dispute which the adversary processes of our courts have never been able to resolve satisfactorily. The advent of community justice centres will mean that those in domestic or neighbourhood confrontations may turn to a conciliatory process conducive to reaching the heart of their problem and providing a lasting resolution.

He emphasised that this was a pilot project Bill and, if the project was successful, subject to the availability of funds, CJCs would open in many more areas. Importantly, he added that the legislation, which represented a novel law-making approach, provided that the operation of the pilot project would be monitored by the Law

Foundation of New South Wales. The evaluation prepared by that body would largely determine whether at the end of the pilot period of 15 months the scheme would continue. He noted that the Bill contained a novel sunset clause reflecting the experimental nature of the scheme which meant that the provisions of the Act expired on 1 December 1983.

He acknowledged the considerable work that had been done by the co-ordinating committee initially established in 1979 to oversee the implementation of the project. From the outset the Foundation's research staff had been assisting the developmental work undertaken by this committee. This committee was chaired by Kevin Anderson SM, who was Deputy Chairman of the Bench of Stipendiary Magistrates. He had been tireless in his efforts to publicise and explain the concept to the community. He had also shouldered the substantial burden of establishing a structure within which to administer the project.

Approximately six weeks prior to the expiration of the 1980 legislation establishing the pilot project, the government in late 1983 introduced the new Community Justice Centres Bill in the Legislative Assembly, with Frank Walker leading the debate for the government. In many respects, this was quite fitting for, although he was no longer Attorney General, he was doing so as the representative of Paul Landa MLC, the then current Attorney General who sat in the Legislative Council. It was normal practice for government legislation to be tabled in the Legislative Assembly by a minister deputising for the minister responsible when such person was a member of the upper house.

As noted in Hansard, Walker said:

> ... the principal bill provides for the permanent operation of one of the State's most successful experiments for the resolution of conflict within the community. Since 1980, community justice centres have been operating at Surry Hills, Bankstown and Wollongong as a pilot scheme under the *Community Justice Centres (Pilot Project) Act*.

> During that time, the centres have established themselves as a truly effective means whereby citizens can seek to resolve disputes they might have with neighbours, family members, friends, work mates and others, without the frustration and expense associated with a court appearance.

He went on to say:

> The operation of the centres was the subject of an extremely detailed evaluation conducted by the Law Foundation of New South Wales, which concluded that it is now possible to say with confidence that it is practical under Australian conditions to institute a programme for the informal, non-coercive, non-punitive resolution of a wide range of relatively minor disputes between parties who knew each other, to deliver this service through lay people recruited from the general community, and for such a programme to be credible in the eyes of the general public and in the eyes of the legal, social welfare and other agencies.

Walker also acknowledged those managing the three pilot centres and the 106 people from all walks of life and representing most ethnic communities who had shown such enthusiasm and dedication in their training to be mediators.

The Foundation's contribution to this major groundbreaking project was the allocation of the time of two research staff, John Schwartzkoff, initially assisted by Jenny Morgan and later by Concetta Rizzo. Their role was to chronicle the progress of the various phases of this important experiment.

Their involvement from the inception of this pilot project gave them a unique opportunity to understand the various outcomes in terms of decisions made and priorities set from time to time. They were also primarily responsible for formulating the methodology of the evaluation on consultation with the co-ordinating committee.

This project was another first for the Foundation. It again demonstrated the confidence the Foundation had built up with both the Attorney General and his department as being capable of undertaking this important research role in monitoring this important new reform initiative.

Community Justice Centres have vindicated the general concept of a dispute settlement alternative that did not depend on coercion, the attribution of blame or the imposition of sanctions.

The success of the scheme was gauged also from the fact that, where parties to a dispute agreed to attend a mediation session, over 80% of disputes were resolved to the satisfaction of the parties. The service was provided free of charge to all sections of the community and mediation sessions were arranged at times convenient to the parties.

The evaluation therefore recommended that the government continue to fund the existing centres. It advocated that consideration should be given to the extension of the scheme by expanding the reach of the existing centres or through establishing some further centres or sub-centres.

Speaking for the Opposition in the Second Reading debate, Opposition MP Tim Moore focused on several key aspects of the Bill and noted with approval:

> The Minister may cause or arrange for an evaluation to be made, at such times and in respect of such periods as the Minister thinks fit, of Community Justice Centres and of their operation and activities. The Opposition applauds the inclusion of that provision in the bill and welcomes the fact that the initial evaluation of the operations of community justice centres under the pilot legislation was conducted by the Law Foundation of New South Wales, an eminently functional and independent body for the conduct of such evaluations.

A Change of Direction

The recognition given to the independent evaluation carried out by Law Foundation staff by both government and Opposition, confirming the success of the pilot scheme of this highly innovative social programme and justifying its permanent addition to the state's dispute resolution processes, was a great reward.

However, such plaudits were lost on the Foundation's then Board. Following a warning from the Law Society that due to adverse economic conditions the Foundation could soon expect a dramatic drop in its 10% entitlement to the Statutory Interest Account Income, the Board, against my pleas, decided to end support of the Foundation's major in-house research projects. The rationale for this decision was hard to fathom and reflected a long-held view of some within the Law Society of the need to rein in the Foundation.

It also coincided with a number of research projects, such as the Community Justice Centres review, coming to a conclusion. The outcome was that this decision effectively put an end to the Foundation's research capacity which had taken years to build up and I, sadly, had to preside over the termination of the employment of a number of highly qualified research staff who were readily snapped up elsewhere.

Within a few months the Board realised that the Foundation's income had not been adversely affected. This meant that it had the money to undertake new initiatives so it was decided that the Foundation should investigate growing community concerns about migrant communities' access to the law. Without any in-house research capacity, responding to such new initiatives became more difficult. However, we continued and, as you will see in later chapters, explored alternative opportunities to implement the aims of our charter – bruised but not beaten!

The Need for a Public Interest Advocacy Centre

During my Churchill Fellowship, I was very impressed with the way the OEO-funded legal services programmes in the US were required to undertake litigation aimed at enforcing or reforming the law, which in turn led to specialist public interest law firms being established. Following the Law Foundation's statutory independence in 1979, establishing a similar public interest law firm was high on my priority list.

Eventually, in December 1981, the Foundation's Board agreed to establish the Public Interest Advocacy Centre (PIAC), which opened its doors in July 1982 and is still in operation today.

The proposal to the Board, which followed on from wide community consultation, was prepared by me in conjunction with Peter Cashman, then a senior researcher with the Foundation. Peter was designated by the Board to establish the new Centre with my strong endorsement.

The Centre was seen by the Board as answering a longstanding need. A specialist legal group was needed to undertake campaigns, either through litigation or lobbying, aimed at bringing about the reform of particular laws and practices as well as initiating test case litigation on behalf of disadvantaged groups.

The Board also recognised that in many areas of government and commercial activity, the public interest is often overlooked to the detriment of the community.

The objects of the new Centre were:

a) to undertake litigation and to arrange appearances before courts, tribunals, enquiries or other forums, in connection with issues of public interest;

b) to lobby for reform of law, policy or practice in the public interest;

c) to consult with groups or individuals on matters of public interest;

d) to encourage and sponsor research and projects in the public interest;

e) to collect and disseminate information and to stimulate community awareness of public interest issues;

f) to monitor existing or proposed laws, policies and practices from the point of view of public interest.

The Centre also had the support of the Legal Aid Commission which agreed to jointly sponsor it. The Foundation's Board agreed to support the Centre for three years and provided initial funding of $125,000 for the first year's operations. The Centre initially operated from the Foundation's premises.

In 1987, to mark the Centre's first five years, it produced a report of its activities during that period entitled *Five Years in the Ring*. In the Foreword, Justice Michael Kirby, then President of the NSW Court of Appeal, nominated three barriers to public interest litigation which PIAC had to overcome when compared to similar bodies in the US.

The first barrier was the cost rules, which gave no relief to those litigating a public interest issue as the named plaintiffs were exposed to heavy cost penalties should the case fail. Having the support of the NSW Legal Aid Commission assisted in some cases.

The second barrier he noted was the law of standing which required a party to have a direct interest in the matter at hand before it could be litigated. As Kirby noted, "the court will not allow the party to test the legal proposition in issue". However, he did note that, in the Commonwealth context, the Australian Law Reform Commission had made recommendations on this issue which would be specifically relevant to PIAC.

The third barrier was that, traditionally in Australia, there was the lack of substantive law upon which public interest cases could be based. Kirby noted that reforms, such as the introduction of human rights and anti-discrimination legislation, provided a basis for important public litigation. Kirby concluded his comments with the statement, "The charter of PIAC is breathtakingly ambitious."

This view was readily seen from the amusingly clever titles given to the chapters of *Five Years in the Ring* which included: *Civil Liberties: rights and fights; Freedom of Information: wrestling for documents; Product Liability and Consumer Interest: perils of life, love and labour; Media and Communications: who's behind the tele?; Discrimination: women, weights and steelworks; The Greek Conspiracy Case: maladministration or malice; The Professions: going a few rounds with doctors and lawyers; The Criminal Justice System: go directly to gaol!* and *The First Five Years: the score.*

The report's author, Peter Waters, was a bright young lawyer who was retained as a project officer to write this report. It was written with both verve and humour, producing a brilliant, colourful and highly readable coverage of PIAC's many cases undertaken in its first five years. Peter Waters has been a consultant with major law firm Gilbert + Tobin for many years and has a stellar reputation as being one of Australia's leaders in competition and regulatory law.

In the final chapter, he said:

> PIAC's accumulated experience shows up a number of other issues which need to be addressed if the legal process is to be an effective forum in which to bring about change in the public interest.

He added:

> The obvious lesson which has been learnt is that Australia is a more hostile environment to a public interest centre than the United States or Canada.

The report also noted that, during the early years, PIAC was largely dependent on the Law Foundation for funding. However, Waters recorded that in 1986 PIAC was put on a firmer financial base with the Foundation securing a capital grant of $1 million for it, the income from which met a significant proportion of the Centre's overheads. What is not recorded is that this funding from the Statutory Interest Account would not have been possible without the active endorsement of then Attorney General, Terry Sheahan, a strong supporter of both the Foundation's work and of PIAC.

The report concludes with a list of all those involved with PIAC during the initial five years. The person who made it all happen was its first director, Peter Cashman, who had an acute legal mind which saw no legal problem as being too big to tackle. Peter also had a unique capacity to attract some of the brightest and best young legal minds to become involved in PIAC's work. At the same time, he was building myriad networks of support amongst special interest groups, as well as with institutions such as the Legal Aid Commission, the Law Reform Commissions and with leaders of the legal profession.

Today Peter is a highly respected Professor at the University of NSW Law School. He is also a member of the Bar, in which latter role he still argues public interest cases in Australia's superior courts. He successfully argued before US Federal Courts, in class actions on behalf of Australian victims of US IUDs and breast implants, that they were entitled to compensation on par with that awarded to US women plaintiffs, a truly groundbreaking result at a time when the pharmaceutical giants argued that foreign plaintiffs were entitled to significantly less. The miracle is, probably, that the Centre has actually survived so long.

A Personal Crusade: The Judicial Accountability Conundrum

Almost certainly my single most important legislative contribution was the establishment of a formal process whereby complaints about the behaviour and performance of judicial officers in NSW could be formally reviewed in an appropriate manner. During my days as a litigation lawyer, I periodically observed behaviour on the part of some judges which caused me to question their suitability to continue to undertake a judicial role. I questioned why there was no process for dealing with complaints about judicial behaviour.

While the great majority of cases I worked on were settled before a court hearing commenced, some others were settled during the course of a hearing and only a very few plaintiffs had their day in court, either before a judge or occasionally a judge and a jury. In the latter two courts the cases were referred to as common law damages claims. These were brought mostly by injured workers who claimed their injuries were caused by their employer's negligence. Less often the cases I worked on involved claims arising from injuries caused by motor vehicle accidents, or due to accidents in public places covered by public liability insurance, commonly referred to as "slip and fall" cases.

As a result of spending a lot of time in or around courts, I saw judges who were misogynists who awarded lower damages awards to women plaintiffs than a male would have received. I also regularly witnessed instances of intolerance and rudeness displayed by judges, particularly when plaintiffs were giving evidence. I saw many judges publicly humiliating barristers or solicitors in open court. There were several judges who sat in the District Court in the late 1960s who had difficulty fulfilling their roles due to illness. One poor judge was reputed to have been kept on the bench, despite suffering the effects of stroke, because he needed to reach the time when he qualified for a pension. There were other stories of several judges being regularly inebriated when sitting in court.

To me this was appalling, as judicial officers seemed to be unaccountable and there was no practical process for dealing with judges on issues of the type referred to.

In 1984, when investigating initiatives aimed at providing access to legal services for people of moderate means in the US, I spent a weekend with Clinton Bamberger and his wife Katharine, then living in Baltimore near Washington. Clinton has been referred to earlier in his role as the first Director of the OEO Legal Services Program. On the social programme for the weekend was a Sunday brunch for a woman journalist friend now living in California and her new husband, whom they had not met but whom they thought was a lawyer.

When they arrived and introductions were made it seemed that his friend's husband was not just any lawyer, but was Justice John Racanelli of the California Court of Appeal and also head of the California Commission on Judicial Performance. Once I discovered this latter role, I expressed interest in knowing more about the Commission and soon learnt that it was the first such body in the US. It was established in 1960 and most other states had established similar bodies since then.

With John's help, I subsequently obtained a large amount of information from his and other such commissions. As the topic fell within the Foundation's courts Target Area, the Board decided that I should investigate the topic of judicial accountability and prepare a discussion paper to be provided to the Attorney General. With issues of possible misbehaviour by several judicial officers having recently been raised in the press, my research was timely.

In August 1985 I was to attend, in the company of Attorney General Terry Sheahan and his departmental secretary Trevor Haines, the UN Congress on Crime Prevention and Delinquency held in Milan. When the itinerary for the trip was being prepared, it was decided that our journey would include spending time learning how the issue of judicial accountability was handled in the UK and in the US. Terry Sheahan had recognised that sometime in the near future a judicial accountability body would be needed, no doubt in part influenced by the recent conviction and gaoling of former chief magistrate Murray Farquhar for conspiracy to pervert the course of justice.

This part of the itinerary started with a visit to the British Lord Chancellor's Office where, during our meeting with a senior officer, she indicated that they were dealing with similar concerns but no clear solution had been identified. In fact, she gave us an example of the quandary they were currently in which arose from a County Court judge being stopped by customs while using his launch to smuggle brandy into the UK. As they had no formal means of dealing with the issue short of bringing the justice system into disrepute, it was likely that pressure would be applied to the judge to resign – a very unsatisfactory outcome all round.

In the US, a number of high-level meetings were held with politicians and those responsible for judicial accountability. Terry and Trevor had a very interesting meeting with the US Federal Court about the steps taken to review the career of a proposed appointee to the Federal Bench. There were also visits to New York state's judicial accountability agency and later and a follow up meeting with Justice Racanelli in California, where additional and very helpful information was obtained.

Following their overseas investigations, this new-found knowledge enabled Terry and Trevor to prepare the ground to be able to provide an immediate legislative response to any such allegations should they arise in NSW. Such preparations included sending several senior departmental officers to the US to carry our more in-depth studies of relevant programmes there. Armed now with this additional information, Terry put in motion steps to introduce legislation for the establishment of a judicial accountability body. Again, the timing of his actions was important as further questions were being raised in the press and in Parliament about certain judges during the early part of 1986.

To ensure that the members of the judiciary were informed of the solution being proposed, the Foundation's Board allocated funds, at the Department's request, to meet the expenses of bringing Justice Racanelli to Australia to meet with and to address various meetings of judges.

With the strong support and backing of Premier Barrie Unsworth, Terry introduced legislation into the NSW Parliament later in 1986 to establish the NSW Judicial Commission whose primary role was to investigate complaints made against judicial officers. The legislation also provided for the education and the provision of other support services to serving NSW judicial officers.

There was a torrid backlash from certain members of the judiciary, led largely by the Chief Justice Sir Laurence Street. The Opposition argued that this was overkill and unnecessary interference with the independence of the judiciary. Nevertheless, the *Judicial Officers Act 1986* was passed by the Parliament and later assented to on 18 November 1986. It enjoyed support from the great majority of judges and magistrates, including the public support of then Chief Judge of the District Court, Judge Jim Staunton QC.

During the latter stages of a prolonged Second Reading Debate in the Assembly, Terry Sheahan took time to acknowledge my seminal role:

> There was much talk about the Californian commission, the 1982 report of the commission, the 1984 report of the commission, and reference to a paper by the Executive Director of the New South Wales Law Foundation, Mr Purcell, on the question of judicial independence of these commissions. I invited Mr Purcell to be present in the gallery today, and he is there. He is a friend of mine. I admire the work he did on this subject. If the honourable member for Lane Cove took notice of it, perhaps he would take yet a different attitude to the bill.
>
> We have learned from the work of the Law Foundation over many years on this subject. The director wrote a letter, a copy of which he sent to me, to the editor of the *Australian Financial Review*, when public controversy on this matter was at its highest.

Being present when the Bill was about to pass into law was a great personal honour. It gave me considerable satisfaction to have played a part in contributing towards a solution to a long-standing conundrum facing the judiciary, governments and Parliaments and those at the time responsible for overseeing the courts. New South Wales was the first jurisdiction outside the US to have such a process in the form of the Judicial Commission amongst all the common law countries whose court systems operated in the British tradition. No other state followed, until Victoria in 2016, some 30 years after the NSW Commission was established.

19

INCREASING COMMUNITY ACCESS TO LEGAL INFORMATION

As mentioned previously, the passing of the *Law Foundation Act* in 1979 by the Wran government, broadened the Law Foundation's charter significantly.

One of the new objects was Section 5 (f), to encourage, support or sponsor projects aimed at facilitating access to legal information.

The Foundation's income, via a set share of the Statutory Interest Account income, allowed the Board to be creative in terms of the types, sizes and time frames of activities the Foundation could now undertake or support. The new Board soon recognised the need to facilitate the community's access to legal information.

Flowing from this new ability to undertake a much wider range of activities were projects such as the publication of *The Pocket Guide to the Law* and assisting Redfern Legal Centre Publishing to produce other community directed innovative and helpful publications and, in time, a Legal Information Access Centre.

The Foundation's annual reports were soon recording many modest grants made to community organisations to support publication of brochures or booklets explaining the law to those they were assisting. Over the years literally hundreds of small grants were made to such organisations for creative initiatives, often employing a variety of media. However, the most consistent and creative applicant for funding to enhance the community's access to legal information came from the Redfern Legal Centre.

From the earliest days it was a Board policy to support the needs of community-based organisations. While the Foundation could not provide operating funding for such bodies, it could allocate funds for projects they wished to undertake, and many requests were received for grassroots projects seeking to provide access to relevant legal information to their audiences.

With the number of grant applications being received following the broadening of the Foundation's role, the Board approved the creation of a new role of Grants Administrator in 1985 and appointed staff member, Dawn Wong, to that role. Dawn oversaw the growing demand for grants and streamlined the processing and approval of such applications. She also provided much assistance to those seeking grants and effectively managed the distribution of a substantial proportion of the Foundation's income.

The Pocket Guide to the Law Project

This extraordinary little plastic covered book, which ultimately sold nearly 500,000 copies Australia-wide, was a publishing phenomenon in terms of reach and cost/benefit and soon proved to be one of the Foundation's most successful initiatives. What was particularly amazing about its popularity was that it was about the law, usually a topic of little interest to most people unless they are amongst the very few who get involved in some legal action.

Its success flowed from a couple of fortuitous events. The first was a gift from a young summer student who, when travelling in France in around 1979, came across a small plastic covered book called the *Guide Juridique de la Poche* and thought it might be of interest to the Foundation. In time it was to provide the answer to a conundrum confronting the Foundation about how to improve access to legal information, particularly for members of Australia's migrant community.

The second was being able to enlist the support and interest of Ita Buttrose, by then the editor in chief of *The Daily Telegraph* and *The Sunday Telegraph*, who, when approached about this innovative guide, took to it immediately and effectively threw behind it the News Ltd. publishing, distribution and marketing might.

This was another significant initiative which flowed from the Foundation's new goal of promoting greater public access to legal information charter which, following an extended Board policy meeting in February 1980, set the directions for the Foundation for the next few years. One of the priorities was to establish a project, Migrants and their Access to the Law. Its purpose was to gain a better understanding of the barriers those born outside Australia faced when confronted by the legal system.

The conclusion reached during an initial exploratory stage investigation undertaken by staff researcher, Jan Bowen, was the need to educate and inform the migrant community about the Australian legal system, while also informing and educating lawyers and other legal personnel of the needs of migrants.

After much consideration of the various options, it was concluded that what was needed was a continuously available access point for day-to-day practical legal knowledge. It was then that I remembered the French pocket guide to the law, which was initially published by a major French transport union for its members.

At the time I received the book it seemed an interesting idea, but I could not see how we might go about replicating it in Australia. However, the Board's challenge made me realise that the pocket guide concept could go a long way in meeting not only the migrant communities' needs but those of the wider community. The pocket guide seemed the perfect solution. Merci beaucoup, France!

The Board agreed and authorised the Foundation to develop a local version of the French pocket guide and Jan Bowen was appointed the project leader. She was the lead researcher, writer and editor of the initial edition which provided information on the legal ramifications of 143 day to day situations. With the development of the first edition, Jan was assisted by Louise Maddison.

From the Foundation's experience with producing publications, we early learnt the need for a distribution channel, particularly in this case, one intended for the mass market. Jan Bowen suggested that we should approach Ita Buttrose, with whom Jan had dealt previously, when Foundation staff wrote a regular column on legal issues for *The Women's Weekly* magazine. As noted earlier, Ita immediately saw the Pocket Guide as a great marketing promotion for *The Sunday Telegraph* and readily agreed to promote it via the papers and ensure that it would be available via newsagencies throughout the state. Ita also arranged its publication by Bay Books, one of News Ltd.'s book publishing companies.

The Guide was launched by the Premier Neville Wran QC on 2 September 1982 with wide media coverage. On 5 September an introductory offer was promoted in *The Sunday Telegraph* and its initial offer of 10,000 copies was oversubscribed within four days. The Foundation's aim was to get the Guide into the pockets of as many people as possible. As we lacked the means to produce, market and distribute the Guide ourselves, a joint venture with News Ltd. meant it took on these responsibilities. It also meant that the Guide would be sold through newsagents at a low cost. It literally became an overnight success when used as a promotional marketing exercise for Ita's paper and 50,000 copies were sold for $2.50 in the first month through newsagencies.

Barely six months later, 130,000 copies had been sold. Based on this response it was decided to produce editions for the other states to be managed through a publishing agreement with News Ltd.'s Bay Books. These editions were published between June and September 1983. The Queensland and South Australian editions sold out almost immediately and reprints were necessary. The Foundation also decided to produce an updated second edition of the NSW Guide.

The acceptance by the community indicated that the Pocket Guide provided an interesting insight into the whole question of community interest in the law. It countered the view that people found the law dull and boring and were not really interested in knowing more about it. The ready acceptance and positive feedback the Guides received discredited these obviously out-dated and ill-informed views, as did the reception of all the Foundation's community-directed publication initiatives which revealed a genuine thirst for knowledge of the law across all ages.

The Foundation's 1984 Annual Report also noted that many members of the community who bought the Guide had made contact to say how useful they found it and, in some instances, made suggestions as to information they felt should be included in later editions. Many of the updates reflected these suggestions.

Over the next few years the Guide sold over 400,000 copies, thus fulfilling the Foundation's goal of reaching the wider community. The last edition was published in 1988 and was written by lawyers Deborah Healey and Margaret White under the editorship of Professor Garth Nettheim of the UNSW Law School.

All those involved in the project can be justly pleased with the huge, unprecedented publishing success the Guide represented. Is there need for one today? Almost certainly. However, with the move away from print media to the internet it would be more logical that it be done as an online publication.

Redfern Legal Centre Publishing

Following the opening of the Redfern Legal Centre in March 1977 its staff soon identified the need for a *Legal Resources Book*. This book would give members of the community and, almost certainly, those who operated in an advisory role but were not trained lawyers, access to an up-to-date statement of the current law on particular topics. When approached for financial assistance by those managing the project to develop the book on behalf of Redfern Legal Centre Publishing (RLCP), the Foundation Board readily agreed to support such a much-needed resource and later continued to support the development of a number of later editions.

High Court Justice and former Law Foundation Board member, Virginia Bell, recorded in her Foreword to the Handbook's 11th edition that she had been involved in the development of the original, unwieldy, loose-leaf volume, *The Legal Resources Book*. She said it had been transformed into the snappier *The Law Handbook*, a comprehensive guide to the law in a single paperback volume, noting that "It has come a long way in 30 years."

Besides the sizeable publishing role of producing periodic updates of the *The Law Handbook*, the RLCP's small staff were regular recipients of grants under the Foundation's General Grants Programme for many other innovative community-directed legal publications. Another relatively early project was a kid's legal comic project, which had the catchy title of *Streetwize Comics* and was seen as a way of reaching disadvantaged under 18-year-olds. It was a long-term success, being published for over 20 years.

Other titles resulting from Law Foundation support included *Death and Dying*, explaining the legal issues associated with dying, an environmental law handbook, a handbook on housing legal issues such as ownership, tenancy, etc., a publication entitled *Surviving Rape*, a handbook on strata titles, a publication dealing with neighbourhood disputes, a guide for women, entitled *Your Body, Your Baby – women's rights from conception to birth*, *Rest Assured*, being a layperson's guide to Wills, estates and funerals and a booklet entitled *If You Are Arrested*.

In addition to community-directed publications, the Foundation also funded another groundbreaking example of a different type of legal publication, also emanating from the Redfern Legal Centre. It was to be directed to sole practitioners and legal aid lawyers with a working title of *The Legal Resources Manual for Lawyers*. It provided detailed guidance on how to handle a wide range of legal matters which could confront a solicitor in general practice.

During my Churchill Fellowship travels in North America, I had become familiar with similar publications in the US which were produced to provide new lawyers with practical knowledge of how to undertake common legal matters. New US lawyers needed these resources as, unlike in Australia, they were not taught practical skills unless they were lucky enough to attend a law school which conducted a legal clinic. Also, before they qualified for legal practice following graduation with a law degree, they needed to pass the Bar Exam which focused on local black letter or statute law and court practice rules in states they proposed to practise in, which meant that they had a great need for published sources of practical knowledge.

While at that time the College of Law provided a six-month practical skills training programme, more was seen to be needed. As a result, I was strongly supportive of a legal resources book for solicitors. The Foundation provided two separate grants. The first was for developmental work, while later, when RLCP had negotiated a publishing and distribution arrangement with the Law Book Co, a more substantial grant was made to meet some publishing subsidies, payments to contributors and editorial cost. The publication, now called *The Lawyers Practice Manual*, was launched at the Foundation's offices by the then Attorney General the Hon Paul Landa MLC on 27 July 1983.

The Manual provided access to the practical knowledge contributed by a wide range of specialist legal practitioners, all of which was located in one large ring binder. According to the *Tenth Year Report* published in 1987 by Redfern Legal Centre, *The Lawyers Practice Manual* was noted as being "one of the most successful loose-leaf publications in Australia." Over 30 years later it is still an important resource for many small legal practices and is available in various formats.

Another important publication supported by the Foundation in that era was *The Independent Social Security Handbook: A Practical Guide for Advisers* edited by Professor Julian Disney of the UNSW Law School and published by the Welfare Rights Centre. It was a much-appreciated resource for those working in the welfare sector.

Legal Information Access Centre

Like several other Foundation projects, this one had a long gestation period which commenced in 1983. The then Board queried, as a cost cutting measure, the possibility of disposing of the Foundation's library, which had been built up over the previous 10 years. It had developed as an essential adjunct to the research and project activities undertaken by Foundation staff during that same period. Because of the unique nature of the collection, the Board sought to have it taken over by one of the major law libraries and maintained separately as the Law Foundation Collection. This attempt, however, proved unsuccessful.

At about the same time, during a discussion with legal centre representatives about the library needs of community-based groups, the role played by legal resources centres in Canada was mentioned. While this idea was later endorsed by the Board, it was not proceeded with at that stage.

Early in 1986 the Legal Aid Commission and the Law Foundation agreed to prepare a joint submission to establish a Legal Resources Centre, and discussions took place to this end. However, once the project was costed it was realised that it was beyond the Foundation's capacity to find funding.

Nevertheless, hope springs eternal. When a new Board was appointed in 1988, its planning meeting was held early the following year, by which time there was a new government and John Dowd QC was the new Attorney General. One of the issues the new Board saw as a priority was law libraries and legal information services.

A discussion paper had been prepared by Foundation staff which stressed the need for a creative, co-ordinating and distributing agency servicing the legal information needs within a multicultural society. The paper also proposed that local libraries had a role to play in providing access to legal information.

While the Board was still concerned about the cost of maintaining such a centre, it recognised the centrality of the issue within the Foundation's statutory objectives. With John Dowd's support, it authorised me to establish such a centre subject to conditions regarding Foundation control and funding. In conjunction with this authorisation, I was also requested to examine the feasibility of developing a public library programme modelled on a similar one which I had seen operating in Vancouver with funding from its local Law Foundation.

As with so many of the Foundation's high impact projects, the main catalyst was usually finding a receptive leader in another organisation who quickly saw an opportunity for their organisation to break new ground by working in conjunction with the Foundation.

State Library of NSW Joint Venture

While with some projects, there were obvious organisations to partner with, but with a community legal information project there were few guideposts. I decided that a starting point was to call the State Library to see what I could find out from them about how we might go about getting such a facility up and running. My initial contact, in the latter part of 1989, resulted in my being directed to an officer with responsibility for special projects who seemed to have difficulty in dealing with the concept of the Foundation, or with what we were trying to achieve.

However, word of my approach soon reached the State Librarian, Alison Crook, who invited me to meet her at the Library for a discussion about our ideas. When she realised what we were trying to achieve was a place where a member of the public could readily access legal information, she immediately saw the benefit of our two organisations working together. The main opportunity for the Library, besides cost sharing, would be making greater use of its own extensive legal collection. It was spread around various behind the scenes locations which could now be re-located in one place in the Library. Another plus was that it would attract a whole new class of visitors to the Library.

By September a jointly formulated proposal was put by Ms Crook and me to the Board, which was readily endorsed. By early 1990, the establishment of the Legal Information Access Centre (LIAC) was well underway, and was officially opened by Attorney General Dowd on 30 April 1990 at the start of Law Week. With Alison's guidance, the Centre's management board appointed a senior librarian manager, Kathleen Bresnahan, as the initial centre manager. Her enthusiasm for this exciting new project and extensive knowledge of those involved in the management of local council libraries put LIAC on the map.

The Legal Information Access Centre was the coming to fruition of a long-held goal of the Foundation's then Chairman, Trevor Haines, who had recognised from the outset the need for a legal resources centre.

However, the end result, and the speed with which it was achieved, was probably far superior to anything Trevor or I could have anticipated. And it all flowed from one tentative call I made to the State Library seeking guidance on how one would go about establishing such a resource centre for law related materials. One of my strengths has always been my ability to look outside the box and to visualise where we might find the right joint venture partner. Alison Crook was to be the latest of such partners who shared a common vision with the Foundation.

Trevor was rightly proud that such a valuable and much-loved resource was so readily accepted by the community. Access was available to the wider community through links with local libraries throughout the state. Combined with the Foundation-funded Legal Toolkit, made up of a collection of dozens of community-directed legal publications, plus online communications between such libraries and LIAC, it soon ensured that a further goal of the Board was also achieved. This goal was to give access to legal materials and legal information to those living in country NSW. Dawn Wong was the main liaison person with LIAC and its staff, and one of the great privileges she and I enjoyed was being invited to accompany Board members to the opening of such facilities in local libraries. Gordon Samuels QC, later Governor of NSW, when on the Foundation Board, happily participated in several such openings, as did Trevor Haines.

20

LAW FOUNDATION: MODERNISING COURTS

In 1983 the Law Foundation embarked on the Model Court Project, aimed at demonstrating, testing, and implementing reforms with a view to breaking down the fear and intimidation members of the community faced when having to venture into a local court.

This was made possible when the Board decided that the Foundation should devote substantial resources to those parts of the law and the legal system, particularly the court system, which had long been neglected and overlooked, and yet had a significant direct impact upon many members of the community.

One area which the Board was interested in was identified as being Court Management and Delay, with a particular focus on local courts, because they had the greatest level of contact with the community.

To investigate this issue, the Board, at the suggestion of Board member Clare Petre, a social worker with Redfern Legal Centre, appointed an Ad Hoc Committee on Court Management. The members were myself, Clare and Peter Webb, an Assistant Secretary of the Attorney General's Department. The committee explored the ramifications of establishing a prototype court and the idea was discussed with representatives of the Local Courts Administration, the Department and a number of magistrates

These discussions revealed concern with the way such courts operated from both community service and administrative points of view. As a result of these discussions, the Local Courts Administration was keen to enter into a co-venture with the Foundation to undertake the development of a model court. The Board agreed, in December 1983, to provide $35,000 to fund the evaluation phase.

The aims of the project were to be the development through

research and usage of a Model Court, which in turn was to be complemented by reforms in a number of aspects of the operation of the court process which might be translated into the operations of all local courts

This highly significant and groundbreaking project was seen as enabling members of the public who came into contact with the Court to obtain efficient, responsive service and a feeling of satisfaction that, as far as possible, their needs had been met.

Primarily, the goal of the project would be achieved through the provision of better material facilities, staff resources, environmental improvements, more informative and contemporary documentation and an improvement in the information available from the court, both prior to and after the hearing. The project was not directed to any alteration of the role of the presiding magistrate.

An evaluation stage involved a three-month research phase by a two-person working party made up of Dr Rick Mohr, a social researcher, and Rod Pickup, an experienced senior officer with the Local Courts Administration. The purpose of this study was to identify and research deficiencies in the relationship between the local courts and the members of the community they served.

In September 1984 the Board approved the recommendations flowing from the evaluation stage. This meant the commencement of the developmental phase of the project, the objectives of which were "to implement, test and demonstrate reforms which improve the accessibility and service which Local Courts offer the public."

The Model Court Project's "Test Bed"

Blacktown Local Court was nominated by the Attorney General's Department as the site for the project, as it was agreed that the project be conducted in a busy court operating from a relatively modern building.

Blacktown Court turned out to be an inspired choice as it was one of relatively few modern court buildings in Sydney. It offered flexibility simply not found in the vast majority of older courts in most other suburbs and country towns. Many of these were modelled on designs developed in the early part of the 19th century and with few exceptions were small and offered few creature comforts for the magistrate and staff, let alone those attending court.

The Model Court Project continued to break new ground over the next 12 months, and this led the Board to provide another two years' funding with a special allocation from the Statutory Interest Account of $512,490. This very important project was destined to be the blueprint for all future upgrades of existing local court facilities and for new local courts.

This next stage also obtained the full approval and strong support of the new Attorney General Terry Sheahan in November 1984. This coincided with the appointment of a Project Manager, Peter Schell, who had a long background in Local Courts Administration. An Advisory Committee was established in January 1985 to assist the Project Manager. It included representatives of government agencies dealing with the court, local community groups, various representatives of solicitors including legal aid lawyers, etc.

Significant changes already underway included the appointment of additional staff, building alterations, explanatory brochures, improved technology, including photocopiers and improved records storage.

The project also opened up the opportunity to apply other cutting-edge communications technologies such as touch screen information technology and adapting airport flight screens to inform those waiting of the progress being made with the court list.

Considerable attention was given to improving consumer comfort through the provision of additional air conditioning, seating, symbolised signage, the installation of drink vending machines and multi-coin telephone facilities. The practical outcomes were recorded in a widely distributed newsletter published periodically during the project's life.

Once the exploratory part of the project was finalised and the Blacktown Local Court had been chosen by the Department as the site of the Model Court, there were a number of clear goals. These included changes to the public areas, the court registry and the court rooms as well as providing those required to attend court with better information and facilities.

Another early priority was to improve sources of information for the public which started with the stationing of an enquiry officer in the foyer to direct people coming to the court building for the first time. Considerable effort was put into creating explanatory brochures to help people understand how the court worked, which in time would be complemented by Courtguide, a touch screen kiosk which quickly and in plain language, offered guidance on a range of issues. Also on our wish list was the installation of suspended screens as seen in airports to display current court lists and progress being made. These were supplemented by a public address system for announcements and warning alarms.

Several meeting rooms were built to ensure that those appearing in court could have confidential discussions with their legal advisers

Radical changes were made to the way the court office looked and functioned. Changes included a new modular counter system which incorporated private interviewing booths for those wanting to discuss sensitive matters with court staff. Computers were also introduced in the court office to aid efficiency and help manage the large amount of information passing through the court.

Other changes were trialled inside the court rooms including the installation of a voice activated recording system, the testing of different methods of protecting the privacy of children and juvenile witnesses via screens and interactive video systems. Another innovation was a mobile rostrum in the court room for unrepresented parties or interpreters, with microphones built in. A significant challenge with the court rooms was improving the acoustics to improve audibility.

Once these changes to the court rooms were operational it meant that more than one court room could now be operated at the same time, and, later, weekly night courts were experimented with. Court management changes included daily callover lists, including consideration of bail and adjournment applications by the Clerk of the Court. Also introduced were weekly hearings by the Registrar to deal with civil matters where only one party was in attendance.

It was recognised that the longstanding and important service provided by the Chamber Magistrate needed greater support and, besides a new appointment system, those seeking help had a separate waiting room away from the main court area. Complementing these court services was a telephone conference service to assist non-English speakers by having a phone connection to the interpreter service. A further addition to the court's service was the attendance of a duty probation officer on a daily basis to assist court officers.

The physical improvements went a long way to make someone's day in court more comfortable and less threatening, while from the Foundation's point of view, the opportunity to test technology seen in US courts in an Australian setting was a high point. It led to more efficient servicing of those attending court as well as giving them instant access to relevant information via the Courtguide interactive video booths and by the display of court lists on airport type screens.

The Model Court Project was another excellent example of how the Foundation's access to discretionary funds provided a catalyst to enable significant reforms to the legal system to be pilot tested and the opportunity to build a case for improvement and reforms. This then enabled government agencies successfully to establish a case based on solid evidence, for the allocation of significant funding for the upgrading of these important public facilities.

I always got a thrill out of visiting new court complexes to see how quickly the ideas and technology pioneered at Blacktown made a difference in the real world of those attending court in other places such as the then new Downing Centre Local Court or the new Campbelltown Local Court.

The Law Foundation Board's initial concerns about Local Courts in 1983 were vindicated by the widespread needs and inefficiencies uncovered by the project's exploratory stage. They justified the timely re-think of such inappropriate public facilities and its expression of concern readily found willing listeners amongst the Department's senior management. As the project moved forward, Terry Sheahan's appointment as Attorney General in 1984 helped to ensure that adequate funding was made available from the Statutory Interest Account to make this important experiment possible.

Looking back, it was one of the most significant projects the Foundation was involved in and demonstrated how a comparatively small amount of discretionary funding had such a major influence in convincing the NSW government of the multi-level advantages flowing from this project.

Because of the collaborative nature of the project, made possible by the co-operation of a number of courts using government agencies, a joint report marking the completion of the main elements of the project was prepared by the Attorney General's Department and the Law Foundation and published in late 1990. In his introduction, Trevor Haines noted:

> The Model Court Project is a unique concept inspired by the realisation that the adoption of a consumer oriented perspective by court management may better serve the needs of the client public.
>
> The Law Foundation and the NSW Attorney General's Department jointly ventured into this new and unexpected terrain to discover deficiencies then existing in the court environment and embarked upon remedial action through improved procedures, practices and technology to more appropriately cater to the court's client base.
>
> Unlike many changes wrought in the administration of the court system, the Model Court Project was driven by de-

termination to improve the lot of consumers, rather than achieve efficiencies.

Nevertheless, and this may be a valuable lesson to us all, the outcome of the Project had provided efficiencies and effectiveness as by-products of the service improvements achieved for the "consumers" of justice.

The Civil Justice Research Centre

The completion of the Model Court Project enabled the Board at its 1989 policy retreat to consider what contribution the Foundation might make to answering the need of court administrators, the Attorney General's Department, and other policy makers for better information. Concerns arose from the stresses being put on the court system by an ever-increasing volume of matters coming before the courts since the reforms of the Supreme and District Court's rules and procedures 20 years earlier.

With the new Greiner government installed, the Foundation's status took another leap forward via collaboration with the Attorney General's Department, with a view to establishing a new research body to be known as the Civil Justice Research Centre (CJRC). Court administrators and departmental policy makers were confronted by a lack of information about the state's higher courts' ability to manage their increasing caseloads and the associated pressures on the resources of those courts.

The conclusion reached, assisted by the input of then Attorney General John Dowd QC, gave the highest priority to the need for an empirical research approach to understanding how the civil litigation process worked. A discussion paper prepared for the retreat had raised the question of whether the Foundation should establish a multi-disciplinary research centre which would undertake policy relevant research to provide a better understanding of the civil litigation process.

The paper referred in some detail to the Institute for Civil Justice within the RAND Corporation located in Santa Monica, California, which I had visited when in the US the previous July. I had spent several days being briefed on the Institute's role and research approach. The Institute had developed a high reputation for producing policy relevant objective research findings on various aspects of the US civil litigation process.

The Board greeted the idea with enthusiasm, recognising that having such a facility in NSW could contribute to the solution of a considerable number of problems for court managers and policy makers. This was viewed as being particularly relevant to current policy debates as to the causes of delay which relied mainly on speculation and not hard facts. Reference was made to the value of such a body within the overall law reform process.

The Board unanimously agreed to fund a permanent independent multi-disciplinary research centre which would examine the workings of the civil litigation process with a view to producing policy relevant data and recommendations. Its role would be to find solutions to policy questions rather than conducting research for academic or private purposes.

I was requested to explore with the relevant industries and professional groups their interest in supporting the development of such a body.

When the dust settled, I realised that such a centre was clearly an ambitious goal. While we had operated with a small research staff in the past, what was proposed was significantly different. My first call was to Dr Terry Beed, a former Board member and a valuable resource when major research questions came up at the Foundation. Terry had been involved previously as a researcher or consultant on a number of research initiatives during the past dozen years or so. At this time, he was working with KPMG Peat Marwick Management Consultants and introduced me to Peter Truda, the partner in charge. Peter would later work closely with me on the Tomorrow's Legal Services project, another major research initiative.

I recognised that two types of assistance were needed. One was broad strategic planning including industry consultation. The second element was the need for advice on the establishment and management of an empirical research centre. I felt Terry Beed's experience in establishing and managing such research centres would be vital.

With their assistance, a submission was put to the Board for the Foundation to undertake a scoping exercise to address such issues as the Centre's structure, likely appeal to outside funders, appropriate staffing for such a centre, and a preliminary research approach. Their submission to the Board in September 1989 added that the outcome of this phase would be options for the full-scale development of the proposed Centre.

One early initiative proposed was that we take immediate steps to invite the recently retired founding Director of RAND's Institute for Civil Justice, Gus Shubert, to visit Australia as soon as was practical. Based in Santa Monica, California, RAND is an independent global policy think tank established in 1948 to offer research and analysis to the US Armed Forces and is now largely funded by the US government. RAND's defence intelligence role, brought to public attention by the release of the top-secret Pentagon Papers by RAND researcher Daniel Ellsberg in 1971, also had a long-standing interest in social policy.

It was thought that we should consider modelling our new research initiative on the work done by the RAND's Institute for Civil Justice.

It was anticipated that Shubert's visit would help promote the concept of the Centre to its potential constituency, as well as assisting the project team with taking the first steps towards establishing the Centre's research agenda. The submission also anticipated that a first operational phase would take place between January and December 1990 and would be aimed at starting several major research projects, hiring suitable staff and settling the Centre's organisational structure.

The Board accepted the proposal and agreed with my recommendation to work with the assistance of KPMG for the first 15 months, with Gus Shubert's visit to be accelerated. Fortunately, he was able to accept our invitation and he was the catalyst for an intensive programme of events, meetings and seminars at which the concept of the Centre was explained and support generated. Shubert met with Premier Greiner and other key ministers, members of the judiciary, lawyers, insurers, trade union officials and industry leaders.

The comparatively quick start time in getting this new Centre operational was due directly to the Foundation being able to draw upon the experience of advisers such as Professor Beed and Peter Truda, both of whom were keen to tap into the trail blazing experience of RAND's Institute for Civil Justice and of Gus Shubert. By the time Gus left for home, the relevant institutions including the courts, government agencies as well as insurers had effectively signed onto the need for such a centre in NSW.

By the December 1989 Board meeting, a detailed programme of research, based on the process of consultation during Shubert's visit, had been established. Initial indications were that there was considerable interest in a major survey of accident victims, but this was considered to be too ambitious and expensive.

As was the case with RAND's Institute in its early days, one of the main aims of this new Centre was to initiate data gathering exercises which were capable of being continued by the institution in question. This would ensure that besides the benefits flowing from results of the particular piece of research, there would be the opportunity for policy relevant data to be collected on a permanent basis.

The Centre's research agenda was formulated and supervised by a committee, which included Beed, Truda, Brian Thornton, a recent President of the Law Society, Peter Cashman, former PIAC director and pioneering class action solicitor, Trevor Haines, the Foundation's Chairman, and me.

The emerging role of the Centre was seen as examining the policies that shape the civil justice system, the behaviour of the people who participate in it, the operation of its institutions and its effects on the community's social and economic systems.

Civil matters were traditionally the poor relations of the justice system. They frequently took a back seat to criminal matters in terms of resource allocation. While a number of bodies, both government and private, conducted systematic research on the criminal justice system, the debate on issues to do with the civil side consisted, until this point in time, of anecdotal evidence often obtained from parties with a stake in the operation of the system itself. The CJRC was needed to provide objective, policy relevant data and recommendations for the improved efficiency and cost effectiveness of the civil justice system.

Within its first 12 months the Centre had completed a number of studies carried out by its small staff of researchers, Deborah Worthington and Tania Matruglio, assisted by Beed and Truda. The first, a report of the study of the WorkCover Authority's conciliation process, was published by the Centre under the title *The Role of Conciliation*. The Centre's second report was entitled *Lawyers in Civil Litigation*. It was based on a re-interpretation of data previously collected by the National Institute of Labour Studies and was timely as the cost of litigation was the focus of an inquiry by the Senate Standing Committee on Legal and Constitutional Matters which received more than 100 submissions.

With these studies completed and widely circulated, the Centre's staff were engaged in several new projects. One was a major study of GIO third party accident cases still awaiting court hearings. The aim of this study was to quantify the delays experienced in these matters and to identify factors associated with the delay. It also examined a number of other features of the way such cases are processed.

This study was completed and a report, *The Pace of Litigation in New South Wales: Lessons from the Tail*, was published in late

1991 which confirmed the need for a systematic approach to the causes of delay. Its release was timely as there had recently been a heated debate about the causes of delay in personal injury cases and the report's findings enabled the issue to be considered on an empirical basis. The success of the study could be seen in the encouraging number of requests locally, interstate and overseas, for the report.

Building on the foundations laid by this report, the Centre proceeded to undertake a survey of plaintiffs' solicitors.

Also, during the year, the Centre published the first issue of its statistical bulletin *Civil Issues*, which shed further light on matters unresolved by the WorkCover Authority's conciliation service. The Centre was also considering the cost of litigation based on information collected from law firms. This information would allow it to follow up on a range of issues including how much litigants were charged, a comparison of costs against amounts recovered and the types of fee arrangements. All of these issues would now be able to be considered on an empirical basis.

In December 1992 Dr Deborah Hensler, Senior Social Scientist at the Institute for Civil Justice, was invited to visit the Centre. As well as participating in an intensive round of meetings with insurers, academics, court personnel and government officials, Deborah gave a seminar at the Law Society titled *Uses and Abuses of Civil Justice Research* which was well received. Dr Hensler was based in the Centre during her stay and participated in discussions with Centre staff and its board of management and commented favourably on the standard of work being undertaken.

The Centre participated in an Accessible Justice Summit held during Law Week in May 1993 and released several reports, namely *Costs Incurred by Plaintiffs in Third Party Litigation*, *The Other View of Activities* which mapped out the activities of the parties in processing third party claims and *The Cost of Civil Litigation: Current Charging Practices*. This latter report provided empirical data on the operation of the current NSW legal system and enabled a more informed debate. It was used by the Foundation to undertake actuarial modelling of the feasibility of its proposed litigation support scheme.

In recognition of the growing demand for the Centre's research and its expanding agenda, the Foundation Board authorised additional expenditure to enable the Centre to recruit more staff and move to the planned fully operational stage with a full staff complement of a Research Manager, four researchers and an assistant.

After several years' operation, the Foundation endorsed a charter which the Centre's Board of Management and staff developed, and which appeared in each of the Centre's research reports published by the Foundation from 1993. It read:

> Charter of the Civil Justice Research Centre
>
> The principal purpose of the Civil Justice Research Centre is to help make the process for resolving Civil Claims in New South Wales more efficient, more cost effective, and more accessible to the public.
>
> The Centre examines the policies which shape the civil justice system, the behaviour of the people who participate in it, the operation of its institutions, and its effects on the community's social and economic systems.
>
> The Centre adopts an interdisciplinary approach to the study of public policy issues; widely disseminates the results of its work to government official, legislators and judges; the unions; the business, consumer affairs, legal and research communities; and to the general public.

During my tenure with the Foundation, the establishment of this Centre filled a massive void in relevant policy related information. A comparison of the situation before the Centre's establishment and after its operation commenced was stark. The extraordinary range of hitherto unavailable information and data now flowing from its research team was widely appreciated by its constituency. We were finally catching up with other advanced economies.

In the second half of 1993, the Centre published two reports on the Compensation Court. The first was an initial study which provided a basis for further research on the demands on the court and issues arising from its current procedures. The second, later in December, was a publication *So Who Does Use the Courts?* by staff researcher Tania Matruglio, which interpreted information collected during the Supreme Court Special Sittings in 1992 to establish a profile of users of the court's Common Law Division.

In this report's Foreword, I wrote:

> So, who does use the court? Many would immediately suggest the courts are the domain of the rich. If pushed, they may also suggest that the very poor have some access to the courts through legal aid and other forms of assistance. However, there is a common belief that those in the middle, the majority of Australians, simply cannot afford the remedies offered by the civil justice system ... the Centre decided to test this proposition and has come up with what for many will be a surprising results ...
>
> This study is really the start of a profile of the NSW court users generally. However, this study demonstrates how little basis there is for many of the commonly held misconceptions about our legal system.
>
> It is hoped that this study will lead policy makers to ask more questions like 'who do use the courts', rather than assume answers ...

Released at the same time was another report, *The Costs of Civil Litigation,* by the Centre's Research Manager Deborah Worthington and researcher Joanne Baker. In the report's Foreword I noted:

> There had been something missing from the current debate of the costs of justice. The recent Trade Practices Commission inquiry into legal services is only the latest of many inquiries and reviews into this issue.
>
> However, Professor Fels and Professor Hilmer's reports

clearly demonstrate that little empirical research had been conducted, despite heated arguments and much media controversy.

This report represents the beginning of a response to a serious gap in the information available to policy makers in New South Wales and Victoria, and indeed, the rest of Australia.

This study gained added importance because, while the Centre collected data on matters heard in the District and Supreme Courts of New South Wales, the Victorian Law Reform Commission was also collecting such data from a similar sample of courts with the cases being analysed for such factors as the length cases took to completion, the legal costs to both plaintiffs and defendants and the proportion of these costs to overall damages awards.

The importance of this study was due to two factors. Such studies had never been undertaken previously and it offered the opportunity to compare similar cases in the two largest jurisdictions in Australia. The differences may now be of only historical value due to the effluxion of time. However, as much the same types of players are still involved and any changes in the court systems would probably be similar, there may still be lessons to be learned.

The differences which emerged were in relation to the duration of matters, the number of matters proceeding to verdict, the methods used to calculate fees and the amounts charged and recovered. These were recorded as follows:

- it took significantly longer to complete matters in NSW;
- more cases proceed to a hearing and verdict in NSW;
- law firms in NSW were found to base fees on time spent whereas their Victorian colleagues relied on court set fee scales;
- the difference in the legal costs were not statistically different, yet in NSW the trend was that legal costs and amounts recovered by way of settlements or verdicts were higher.

The report noted that such findings gave rise to more questions about what caused these differences and further empirical research was needed.

Included in the highlights of the 1993/94 years was the appointment of lawyer researcher, Gillian McAllister, as the Centre's Executive Director and a visit to the Centre by Pat Ebener, a senior researcher with RAND's Institute for Civil Justice. The Centre's staff benefitted from Ms Ebener's extensive research experience. Also, the Centre had been requested by the Law Society to undertake an analysis of statistics collected by the Family Court. These showed that there were different disposition patterns between different court registries and a report was finalised during this period.

Another new study was undertaken of alternative dispute resolution in the District Court which was intended to provide a plaintiff's perceptions on the various procedures being trialled. The Centre also received commissions from WorkCover and the Department of Courts Administration, and discussions were underway with the Motor Accidents Authority for a study of cases resolved under the NSW Motor Accident Scheme.

Reports published later in 1994 included *Who Settles And Why? - A Study of Factors Associated with Case Disposition* by Joanne Baker, another report flowing form the 1992 Supreme Court Special Sittings, *Compensation in an Atmosphere of Reduced Legalism - a study of workers compensation claims made under the NSW WorkCover scheme* by Deborah Worthington, *Plaintiffs and The Process of Litigation - An Analysis of the Perceptions of Plaintiffs Following their Experience of Litigation* by Tania Matruglio.

In 1995 reports published included *Awards under The Motor Accidents Act 1988* by Deborah Worthington and researcher Marie Delaney, a report commissioned by the Motor Accidents Authority which was intended to shed light on how judges and arbitrators were applying the Act in determining levels of compensation; and *Economic Evaluation of Differential Case Management* by Chris Guest and Tom Murphy, which was commissioned to provide information about the newly introduced differential case management in the NSW Supreme Court.

The Civil Justice Research Centre was another groundbreaking Foundation initiative which revived its initial strong interest in applied social science research which began in the early 1970s. This was all being undertaken within a comparatively modest annual allocation of $350,000 for 1993/94.

21

LAW FOUNDATION: YOUTH AND THE LAW PROJECTS

Through its High School Education Law Project, the Foundation had extensive experience of assisting teenagers to gain a better understanding of the law through introducing legal studies as a high school subject. The Foundation had not previously had the opportunity to explore other ways of assisting young people relate to the law and the legal system. However, in the lead up to the UN's International Year of the Child (IYC) in 1979, such an opportunity presented itself which resulted in the Youth Forum initiative.

This and later youth-oriented initiatives allowed the Board to adopt a unique leadership role in pushing the boundaries beyond education into cutting edge areas of youth crime and delinquency prevention, building important links with the NSW police, local government and legal services providers. The success of this initiative was the subject of an Australian contribution to the UN Congress on Crime Prevention and Delinquency held in Milan in 1985.

Later, the Foundation seized the opportunity to intervene in the vexed area of juvenile justice in NSW when an expert group sought its assistance to undertake research as part of a major push for law reform in this long-neglected area. The work of this committee resulted in the NSW government changing its policy in adopting the project's findings.

Youth Forum: Marking the International Year of the Child 1979

In the lead up to the IYC, the Foundation was approached by Ms Anne Gorman, director of the IYC Secretariat in the NSW Department of Youth and Community Services. The Secretariat had been established by the NSW government to organise a programme of events to mark the year.

One of the initiatives the steering committee was interested in was finding a way to focus on the way the law related to children. From this came the idea of holding a youth forum over several days and involving children from all over the state. Anne approached the Foundation, and the Board thought that it was a good initiative and agreed to make a grant to meet the cost of the event.

It was decided to hold the event at the Sydney Teachers' College on the Sydney University Campus during September 1979 with around 400 school students attending, with many from the country being billeted with Sydney families. An extensive agenda of issues to be discussed was planned with a mixture of small groups reporting back to plenary sessions with a view to a final report of the conclusions reached.

The event was opened by Premier Neville Wran QC, who made a wonderful speech welcoming the delegates and speaking to them as equals. Each child felt the Premier was speaking to them personally about the importance of their views being heard, particularly during that important year. As one of the organisers, I was as excited as the participants were by Wran's thoughtful and sensitive speech. At the end of it, he was treated to applause normally reserved by teenagers for rock stars, not politicians. It was an extraordinary event to witness. I am sure that for every one of the young people present, the IYC Youth Forum was an unforgettable experience and 40 or so years later in their life, they would probably recall it as a high point of their teenage years.

After such an inspirational start, the event went like clockwork over the next few days. On the last day, Rex Jackson, the Minister for Youth and Community Services, whose Department was the lead organiser of the event, was due to make the closing address. He came looking like a man who wished he was anywhere else but there and opened his address by saying that this event was far more significant for the country than the ACTU Congress then also being held in Sydney.

After his short address, he asked if there were any questions. A bright female student asked him if this event was so important how come he as the relevant minister had waited until the end to come and join them. Similar questions followed and eventually the officials had to usher the seething Rex out of the hall before he jumped down from the stage and belted some child as he was so enraged at being ridiculed by "children". I am sure the episode did not help Anne Gorman's career in the Department, but nevertheless as an event was a brilliant success. It was apparent that the participants got a lot out of it and voted unanimously for a similar Forum to become an annual event for others to experience.

In fact, the Foundation Board and the Attorney General were so pleased by the event, similar successful forums were held with Law Foundation funding for the next few years at Mitchell College of Advanced Education. These later events were sponsored by the Commercial Banking Company of Sydney, and later by the National Australia Bank and Esso Sydney. The approach taken at subsequent events followed the format developed for the first IYC event. Students participated in group discussions resulting in a series of action plans being adopted. The participants were taught skills to implement selected plans in their own schools. A number of local Youth Forums were also held in high schools throughout the state with the assistance of the project team, led by Julia Young, who was a very valuable consultant to the Law Foundation on this and similar initiatives.

Campbelltown Youth and the Law Project

Forty years ago, Campbelltown was one of the fastest growing urban areas in Australia, containing many young and single parent families. In March 1985, a citizens' committee was formed in response to what was perceived to be an increase in youth crime. The result was the establishment of the Campbelltown Youth at Risk Program. The goal of this initiative was to implement a preventative programme aimed at juvenile and early adult offenders and other youths at risk. A longer-term diversionary programme was also envisaged through the establishment of a drop-in crisis centre.

Following an approach for assistance by the Youth at Risk Program, the Foundation's Board decided to investigate whether there was a role for the Foundation to play in dealing with youth crime in the Campbelltown area.

To assist it in this task, the Foundation turned to Professor Duncan Chappell, an internationally renowned Australian criminologist, to carry out a preliminary assessment of the Campbelltown youth problem. Following completion of the assessment, Chappell's study provided a remarkably comprehensive overview of the Macarthur region, and, while one could have easily become depressed about the picture he drew, there was a thread of optimism running through his report, *Growing Up in the Macarthur Region*. His recommendations were directed towards the raising of community aspirations in the area, particularly in the focal group of his study, the 10-18 years age bracket.

Chappell concluded that, in the particular social context of the Macarthur region, with the high proportion of young people in its population, it was likely significant levels of criminal and related conduct would soon start to become apparent. He felt that possible responses to the problem must be planned and implemented in a short time span if a severe increase in anti-social behaviour, spawned by the social conditions surrounding wide unemployment, were to be avoided.

Professor Chappell accordingly urged the Foundation to become the initiating force behind a "crime prevention model" which would be guided by proactive strategies designed to prevent, or at least to mitigate, the occurrence of anti-social behaviour by the youth of communities such as Macarthur.

He further recommended that the Foundation should take an

initiative which would build upon the activities associated with the UN's International Youth Year (IYY) currently underway and give credence to the philosophy of encouraging youth to be involved in identifying and developing their own resources. This would involve a comprehensive study of the expectations and needs of young people growing up in Macarthur, focusing particularly upon, although not limiting itself to, those issues believed to be most critical in reducing anti-social behaviour by youth.

It was felt that the results of such a study would provide policy-relevant information to decision-makers concerned with the development of youth crime prevention strategies, as well as allowing continuing assessment to be made of the extent to which these decision-makers took account of established youth needs and concerns.

Chappell also suggested that the youth of the region be actively involved in the survey and largely responsible for carrying it out. He believed that the Law Foundation's youth project, Youth Forum, could become involved in respect of the dissemination, discussion and implementation of results. It could apply its extensive experience of working with the target age group to assist the young people in Macarthur to learn the skills required to be proponents of social change and to impact directly upon crime prevention measures affecting youth.

Although encouraging the Foundation to become actively involved in the Macarthur region through Youth Forum, Chappell recommended against funding the application from the Youth at Risk Program, on the basis that it already fitted within current reforms being introduced by the government in respect of the handling and processing of juvenile offenders and thus was likely to be addressed best by those reforms rather than needing Foundation support.

Growing up in the Macarthur Region was considered and its recommendations were adopted by the Foundation's Board in April 1985. Approval in principle was given, subject to more detailed development of the methodology to be used in the project. The project promised to be a major IYY activity and was widely recognised as such.

With the Campbelltown Youth and the Law Project, the Board accepted Chappell's recommendation and invited the Youth Forum team in April 1985 to submit a proposal to carry out all stages of the project. The project commenced operation in late August 1985. While this was occurring, the Chairman of the Law Foundation, Trevor Haines, and I, as noted previously, attended the five-yearly UN Congress on Crime Prevention and Delinquency being held in a special conference centre outside Milan, where he delivered a paper describing the new initiatives being taken on the advice of Professor Chappell. The paper drew considerable interest from representatives of other countries attending the Congress.

It was my first experience of such a huge event with representatives from over 150 countries. I heard about the magnitude of the problems confronting officials in a host of third world countries. Our concerns about the youth of Campbelltown gave real meaning to the current throw-away line "such a first world problem"!

The Australian delegation was led by Lionel Bowen, the then federal Attorney General, who was travelling with his wife. Like most of the other delegations, we were booked into Milan's deluxe hotels. However, being summer and normally a tourist dead zone for Milan, the hotel rates were approximately one-third the cost during the rest of the year and the room cost was easily covered by the normal Australian allowances. Plebs like me had a once in a lifetime opportunity to stay in the Hotel Principe Di Savoia!

One afternoon was free of Congress events so, with Terry Sheahan, Trevor Haines, Chris Guest (Terry's senior adviser) and Cathy Lyons, a public defender who was visiting Milan as an observer at the Congress and staying with friends nearby, I travelled by ferry up Lake Como to Bellagio. It was a magic day. The weather was warm and sunny, and we spent the afternoon wandering the narrow steep streets of, I believe, one of the more gorgeous places in the world. I learned that the Rockefeller Foundation maintains a centre of learning in an old Bellagio Palazzo and I was deeply envious when I learned on my return to Australia that my former

Foundation colleague, Dr Roman Tomasic, had spent some sabbatical leave there as a visiting scholar.

Back in Australia the Campbelltown Youth and the Law Project continued to gain momentum with increasing public, as well as political, support. Considerable publicity arose from a project organised by a group of schoolgirls associated with the project. They decided to try to change the unhealthy attitudes many of their peers held towards the police. They hit on the idea of "Say G'day to a cop … today" which garnered considerable media attention. Another group associated with the project decided to write a law booklet, *Get it Right the First Time*. It was intended to tell young people how they should act when approached by the police. It used a backdrop of "do's" and "don'ts" in a style, and using language, teenagers would identify with. It was launched by Attorney General Terry Sheahan on a visit to the Campbelltown Project.

At the Board retreat in early 1987, considerable time was devoted by the Board to discussing whether it should continue to fund the project. The Board had invited the Deputy Director of the Bureau of Crime Statistics and Research, Dr Don Weatherburn, to provide his views on the project's impact. Like Professor Chappell, he saw considerable merit with the approach being taken with the project and felt the Foundation should support practical interventionist projects. He also could see benefit in the initiative being replicated in other parts of the state. After hearing Dr Weatherburn's views, the Board agreed to continue support for the project and the Attorney General agreed to bring the project to the attention of the ministerial task force on juvenile crime, as well as its members individually.

Over the next few years, the project continued to be effective and enlisted wide community support and assistance from other agencies, including the Federation of Police Citizen and Youth Clubs, the federal government and Campbelltown City Council, which meant that financial dependency on the foundation decreased. The success of this project was due to a group of young project leaders, such as

Robert Oerlemans and Rod Smith, who were ably assisted by long-term project consultants Julia Young and John Engel.

The great importance of the project was its significant and verifiable direct influence on many thousands of Australians who are still benefitting today from this initiative. Its influence on front line service providers, such as the police and other mainstream government and non-government organisations dealing with young peoples' issues, was enormous.

It was another of the Foundation's impressive success stories, having a greater influence than might have been expected from the relatively modest funds allocated to it over the years.

Youth Justice Coalition: Kids In Justice Project - A Game Changer

This project was initiated by Michael Hogan, a Public Interest Advocacy Centre lawyer, and later its director. It involved a 12-month research project aimed at examining the non-government sectors involved in a number of spheres of the juvenile justice system, including the policing of young people, advocacy and representation in the children's court and correctional services for young offenders.

The underlying rationale was to subject the juvenile justice system to detailed independent scrutiny of its general operation. The project was to document and review existing problems and gaps in the youth justice system and to develop a blueprint for future directions to be followed in finding solutions to the identified problems.

While the Board was interested in the concept behind the Kids in Justice Project, it had reservations about the proposed methodology and scope of the project. Several months of negotiations ensued, supervised by the Foundation's Grants Administrator Dawn Wong, which led to a revised proposal being considered at the December 1988 Board meeting. The Board approved a sum of $12,500 to undertake a three month pilot project, during which a more comprehensive plan would be developed.

I have a strong recollection of Dawn Wong and I participating in several meetings with the proponents of this scheme, Michael Hogan, Professor Helen Gamble, at the time Chairman of the NSW Law Reform Commission, and Elaine Fishwick, from the School of Social Work and Social Policy, drawing on our extensive experience of overseeing and guiding many similar projects. Once the project got moving, we were assisted by a steering committee including representatives of the Police, UNSW Law Faculty, legal centres, the Aboriginal Law Centre at UNSW and the NSW Law Reform Commission. In addition, two key researchers, Julia Tresidder, project co-ordinator, and research consultant Dr Rick Mohr, were engaged and supported by several short-term research assistants.

In May 1989 the Board accepted the methodology arising out of the development phase and, based on detailed costing submitted, made a special allocation of $95,000. This enabled the project to proceed to completion.

The project delivered two impressive reports. The first was an *Overview Report* of around 80 pages with a summary and a list of recommendations. This was intended to assist the media and the policy makers whom the project was seeking to influence. The second, entitled *Kids in Justice A Blueprint for the Nineties*, was 350 pages long and packed with data and findings.

The reports were successfully launched by the highly respected NSW Police Commissioner John Avery at the Police and Justice Museum. With the Foundation's assistance, every television channel and key radio stations, as well as the major newspapers, were represented at the launch. The story was first or second news item in every state and territory and was picked up by *4 Corners* and the *7.30 Report* on consecutive nights. It was also covered on *The Investigators* and *Good Morning Australia*. Articles in *The Bulletin* and other magazines followed.

The demand for the Overview Report was unprecedented for the Foundation, with some 2,000 copies being sold or distributed, a 100% increase on the number originally planned. The print run on the full report was extended from 300 to 500 copies.

The launch of the report had a huge impact on policy makers and on the NSW government which, with the report having been effectively endorsed by the Police Commissioner, had little option but to agree to the proposed reforms. It was a classic example of a well planned and executed project completed on time and within its budget. This, combined with a joint acceptance by the project team and Foundation staff that a well-planned media campaign would give it the coverage it deserved, left the government no option but to respond appropriately and agree to implement its findings.

According to Michael Hogan, this project demonstrated the benefits and effectiveness of innovative and independent research and evaluation in a complex and controversial area. The report was policy focused yet drew substantially on the views and experience of clients, staff, families and community workers. Almost 100 young people were interviewed, as well as families, members of the public, community workers and the staff of the agencies involved in the juvenile justice system, namely the police, family and community services personnel and the courts. To this, the project added information about the emerging trends and lessons in laws, policies and programmes throughout Australia and overseas. Issues papers were distributed, and policy workshops held on specific areas. Theatres, comics and radio sessions were used to involve young people in innovative ways.

The aim of the report was to provide a blueprint for reform of the juvenile justice system for the 1990s. It laid out a comprehensive package of proposals. There were more than 230 recommendations. New government expenditure of $13.8 million was proposed, to be offset against savings in courts, policing and detention centres. The report also aimed to inform the debates about juvenile justice issues, giving the users of the system a say and creating dialogue between the various people interested or involved in the juvenile justice system. It was another model of how a relatively modest, well targeted grant from the Foundation produced maximum benefit for society.

22

LAW FOUNDATION GRANTS PROGRAMME

From its earliest days the Board saw the best way to implement the Foundation's charter as being to initiate research and projects which would be undertaken by Foundation staff rather than to be a typical reactive philanthropic trust, periodically making grants to worthy recipients. However, the Board did recognise that some funds should be available for grants to individuals or organisations to undertake activities which fell within the Foundation's objects.

As noted elsewhere, from 1973 to 1978, funds were limited due to the Board's commitment to meet the establishment costs of the College of Law and the initial running costs of its continuing education activities. However, once the establishment phase was completed and the College's ongoing costs were being met by the federal government with it having been accepted as a tertiary institution, the Board was able to fund its internal research and project activities and consider requests for grants.

The passing of the *Law Foundation Act* in 1979 ensured the Foundation would have a more certain income and a broader charter. While succeeding Boards and Attorneys General saw the Foundation's main role as supporting major research and reform initiatives aimed at improving different aspects of the state's legal institutions and processes, they also recognised the need and the opportunity to provide funds for activities relevant to the Foundation's charter being undertaken by a range of external agencies, organisations and individuals.

That process became to be known as the General Grants Programme and in its first formal annual report in 1980 the Board noted that 34 grants to external bodies were made, with a total of $132,338 being allocated. These included a large grant of $28,225 to the NSW

Council of Social Service to investigate the legal information and legal education needs of social workers, while at the other end of the scale an amount of just $402 was to be one of the first of many grants made to Redfern Legal Centre which needed it to publish a booklet entitled *On and Off the Dole*. Amounts allocated were at a similar overall level for the next few years, but by 1985 with the Foundation's income steadily increasing, the amount allocated for grants jumped to over $350,000.

The Foundation's annual reports in the 10 years prior to my departure, namely from 1985 to 1994, recorded how 542 organisations, groups and individuals benefited from just over $8 million allocated to grant recipient projects, which amounted to 24% of total revenue received by the Foundation in that period, namely $33,432,984.

An Overview of Applicants

With so many worthy projects, the great majority of which had successful, groundbreaking outcomes benefiting the people of our state, I would like to convey some understanding of the variety of applicants assisted and the benefits flowing to their particular constituency.

A grant of $18,025 in 1985 showed how willing the Board was to be at the cutting edge of emerging issues which shed light on the adequacy of the relevant legal processes. This grant was made to Professor Kim Oates, Professor of Paediatrics and Child Health at Sydney University. Professor Oates had sought funds to study 206 cases of child sexual abuse managed at Royal Alexandra Hospital from January 1981 to December 1983 by reviewing the families of those children and the impact on the families and the affected children, of their experience of the legal processes.

The Board decided that, in light of the increasing incidence of child abuse and the growing public concern, this would be a timely study, the findings of which would have a direct bearing on influencing policy makers as to the most appropriate legal processes in such cases.

The Foundation was, in many ways, ahead of its time in funding such an inter-disciplinary study, being several decades before the issue of child abuse finally was exposed as a national scandal leading to the establishment of the 2012 Royal Commission into Institution Responses to Child Sexual Abuse.

In 1987 the Board undertook a major review of the grants programme and, in light of significant increases in its own funding, acknowledged that its then limit of $20,000 on grants to external bodies discouraged some applicants and the limit was lifted to $50,000. The review also revealed that there was an encouraging extension of the Foundation's catchment area well beyond legal professional bodies, legal centres and government agencies, which indicated the Foundation's efforts to promote the granting programme more extensively was working. In the previous four years, 62% of applications came from community-based bodies or universities.

While the Foundation had long been a supporter of the application of computer technology to the law, in 1987 the Board funded several somewhat speculative but potentially highly important software development projects. One was the DataLex project being conducted by academics Andrew Mowbray and Graham Greenleaf. They were allocated $48,177 for their project which was focused on assisting lawyers with techniques for computerised legal information retrieval. This project evolved into the Australian Legal Information Institute, a joint venture of UTS and UNSW Schools of Law. This initiative presently operates AUSTLII, the now ubiquitous full text computer based legal information system. It provides public access online to all Australian legislation and case law which, without substantial Foundation funding, may never have become the reality it is today.

The other big technology take up was the rapid recognition of the role of videos by many of the organisations the Foundation had traditionally dealt with, and the following are some examples of how this relatively new technology was put to good use in the second half of the 1980s.

In 1987 The Law Society's Young Lawyers Section received a grant of $20,000 to produce a video entitled *Who Needs a Lawyer* for public dissemination. They also successfully applied for a grant of $21,094 to acquire video recording equipment to tape their continuing education seminars and so create a video library for young lawyers.

Kingsford Legal Centre, attached to the UNSW Law School, also successfully applied for a grant of $16,610 to produce a teaching video about its clinical education course, and for acquisition of a video player and screen.

The 1987 Annual Report also recorded a grant of $36,000 being made to the Working Group on Intellectually Disabled Offenders to enable it to produce a staff training video to assist justice personnel in identifying those brought into contact with the justice system who had an intellectual disability. This group was established following a review by the government of the roles of departments providing services to intellectually disabled offenders. It was made up of representatives of a number of government agencies and organisations dealing with the intellectually disabled, who saw such a video as leading to more appropriate treatment of intellectually disabled offenders within the justice system.

The end result was a video titled *Appearances Can Deceive* and it was intended to play a vital role in the formal training of police, magistrates, lawyers, parole officers, welfare workers and prison officers.

A grant was also made to the Intellectual Disability Rights Service to enable it to publish a manual directed at intellectually disabled people, setting out their rights and responsibilities in the workplace. It was intended to be a valuable component of the Service's *Rights at Work Kit*, a first in the area of educating intellectually disabled people about their legal rights and obligations.

In 1988 the Board, recognising the continuing needs of the over 150,000 people with intellectual disability in the state, made several more grants to the Intellectual Disability Rights Service. One was to meet the cost of developing *Rights in Residence*, a manual on legal and human rights of intellectually disabled people living in residential facilities. The Board later made a grant of $13,300 to enable the publication of the manual.

After the positive reception of the *Rights in Residence* manual among social workers and others, the Board endorsed a further application from the Service and allocated $11,940 to enable the development of a manual for lawyers.

In the early years following the Foundation's incorporation, there had been little contact from Aboriginal organisations other than from the Aboriginal Law Research Unit at the UNSW. The unit had received several quite small grants, but in 1985 it sought a grant of $20,000 to enable it to prepare legal resources for Aboriginal Land Councils which wished to enter into commercial arrangements with respect to issues such as mining and tourism. The Unit wanted to prepare and provide manuals, data and model agreements. The Board thought that this grant should be made in light of the lack of resources most Land Councils had available. Land Councils also needed the assistance of the Unit with making claims under the land rights legislation.

The next application for assistance relating to Aboriginal Australians came from a group associated with the Aboriginal Legal Service, which was concerned about the high proportion of Aboriginal children aged between 12 and 16 amongst young people in juvenile detention centres. The Service pointed out in the application that such children often had difficulty understanding basic legal concepts, resulting in alienation and a loss of identity.

They saw the need to give these children the opportunity to use their talents and express themselves through their own culture. The proposed programme was aimed at encouraging these children through mediums of dance, drama and video workshops. Video workshops were aimed at creating a 30-minute video dealing with issues relating to Aboriginal youth and the law. The Board readily endorsed this application and the requested amount of $49,951 was allocated.

Another application came from the Aboriginal Law Centre seeking a grant of $39,237 to employ a Research and Information Officer for cataloguing a collection of materials on the Indigenous peoples of Australia and elsewhere. The cataloguing had commenced under a previous small grant from the Foundation and the centre now wanted to put the catalogue into a computer database. The Board thought that this was an important project and allocated the requested amount.

With the coming of the 1990s and the increasing cost of maintaining law libraries, the Board allocated significant funds to those organisations responsible for maintaining such libraries including the Law Society, the Bar Association, the Law Courts, the Attorney General's Department and the four main University Law Libraries. The total being granted to these organisations was over $370,000 in 1990 alone.

On a different level, in 1991 the Foundation Board decided to allocate $25,000 to the St James' Ethics Centre, now the Ethics Centre, so it could appoint an Executive Director. It retained Dr Simon Longstaff, who still holds that position at the Ethics Centre, which under his leadership has carved out a very important role in Australian society – another important seeding grant.

The more than $8 million distributed during the 10 years to 1994 under the General Grants Programme included hundreds of grants to local suburban or regional organisations for whom even a small grant of a few hundred dollars enabled them to undertake some law related activity which furthered the Foundation's statutory objectives. For example, in 1994 the National Association of TAFE Child Studies Teachers needed $350 to meet the travel costs of a noted legal academic to speak about issues relating to the law and the childcare industry.

In 1993 the Public Defenders Chambers needed $764 to meet the travel costs of a speaker on the subject of *Aboriginal English and the Law*. In 1992 a grant of $5,000 was made to the Illawarra Legal Centre Inc for supplementary funding for community legal education workshops as part of its Youth Education Programme. In 1991 a grant of $1,600 was made to the AIDS Council of New South Wales to enable it to purchase basic legal texts to assist in the establishment of a specialist legal practitioner's library which was intended to serve both solicitors helping those people with HIV/AIDS, and the ACON legal working party. Also, in 1991 a grant of $2,500 was made to the Blue Mountains Community Legal Centre Inc to cover cost of the production of a pamphlet and poster for the promotion of the Centre's services locally.

Managing the Grants Programme

Before ending this overview of the Foundation's General Grants Programme, it is appropriate to comment on the responsibility which went with managing such a substantial funding programme. No grants were made without the formal submission of a request which met the Foundation's published criteria. As demand grew for funding, the Foundation formulated a new application form which put considerable onus on the applicant to effectively address a range of issues.

Foundation staff headed by Assistant Director Dawn Wong developed the application form, the completion of which often told an applicant whether they were ready to undertake a major project in addition to their organisation's day to day activities. Often Dawn would review applications where doubts existed based on our past experience and arrange to meet with representatives of the applicant organisation. This frequently resulted in advice as to how their application could be improved if they took more time to gather supporting evidence and bring it to a level at which the Foundation would then have little difficulty in supporting the request.

This collaborative approach more often than not resulted in

projects achieving their goals and with the funds allocated, as noted with the Kids in Justice project. This represented a high water mark in having the right project team submitting a professional application which ticked all the boxes and, ultimately, when completed, the findings were so powerful and well documented the government of the day accepted the report's entire recommendations and effectively changed its management of juvenile offenders overnight.

Finally, in cases where more than a few thousand dollars were sought, we always required the submission of a payment programme. Individual payments were only made on submission of evidence that the grantee had made progress in accordance with the plan they submitted, and that funds had been expended as proposed.

We never transferred significant funds to a grantee in advance. Yet in only a very small percentage of cases were funds never released because the successful applicant, whether an individual or an organisation, simply never got their act together and never proceeded to implement their project. Even with over 500 applications approved, this was a very rare event.

In many ways, conducting the Foundation's General Grants Programme was enormously satisfying as it helped so many, often grassroots, organisations take steps for their constituents to help them get access to legal services or legal information when they needed it. Studies undertaken by Dawn Wong of leading foundations in the US with a similar mix of major in-house projects and grants programmes, revealed that the modest percentage of the Law Foundation's income spent on administrative overheads was comparable to that spent by those foundations and well below 20%.

23

The Hawke/Keating Era: Transforming the Economy

There were striking differences between the Hawke government and the Whitlam and Wran governments in terms of the challenges all three faced on winning government. As with my review of earlier governments with which the Law Foundation had dealings, I also looked at Hawke's legislative record. This quickly revealed an extraordinarily different story. During the Hawke era the government had few pieces of legislation on the reform scale of the other two governments.

This is not to say that Hawke's government had a poor record in passing legislation, it was just that most of its legislation consisted of amendments to Acts already in place, the usual money acts funding the machinery of the federal government, or tied state grants – in other words a lot of fine tuning but no dramatic litany of groundbreaking legislation which was the case with the Whitlam government.

I was initially confused by this finding as my recollection was a very busy government which hit the ground running after being sworn in on 11 March 1983. However, reviewing various accounts of the Hawke era, I soon recalled that this new government faced significantly different challenges because of the state of the economy to those faced by the Whitlam government, which inherited an Australia where the previous government had long neglected the social fabric and had not faced up to the changes taking place in the 1960s largely due to the post-war baby boomer generation. Hawke's government faced an urgent and desperate need to modernise the Australian economy rather than initiating an agenda of legislative reform.

Malcolm Fraser's decision to call the 1983 election early was because he was aware of the rapidly deteriorating state of the economy. Before the election, Fraser's Treasurer John Howard had indicated that the 1983/1984 deficit would be $6 billion. Hawke relied on this estimate and made spending promises of only $1.5 billion, which he considered affordable in that context.

However, on the Sunday after the election Hawke and Keating learnt that they had been left with "… a fiscal imbalance unprecedented in Australia during peacetime, as is the level of government spending."

Hawke realised that the actual deficit, including his modest promises, would be nearly $12 billion. Either Fraser was economically illiterate, or his Treasurer John Howard kept him in the dark.

At a press conference held shortly after these revelations Hawke said that, to deliver on his election promises in this context would be irresponsible and he would put them on hold until a review could be carried out. Nevertheless, the establishment of Medicare would still proceed, it being a pillar of the Prices and Incomes Accord which Labor had committed to prior to the 1983 election.

As Hawke's Treasurer, Paul Keating had a significant role in the development of the government's response to the economy. However, the urgency of the prevailing economic circumstances prompted Hawke and Keating to take the immediate and momentous step of floating the Australian dollar and breaking the nexus with the US dollar, a move supported by the Reserve Bank but made against the wishes of Treasury Secretary, and later Coalition Senator, John Stone.

The stability of the new government under Hawke meant that foreign funds were quickly flooding into Australia with speculators betting on a revaluation of the dollar, hence floating the dollar would stop such speculation. Keating also argued that floating the dollar would make it easier to attack inflation, a high priority with the new government.

As *The Sydney Morning Herald* editorial marking the event's 30th anniversary said:

> Thirty years ago this week, Australia took a leap into the unknown. In one of the most dramatic changes in our economy's history, global financial markets, rather than government officials, set the value of the Australian dollar from December 12, 1983.
>
> It can be easy to forget the significance of this change when the dollar's movements are a routine part of news bulletins, just like the weather. But the country's experience since then shows that Treasurer Paul Keating's move to float the dollar was a critically important decision that continues to benefit the nation.

The floating of the dollar was the first step along a 10 year path of economic reform and deregulation which resulted in Australians today benefiting from our nation's more than a quarter century of uninterrupted economic growth.

Troy Bramston's definitive biography of Hawke, *Bob Hawke: Demons and Destiny*, Viking, 2019, pp. xxv-xxvi, notes that Hawke:

> ... eschewed the class war and the politics of envy and worked with business and unions to turn Australia in a new direction. He saw opponents as adversaries, not enemies. The nation became more confident and optimistic, dynamic and brave, with a renewed sense of identity and purpose in a rapidly changing world. The Hawke government smashed the established policy settings and introduced vast economic, social and environmental reforms.

Another interesting comment Bramston quotes about the Hawke government was one told to him by former Attorney General Gareth Evans in an interview, that Hawke had "no interest whatsoever in the law reform agenda, human rights, civil liberties."

This in part explains the absence of any legislative record of dealing with issues unrelated to sorting out the economy until Hawke later acceded to Attorney General Lionel Bowen's plans to undertake a comprehensive review of the efficacy of the Australian Constitution with a view to having constitutional reforms to put to a referendum in conjunction with the bicentennial celebrations being planned for 1988.

When Hawke became the new Prime Minister in March 1983 he was, in parliamentary terms, one of the least experienced leaders, having served only one three year term in the national Parliament, and then holding the role of Leader of the Opposition for only a few weeks during the election period. Hawke was blessed with luck on his side. On 3 February 1983, at the meeting of the Shadow Cabinet in Brisbane, Bill Hayden was convinced to resign and Hawke, the most popular politician in the country, was appointed leader.

At almost the same moment, Malcolm Fraser was visiting the Governor General to take the steps to call an election, thinking he would be facing Hayden. Hawke easily won the election with a majority of 25 seats, which some commentators classified as one of the great Labor electoral victories, second only to John Curtin's win in 1943.

His ministerial colleague Neal Blewett, in an interesting contribution to Michelle Grattan's *Australian Prime Ministers*, wrote:

> While Hawke's charisma contributed to his electoral success, his talent for bureaucracy gave his government cohesion, stability and authority. Hawke possessed an unusual combination of qualities, for the charismatic politician tends usually to be slipshod, relying on wits and charm rather than organisation. Not so Hawke, indeed his great attention to process has been seen as a substitute for his lack of any political philosophy. It was soon apparent this was an orderly Labor government working in co-operation, rather than in conflict, with the public service, which recognised that it had a sympathetic prime minister. In deliberate contrast to the Whitlam regime, Hawke gave process prime place in structuring his government and his style was to concentrate on a few major strategic concerns while leaving policy making up to Ministers.

The major challenges confronting the Hawke government included the immediate one of the cyclical economic downturn of the early 1980s which confronted the new government with high levels of inflation and unemployment. The other was long-term and deep-rooted, namely the structural malaise in the Australian economy which made it increasingly uncompetitive in a globalising world.

Compounding this was the Labor Party's traditional ideology which offered no solutions to problems which were "globally transmitted", such as protectionism, industry subsidies and, to quote Blewett, adding to the list of obstacles were, "inefficient public enterprises, the sclerotic grip of financial regulation and the rigidities of the labour market". In these unpropitious circumstances, Blewett saw Hawke was an ideal leader, being an extreme optimist with unquestionable faith in his ability to negotiate his way through intractable problems which, while naïve, helped sustain the government through many a dark hour.

Hawke's extensive exposure to industrial relations and his membership of several major inquiries into Australia's manufacturing industry would have made him thoroughly conversant with the elite consensus on the structural flaws in the Australian economy and the need to create a more open, competitive, less regulated market economy. Thus, in the lead up to the 1983 election, Hawke was more fully across these issues than anyone else in his government and made an election promise to hold a National Economic Summit Conference within a short time of being elected.

Besides his own experience to draw on, Hawke was greatly assisted by having a ministry which was probably the best qualified and most experienced Australia had ever seen. While there were sections of the party still hankering after worn out policies and practices, there was now openness to alternative ideas and the need for serious rethinking. The Prices and Income Accord was the first step in that direction and was designed to tackle the problem of stagflation and to reduce the number of industrial disputes. The Accord was a creation of Bill Kelty, ACTU secretary, and Ralph Willis, while he was Hayden's shadow Treasurer.

The Accord depended on the unions agreeing to limit wage demands on the basis that the government promised to reduce inflation and spend more on education and welfare to maintain living standards. Most people agree that Hawke's role in getting the Accord across the line should never be underestimated.

In 2012 Hawke was interviewed on ABC radio's AM programme and referred to the National Economic Summit, saying:

> I'd promised we'd have that summit within a month of me coming to office. We did and we had the representatives, Federal government, state government, local government, large employers, small employers, trade unions, churches, welfare organisations. They were given by Treasury all the information that we had and so you had the people of Australia through their representative organisations informed in a way that they had never been before.
>
> So I think that was the great thing because it was out of that that I got a unanimous communiqué except for one person, Joh Bjelke-Petersen, agreeing with the analysis and accepting the things that had to be done, getting a constructive relationship between employers and trade unions, reducing the increase in money wages in return for acceptance of the social wage.
>
> Virtually all of the success, the economic success of 1983 stemmed from the summit.

With the formal adoption of the Accord by the government following the Summit, itself a massive break with traditional union resistance to wage restraint, the changes it secured for all workers were a 4.3% pay rise in September 1983, a 4.1% pay rise in April 1984 and a deferred 2.6% pay rise over the initial three-year period, as well as improvements in family payments and childcare and the introduction of Medicare.

With the Accord in place, the Treasurer Paul Keating took aim at the banks and announced plans to break up the local banks' monopoly by issuing banking licences to foreign and local qualifying institutions to bring more competition. He had long resented the conservative lending policies which impacted at the small business levels where his father suffered a business setback due to rigid lending policies. As shadow minister for national resources and overseas trade in the late 1970s he also fumed about the banks' unwillingness to fund the development of Australia's massive mineral endowment.

Taxation reform was the next issue confronted in 1985. This represented a fracture in the relationship between Hawke and Keating and, in the lead up to the December 1984 election, Hawke announced a Tax Summit on the return of the government.

When it came to the Tax Summit, Treasury staff had prepared three options. A consumption tax was included in the two options which Keating was pushing but was unsuccessful. Keating was reported as lamenting that "his tax cart had lost a wheel" when the consumption tax was rejected by the Summit. However, the changes were considered to be the most significant since the Second World War as taxation of capital gains and fringe benefits was introduced, tax shelters were shut off, dividend imputation was brought in, and the top marginal tax rate was reduced to under 50%.

Another bogey which ultimately needed to be dealt with was the phasing out of tariff protection for all industries by 2000, except for cars, textiles and footwear, which were subject to substantial reductions. This was done in two later statements, one in 1988 and the other in 1991.

In a move to adopt micro-economic reform in 1988, Cabinet supported partial privatisation of Qantas and Australian Airlines which both needed substantial capital injections. This move was against party policy but eventually Hawke's negotiation skills prevailed. Similar steps were taken to open up telecommunications to competition and to privatise the Commonwealth Bank. The aim of these moves was to free up capital to be applied to improve infrastructure, particularly the ports, due to increasing use of containers.

The Hawke government's transformation of the Australian economy marked a watershed in Australian history, having inherited a cossetted economy characterised by all-round protection with an associated rent-seeking culture. It was an economy that was uncompetitive internationally and overly dependent on commodity exports, inefficient public enterprises, a rigid labour market and low productivity. While the government did not cure these ills, it did tackle most of them and gave Australia an entirely new development trajectory. It also left the hope that Australia might ultimately be able to pay its way in a globalised world.

As to Keating's contribution to these reforms as the driver of the government's micro-economic reforms, the Grattan Institute has identified 10 such reforms that have contributed most to Australia's sustained period of economic growth; eight of which occurred while Keating was Treasurer or Prime Minister.

Keating Takes Over December 1991

Eventually Paul Keating replaced Hawke and became Prime Minister on 20 December 1991. He was worried that Labor's political capital was severely diminished after four election wins and a crowded eight years of reform and yet Keating still wanted his chance to put his imprint on the government.

When Parliament resumed, Keating quickly established his dominance and brought his divided troops behind his leadership. This he did in his first parliamentary week and his colleagues were heartened by his aggressive leadership and encouraged by his recently released economic statement titled *One Nation*.

In response to the intractable unemployment level, particularly amongst young people, Keating, unlike his predecessor, used Parliament to address the issue by legislating to establish the Australian National Training Authority, an agency to coordinate training opportunities, increase workforce skills and provide for a youth training wage. This was complemented by the *Disability Discrimination Act 1992* which provided a uniform base for the elimination of employment discrimination against disabled people. Keating also continued to address the escalation of welfare costs by continuing moves to limit the cost of social security spending by turning this expenditure into a productive investment through job support.

Keating also recognised the importance of the High Court's recognition of native title in the 1992 Mabo decision. This gave him another opportunity to break with the past through proposing to legislate once and for all remove from the law the outrageous notion of terra nullius, which Keating saw as the greatest barrier to reconciliation with Australia's First People.

His solution was the *Native Title Act*. However, before he could achieve this, he needed to win the election due no later than March 1993.

Keating's Redfern Speech

In the lead up to that election Keating decided to give a speech at Redfern Park on 10 December 1992 to launch the International Year of the World's Indigenous People. This became a landmark speech and was a highlight of Keating's time as Prime Minister.

In the speech Keating, acknowledged the great wrongs done to Indigenous Australians and the failure, up to that point, to extend opportunity, care, and dignity to the Indigenous peoples of Australia. He went on to say that the starting point might be to recognise that the problem started with non-Aboriginal Australians. He also saw the Mabo decision as an historic turning point a basis of a new relationship between Indigenous and non-Indigenous Australians.

On winning the election, Keating declared that it was a victory "for the true believers", and "the sweetest victory of all". However, the economy was not great and his chances of implementing his most expensive promises were in the balance. Yet he was determined to put his stamp on his prime ministership. On 21 April 1993, shortly after winning the election, at a meeting of company directors in Melbourne, he announced probably the most radical departure from long-term Labor Party policy, namely, that the labour market would be de-regulated so that individual companies could negotiate wage agreements based on productivity improvements.

He said this move was designed to increase flexibility and would be achieved by a continuation of co-operation rather than a return to conflict. He was quoted as saying:

> The success of economic policy depends on the success of business. We should work together for economic and social ends.

This, like other major reforms of the labour market, were made possible with the support Keating got from the ACTU's Bill Kelty and built on the progress made in the previous decade with the series of Accords.

Keating continued to make waves with another announcement following the election victory in which he appointed a Republic Advisory Committee to examine options for Australia's development as a republic. This was part of a national "big picture", a shared commitment to shaping the nation as an independent republic, with progress towards social justice as its foundation.

The *Native Title Act 1993* and the *Land Fund Act 1994*

The Mabo decision was also causing uncertainty and, after months of negotiation with a wide range of affected stakeholders within the Labor Party, with key stakeholders and with the broader community and, after a year of negotiations, Cabinet agreed in October 1993 with the enactment of the *Native Title Act 1993* and the *Land Fund Act 1994*.

These provided the first national recognition of Indigenous occupation and title to land in Australian legislation. The *Land Fund and Indigenous Land Corporation (ATSIC Amendment) Act 1995* amended the *Aboriginal and Torres Strait Islander Commission Act 1989* to establish the Aboriginal and Torres Strait Islander Land Fund and Indigenous Land Corporation.

In May 1994 Keating presented *Working Nation* to Parliament. This was the government's five-year programme for expanding employment, particularly for the young unemployed, by creating two million jobs. With reduced inflation and good growth in 1994, recovery from the recession seemed to be at hand. By the end of 1994 unemployment dropped to 9.3% and economic growth continued to improve. John Edwards, in his account of the Keating government, *Keating: The Inside Story*, recorded that *Working Nation* included funding for training and job creation programmes for the long-term unemployed.

Although Keating had pursued his grand vision after he won the 1993 election and brought in significant changes on various fronts, in his second term basically he did not have enough time for his radical economic reforms to take effect. He also had problems in his ministry, not unexpected after 13 years in government.

The end to the Hawke/Keating era, which had begun in March 1983 with the resounding election of the Hawke government, came in March 1996 when the Coalition won a similar overwhelming victory. The electorate accepted their three-week campaign pitch, "Enough is enough", despite Howard not releasing any detailed programme until the last minute. The electorate was very significantly divided into two camps, those who considered Paul Keating to be Australia's saviour while others were either over reform, or like many, took umbrage at Keating's style and, from time to time, his brutal approach to politics.

Yet in, many ways, the Howard government's ready acceptance of virtually all of the major changes to the nation's economic foundations made by the Hawke-Keating governments ensured that there would be long-term benefits flowing to the nation from their hard-won changes.

For many Australians today, the most visible of Keating's reforms is his establishment of a superannuation system for working Australians. Previously superannuation had largely been the preserve of corporate executives and public servants. The various Accords had included superannuation contributions in the various awards re-negotiated as part of the Accord process.

24

THE HAWKE/KEATING ERA: LAW FOUNDATION OPPORTUNITIES

Unlike the extensive contact the Foundation had with the Askin, Whitlam, Wran/Unsworth and Greiner/Fahey governments in NSW, direct involvement with the Hawke/Keating governments was relatively limited.

My first dealing with the new Hawke government flowed from being appointed by it in early 1983 to the Advisory Council on Inter-Governmental Relations (ACIR).

The other significant engagement with the Hawke/Keating governments was through the work of the Communications Law Centre. This was an initiative of the Foundation established in a response to pleas from the Public Interest Advocacy Centre which was being overwhelmed by requests for assistance from community groups. They needed specialist assistance with responding to the major changes mooted by the government in the areas of telecommunications and the mass media which was beyond the resources and capacity of PIAC.

Advisory Council for Inter-Governmental Relations

My appointment to ACIR as one of five community representatives had been mooted during the latter days of the Fraser administration. This was largely because Terry Sheahan, along with Gareth Evans, had been early parliamentary appointees to the new body and Terry thought that my background would enable me to make a useful contribution to the work of the Council.

The Council had been established following approval of a Charter for the Council at the Premiers' Conference in April 1976. That charter stated that the purpose of the Council was:

> ... to bring together representatives of the Federal, State and local governments and private citizens ... to give continuing attention to intergovernmental problems.

The Council's chair at the time of my appointment was Professor Ronald Gates, then Vice-Chancellor of the University of New England, who was one of five citizen members from whom the chair was required to be appointed. The politician members of the Council included five senior backbenchers from the federal Parliament, with three from the government and two from the Opposition, while the states and territories were all represented by ministerial nominees. They in turn were complemented by each state and territory's Local Government Associations being represented by senior experienced local government leaders.

At the first meeting I found myself being elected deputy chairperson by the Council, which I suspect was simply because of my experience of being head of a body with wide ranging research experience.

At the next meeting Professor Gates announced that from the end of that meeting he intended to retire forthwith from the Council to pursue other interests and proposed that I become the chair. This unexpected and extraordinarily rapid elevation seemed to be warmly welcomed by the various politician and citizen councillors. At the time, I looked at this in a positive light on the basis that Gates felt the leadership of the Council was in safe hands.

However, it was a large council with 25 members and I was apprehensive about controlling the meetings of such a large group, none of whom one could accuse of being shrinking violets. Thankfully, it quickly became clear that all the members were very experienced in working on committees, and being busy people meant that the role of Chairman was not as challenging as I thought it might be.

I was also helped during the initial period by knowing some of the politician members, including my friend Terry Sheahan who, as NSW Minister for Housing, attended meetings as the state's representative. Looking back, I now realise that having been a Board member of the Law Foundation for nearly five years and worked closely with some very experienced chairpersons such as Ken Smithers and John Ellard during my time at the Foundation, I was pretty well equipped to handle the task.

The Council had a small research staff based in a rather grand 1930s mansion on the heights above Battery Point in Hobart. It housed a staff of around seven or eight, including a small research staff headed by the director Dr Colin Balmer. It had some excellent researchers including the now prominent economist Saul Eslake, then a young, local honours graduate in Economics from the University of Tasmania.

My appointment coincided with the completion of the last of 12 groundbreaking reports on issues relating to various aspects of Australian local government. In addition, a very large project, which was a major study on *Resource Development Infrastructure and their impact of State and Local Government*, was also nearing completion, all of which meant that there was an opportunity to undertake some new inquiries.

However, before settling on any new projects, I suggested that we should do a survey of the various state governments and Local Government Associations represented on the Council to find out what issues they thought the Council should be investigating. This in turn led to a small delegation including the Director and myself travelling around Australia to meet with representatives of each constituent state government and Local Government Association.

The Council considered the feedback and noted the concerns expressed by state governments that the Commonwealth government adopted policies and introduced programmes, especially relating to immigration, with virtually no consultation with the states. This meant that such policies were often implemented without fully realising the stresses and demands these imposed on state and local governments. The Council readily endorsed the need for the study and authorised an inquiry to be undertaken.

The aims of the inquiry were to review the roles and contributions of the three spheres of government in the provision of post-arrival services for immigrants and to make recommendations designed to improve intergovernmental co-operation in this field.

These aims were set with regard to ACIR's terms of reference, which required it to examine and keep under review matters relating to intergovernmental co-operation and to make an examination of the relationships which should exist between federal, state and local governments.

The inquiry found that the mechanisms intended to facilitate consultation between the Commonwealth and the states were not as effective as had been assumed. The inquiry also found that there was some degree of overlap and duplication among the programmes of the three spheres of government and the non-government sector. Some needed services were not available and immigrants sometimes were unaware of services being provided. These inadequacies in service provision arose from poor co-ordination and communication resulting in a lack of awareness.

While the report acknowledged that several reviews of the services for immigrants had been initiated by the Commonwealth, with new programmes introduced and state Ethnic Affairs Commissions having been established, the success of such measures had been limited by insufficient recognition of the fact that the states and the Commonwealth have complementary tasks and goals. The Commonwealth saw immigration in terms of annual intakes, initial settlement and post-arrival programmes while the states needed to adopt a longer-term view of immigration particularly in relation to the provision for housing, education and community services. Yet the Commonwealth's variations in annual immigration intakes continually created difficulties for the states.

The Report considered these matters against a backdrop of broader issues such as constitutional and jurisdictional issues, consultation in the development of immigration policy, provision of services, roles of government and non-government organisations and co-ordination arrangements.

It also reviewed the available information under each of those headings in considerable and objective detail and, taking into account available data before the Council, made a series of detailed recommendations. A draft copy of the 79-page report incorporating details of the study's methodology and the data and references relied on, was widely circulated to all stakeholders with the intention, prior to the release of the final report, to hold a National Workshop.

The workshop was held on 17 May 1985 at Essendon Civic Centre to consolidate government and non-government responses to the draft report. More than 50 participants from the three spheres of government and non-government bodies spent a full day reviewing the draft report in detail. Those invited to speak included the Victorian Minister for Ethnic Affairs and the Commonwealth Minister for Immigration and Ethnic Affairs, Chris Hurford.

I chaired this meeting, and we had several speakers from the non-government sector as well as individual experts who applauded the approach taken in the report. Later in the day we were joined by Chris Hurford who wasted no time in attacking the report and then personally attacked the members of the Council for approving the project and effectively damned the document and those associated with it.

Despite this unexpected assault on the organisation, its staff, those state and local governments and the non-government sector which encouraged the Council to undertake the project, the minister's views were not supported by anyone else in the room and he soon departed. He had been clearly sent to this meeting for the sole purpose of discrediting the report as his departmental personnel disagreed with the findings. It was an incredibly disappointing experience. However, worse was to come.

Within 12 months the bureaucrats in the Immigration Department somehow convinced the Hawke government that ACIR was a relic of the Fraser government and a waste of time and money. As a result, the highly credible body was shut down with little notice, by the simple expedient of its funding being removed. As Chairman of the Council and, indirectly, as an agent of the federal government, I had the unenviable task of breaking the bad news to the staff and then to the stakeholders. I also felt I owed it morally to the staff and other stakeholders to spend considerable time carrying out this onerous duty with the assistance of an extremely disappointed Colin Balmer, all on behalf of the federal bureaucrats who killed off a very worthwhile and accomplished organisation.

The losers were the various state and territory governments with the biggest loser being various Local Government Associations which had benefited enormously from the large number of studies which ACIR initiated and which, for the first time since Federation, addressed a large range of issues faced by local government bodies across the country.

Malcolm Fraser had had the foresight in this instance to create an influential forum at which they participated on an equal basis with representatives from both sides of the federal Parliament and with ministers from each state. It was also a loss for the citizens of Australia who for the first time participated in a body capable of making much needed and significant contributions to inter-governmental co-operation in our federation.

In an extraordinary act of political wisdom, Malcolm Fraser ensured that the chairperson of this unique body had to be one of the citizens. For a very modest outlay compared with the cost of an inefficient national governance structure, ACIR offered the promise of long-term solutions to a whole range of inter-governmental issues filtered through a body overseen by experienced representatives of all three levels of government.

Prior to this experience, I had long held the federal public service in high regard, particularly as it allowed me to have the chance to find my feet as a young adult and benefit from its affirmative action programme encouraging low level public servants to study and obtain tertiary qualifications.

However, the experience of being part of a good organisation bludgeoned to death because it had the temerity to demonstrate alternative solutions to problems those same bureaucrats were unable to solve left me, and a number of other good, highly qualified and dedicated, mostly young people, scarred for life. Considering the recent behaviour of the Immigration Department under the previous government, it is clear that regardless of which political party is in power, nothing has changed since my 1986 experience. The Immigration Department (regardless of its current label) is still a law unto itself!

To many of my generation Malcolm Fraser was an arch villain, but like all of us he was equally capable of being inspired to tackle a major problem confronting this country. This problem was the cost and inefficiency of inter-governmental relations which, 30 years after ACIR was callously dispatched to the legislative dust bin, still cripples this great country.

Media Reforms: Getting a Seat at the Table

A new project idea flowed from a paper prepared for the 1987 Law Foundation Board retreat by Dr Kate Harrison, then a senior lawyer with the Public Interest Advocacy Centre. It put forward evidence of the need for a Communications Law Centre, a project endorsed by the PIAC Board. This paper reflected a growing need from community organisations to have specialist assistance due to major changes flowing from the Hawke government's proposals to shake up both the telecommunications and the mass media environments. PIAC had been approached for assistance in these specialist areas by members of the public concerned about the government's proposed changes, which seemed to be being made with little input from consumers. The concerns also included public rights of access to government and private data banks brought into focus by the Australia Card.

PIAC's entry in the Foundation's 1987 Annual Report noted that it had continued its work on media and communications issues which had grown in recent times. As a result, it was heavily involved in the establishment of a new media lobbying organisation, Free the Media. PIAC had also been assisting this group to campaign about the increasing concentration of ownership in Australian media. Other activities included presentation of submissions to the Australian Broadcasting Tribunal and the Trade Practices Commission, extensive media appearances and the presentation of evidence to the relevant Senate committee.

The Centre had submitted a formal proposal to the Foundation's Board seeking its support for the establishment of a new Communications Law Centre which would ensure that PIAC's work in this growth area would be undertaken in the future by a specialist body. With the assistance of the Foundation, Kate Harrison travelled to the US in May and June 1987 to review media law centres operating there.

The Foundation's Board duly accepted the proposal and appointed Dr Harrison to head the new Centre. It also agreed to a three year funding commitment of $250,000 per year for the new Communications Law Centre and provided an additional amount of $78,000 to meet establishment costs. Financial assistance had also been obtained via a grant from the Myer Foundation.

The Foundation's support for the Communications Law Centre recognised the need for a public interest voice to be heard in the context of a significant era of change within broadcasting and telecommunications. With the support of the UNSW Law School, the centre was to be affiliated with the University. This involved the Centre's staff participating with the Law School's teaching programme in return for which the University agreed to provide premises on the campus. Interestingly, it was to be housed in the historic White House, most recently used by NIDA and previously used by jockeys when the UNSW campus was a racecourse!

In recognition of the potential contribution of the new Centre, its new premises were opened by the Minister for Transport and Communications, Ralph Willis. His presence confirmed the rapidly growing influence of this important new Centre, with the Chancellor of the University Justice Gordon Samuels and I being amongst the supporting cast.

The pattern of the Centre's activities was set during its first year, with a strong interest in the extensive changes in Australia's telecommunications policy. Its staff participated in a number of high-level policy-oriented conferences and made submissions on aspects of the proposed legislation underpinning the changes. It was also represented on the new Telecom Australia Consumer Council. This later led to Telecom commissioning two major projects from the Centre. One examined possible definitions for Telecom's Community Service Obligations, while the other involved surveying the complex and rather fractured regulatory framework for handling consumer complaints.

The Centre was also a very active participant in the push to reform the *Broadcasting Act*, producing a discussion paper on the inquiry procedures of the Australian Broadcasting Tribunal for the Administrative Review Council. The Communications Law Centre was clearly becoming a very influential participant in the broad communications sector. It also provided submissions on pay television for the relevant parliamentary committee and, later, to the Department of Transport and Communications on a variety of issues such as the viability of a trustee proposal for broadcasting licences and on drafting the new foreign ownership rules for broadcasting.

The Centre also received a major research grant from the Australian Film Commission which funded work on a project on Australian content in television, pay television, short films and cultural policy. The result was later published by Allen & Unwin.

While developing a major role in litigation, the Centre's legal practice also advised on copyright, defamation, complaints about the press, broadcasting licensing, advertising standards, newspaper ownership, the meaning of "fit and proper" requirements for broadcasters, complaints about Telecom, the rights of interviewees and freedom of information and privacy laws.

In relation to the finding by the Australian Broadcasting Tribunal that the licensee companies associated with Alan Bond were not fit and proper persons, the Centre appeared in those proceedings on behalf of the Australian Journalists Association and Actors Equity and was involved right up to the High Court hearing which upheld the Tribunal's finding. The Centre was also actively involved in pressing the government concerning Christopher Skase's status of not being fit and proper.

In the middle of 1990, after more than two years leading the Centre and a similar period at PIAC extending its role into the communications area, Kate Harrison was awarded a Fulbright Scholarship and decided it was time to take the offer and departed for New York to undertake further postgraduate studies. I was personally worried about how we would fill the shoes of someone who had done so much to build the Centre's momentum and high profile.

However, my concerns were short-lived. We were able to attract the interest of Anne Davies, who as well as possessing a law degree was a senior journalist with *The Australian Financial Review's* Canberra Bureau. Additionally, she had specialised in the years prior to her appointment in covering communications and related policy issues. Her first-hand knowledge of the personalities and issues involved in the then current debate over communications reforms, as well as her experience of the media, added greatly to the Centre's already wide range of talent and provided reassurance to the Centre's and the Foundation's Boards. Anne was a successful leader for a number of years before returning to journalism.

25

Constitutional Reform 1: An Interest from Childhood

I owe my interest in, and early knowledge of, the Australian Constitution to my father who was born in 1902, shortly after Federation became a reality. He grew up being a child of this new nation and never lost his interest in the nation's politics. As a child, I was made aware of the significance of the events in 1901 by being taken by my father to see the Jubilee festivities held in Sydney on 1 January 1951 to mark the 50th anniversary of Federation.

As a 25-year-old I was able to vote in the overwhelmingly successful 1967 referendum which led to our Constitution being amended to formally acknowledge Aboriginal people as citizens. I remember the pride I felt that Australia had voted to include them in the Census and that they would now benefit from Parliament being able to legislate for their benefit. It sounds obvious and fair now but it was groundbreaking in Australia at the time.

Further down the track, in my role at the Law Foundation, the Constitution again loomed large in my life. I was part of the leadership of a Law Foundation project initiated by a proposal from Senator Gareth Evans, which ultimately produced the landmark publication *Australia's Constitution: Time for Change?* A year or so later, came my involvement with the Constitutional Commission following my appointment as Chairman of the Commission's Advisory Committee on Individual and Democratic Rights. Thus I joined the rather exclusive club of those who directly sought to change the Constitution and failed.

I continue to be fascinated by the role of our Constitution in Australia's progress and continue to be saddened by the fact that so many do not realise the large role it plays in the amazing nation we all enjoy today.

When I started working in the law in the mid-1960s, the legal landscape in NSW had not changed significantly since the first half of the 19th century, when NSW was granted self-governance in 1855 and inherited laws and a court system from the then British court system.

Sadly for NSW, shortly after 1855, the UK government had made major and rapid reforms of its laws and court system in that period to enable it to manage and benefit from its industrial revolution and to maintain its position as the world's leading economy. When the other colonies later became states, they automatically adopted the modern UK legal system.

The Path to Federation

With the coming of Federation in 1901, the newly independent nation of Australia was largely fortunate in being able to adopt its own locally drafted national Constitution providing an operating framework for our new Commonwealth government. This positive outcome has been attributed to Sir Henry Parkes' Tenterfield address in 1889, following which a draft constitution was prepared and considered in 1891 at a meeting of state parliamentarians, following which the constitutional reform movement appeared to lose its way.

However, in 1893 another attempt was made at an informal constitutional conference held in Corowa made up of a broad range of delegates representing various political and commercial interests. The outcome was the adoption of a proposal moved by Dr John Quick, a prominent Melbourne journalist, lawyer and politician, to adopt a plan and timetable for the establishment of a National Constitutional Convention. Its members, who would be popularly elected members, were charged with producing a draft constitution to be considered by the various state Parliaments with a view to it being ultimately submitted to the British Parliament.

Any such document needed to recognise the continuing role of the states under the new federal structure. This meant the states largely retained responsibility for domestic law, with the new Commonwealth government's responsibility limited to the powers listed in Section 51 of the Constitution.

The Act creating the Australian constitution, the *Commonwealth of Australia Constitution Act*, was passed by the British Parliament in July 1900. Despite some last minute negotiations with the Australian delegation over a few provisions, it became law when signed by Queen Victoria on 9 July 1900. It was one of the last pieces of legislation passed during the long reign of Queen Victoria and by the time of its proclamation on 1 January 1901, the Western Australian government had finally agreed to participate as an inaugural state and joined in the celebrations surrounding the proclamation of the new Australian Federation, a unique first for the 20th century.

Tens of thousands Australians witnessed the proclamation of the new nation by Lord Hopetoun, Australia's first Governor General. The ceremony was held in Sydney's Centennial Park on 1 January 1901, to national jubilation. Lord Hopetoun also confirmed the first federal ministry to be led by Sir Edmund Barton as Prime Minister.

The establishment of the Australian Federation has been referred to by one historian as the first nation state established following a national vote of its people, a unique occurrence which is too readily overlooked by, or perhaps simply unknown to, Australians today.

Sadly, many Australians currently seem to have little pride in our stable constitutional structure and the democratic governance which has flowed from it over the past century. Maybe this is largely because politicians in both major political parties and in both Commonwealth and State Parliaments, often with little historical knowledge of the Constitution, see it as an impediment to their ambitions when in power.

It is at times like this that the wisdom of its drafters comes to the fore, while the same politicians who complain of its limitations today never put the effort into building a political and community consensus behind issues of national importance, as occurred in 1967 and on several occasions earlier.

An important feature of the Constitution is that the Commonwealth government's legislative authority is limited to defined areas deemed by the founding fathers as being appropriate for a national government. As a result of this significant division of powers, the states were left with legislative responsibility for domestic law, or the laws which affected most peoples' lives. This body of laws was largely inherited British law, as noted earlier, and amended piecemeal from time to time by each of the state parliaments.

The subjects studied during my law course were therefore largely based on such English legal cases which then still held considerable sway in our courts. However, much of that has changed over the past 50 years or so, partly because of the ending of appeals to the Privy Council. Another important factor which contributed to the development of a distinctly Australian body of law was the creation of whole new court systems such as the Federal Court of Australia and the Family Law Court system at a national level. This has been matched by the dramatic growth at state level of specialist appellate courts and jurisdictions, such as Land and Environment Courts, in turn complemented by many new specialist state and federal administrative tribunals, which have all helped transform Australian law and procedure.

The formal establishment of the Commonwealth of Australia made all that possible and, ultimately, inevitable.

In May 1951, in Cabarita Park, Concord, I had another exposure to Federation when the bandstand in the park was formally recognised with a plaque as being one of the two pavilions used in 1901 in Centennial Park for the signing of documents confirming the proclamation of the Constitution. That 1951 event marked the 50th anniversary of the opening of the federal Parliament in Melbourne on 9 May 1901 and, according to press reports, there was a crowd of 10,000 in attendance to witness the event.

CONSTITUTIONAL REFORM 1: AN INTEREST FROM CHILDHOOD

For a child, it was another important reminder of the significance the original proclamation had for the Australian people of that era. The event was made more colourful for me because our neighbour across the road, Mr Stanton, who was Mayor of Concord at the time, had escorted the Lieutenant Governor Sir Kenneth Street to the Park where he officiated at the event.

As someone long interested in our constitutional history, I believe we owe a very significant debt to the wisdom of 19th century "Australians" who, in the early 1850s when statehood was being granted to Victoria, South Australia and Queensland, were being strongly encouraged by the British Colonial authorities to federate.

The people of the colonies wisely resisted this pressure by saying that they were not ready for a federal structure imposed on them by a UK government, which clearly wanted to rid itself of the responsibility and associated governance problems emanating from such a remote and, at the time, relatively worthless part of the Empire.

One only has to look at Canada's constitutional structure flowing from the 1839 Durham Report to see how lucky we Australians are. This report, prepared for the British Government Colonial Office by the Earl of Durham, flowed from the international uproar over the brutally suppressed rebellion of French Canadians in Quebec in 1837, when 39 leaders were rounded up and summarily hung. Shortly after, 149 community leaders were quickly tried and transported to Van Diemen's Land and Sydney.

The Durham report made a number of recommendations, including a plan for a national federation, which was eventually put in place in 1867 by the British North America Act, also passed by the British Parliament.

The wisdom of Australian settlers ensured that we avoided being forced to adopt a constitution modelled in broad terms on a comparatively clunky federal governance structure devised by the British early in the 19th century and under which Canadians still live today.

Studying Constitutional Law

My more formal knowledge of the Australian Constitution was acquired during law school lectures when Professor Patrick Lane mesmerised me, as well as several generations of law students, with his encyclopaedic knowledge of the subject. I have vivid memories of him giving lectures without notes and reciting passages from key High Court cases or from the Constitution itself.

By that stage of my studies, I was working in the Commonwealth Deputy Crown Solicitor's office in Phillip Street where there was a constant buzz about important High Court cases my legal colleagues were working on. One of the big issues that Lane was concerned about was the difficulty faced by those wishing to amend the Constitution. The "iron rule" was the need to have a majority of voters in a majority of states approving any change. Lane dwelt on the numerous examples of failed referenda over the previous 60 years or so. Although it was an interesting subject, for someone then about to head back to a small law firm to engage in workers compensation and common law damages cases, it was hard then to see its relevance in the day-to-day practice of law as I knew it.

In fact, the only time in which I strayed into the jurisdiction of Commonwealth law was when, as a young lawyer, the senior partner asked me to seek counsel's advice for a client who was a friend of his. The case involved a claim by the Australian Tax Office against this man who was a partner in one of Sydney's leading engineering consulting firms where he was responsible for managing the firm's finances and tax issues. He used to do this work from his home office and there had been an unfortunate fire which destroyed part of the house, including his office and the records kept there.

I duly sought a conference with an eminent tax barrister and explained the circumstances to him. He said that there being no evidence that the tax had actually been paid, the client simply had to pay the debt. I then pointed out that as the proceedings were in the Supreme Court of NSW, the Tax Office was bound by the normal court rules for cases it commenced there. I further pointed out that as that was the case and the Tax Office being the only party with any records to prove or disprove my client's claim, I questioned what was to stop us from simply applying for an order for discovery under the recently modernised Supreme Court rules, following the passing of the new *Supreme Court Act*, and force the Tax Office to disclose what records they held relevant to the matter.

The look of incredulity on his face was as though I had blasphemed! I simply could not believe that I was the first person to have suggested such a course to a senior barrister who worked in the rarefied fields of tax and commercial work. Maybe it was simply due to my predominantly common law experience, but I was equally as shocked by his reaction to my suggestion. Nevertheless, the partners sought a discovery order which was promptly issued by the court and served on the ATO's lawyers. An interesting side to this case was that there were suggestions that, at that time, some Tax Office staff, for personal gain, took advantage of such genuine defendants whose records of payment had been lost.

However, my first legal case involving a Commonwealth agency was ultimately successful as I was advised several years later by my former colleagues that the Tax Office had withdrawn the claim. One can only assume either that they did not want to have an enforceable discovery order made against them on the public record or that there had been some maladministration they did not wish to disclose. Groundbreaking? Hardly, but a very interesting part of my legal education. The fact that the ATO had to initiate legal actions against taxpayers in the state courts at that time was an example of the limitations of Federation which were ultimately remedied by the establishment of the Federal Court system in 1976, an outcome initiated by the Whitlam government and completed by the Fraser government.

26

Constitutional Reform 2: Time for Change

In August 1981 the Foundation Board decided to support a project proposed by Senator Gareth Evans which involved establishing a consultative committee of eminent Australians to oversee a review of the Constitution and to produce a blueprint for constitutional change in Australia.

The project's application envisaged that a grant be applied to employing a research scholar who was intended to be the main author of the committee's report. This report, which would be written so most Australians could understand it, was to be the basis of a nationwide series of seminars to educate the community about the need for Constitutional reform and to stimulate their interest in it.

Funding would enable the committee to retain a research scholar to produce an accessible report explaining the need for such Constitutional reform which most people could understand. Once published it would be the basis of a nationwide series of seminars to educate the community and stimulate their interest in constitutional reform.

Hitting the Headlines

The announcement of the grant, on 11 August 1981, generated headlines in newspapers across Australia such as the Sydney *Daily Telegraph's* "Bicentenary Overhaul of the Constitution", *The Australian's* "Law Foundation wants to update the Constitution", *The Australian Financial Review's* "$35,000 FOR PROJECT ON NEW CONSTITUTION" and *The Sydney Morning Herald's* "New Constitution planned for 1988". Many regional papers also followed the launch of this important new Foundation project.

This unprecedented whirlwind of publicity was not something which normally occurred when the Foundation announced a new initiative. This was different because the main driver was Senator Gareth Evans, the then young and dynamic Shadow Attorney General, whose "star power" had helped enlist a high level bi-partisan group to be members of the project Consultative Committee. These included leading academics, some with strong constitutional law backgrounds, such as Professor Geoffrey Sawyer and Professor Jack Richardson, then Commonwealth Ombudsman, leading businessmen Robert Holmes à Court and Sir Laurence Muir.

Also, happy to participate were prominent advocates of reform including Professor Donald Horne, Justice Michael Kirby and Dr Ella Stack, a hero of the Darwin cyclone and later its Lord Mayor. From the political arena Evans had attracted Dr Neal Blewett MP, Bob Hawke MP, Franca Arena MLC, Senator Don Chipp, former WA Liberal MHR John Hyde, and Liberal Senators Kathy Martin, Alan Missen and Peter Rae. John Valder, prominent businessman and President of the NSW Liberal Party was also involved.

The Foundation was represented by the Hon John Maddison and me. I filled the roles of Convenor of both the Consultative Committee and of the Supervisory Committee. The Supervisory Committee included Sir Clarrie Harders, former head of the Commonwealth Attorney General's Department, Professor Ron Sackville, then chair of the NSW Law Reform Commission, Senator Evans and Haddon Storey QC, Victorian Liberal politician. A young lawyer, John McMillan, later to be Commonwealth Ombudsman, was retained to undertake the research and produce a draft report.

The first meeting of all involved in the project had been held in Sydney at the Law Foundation's offices on 11 February 1982 and it also received a high level of national press coverage. This in turn earned a stern rebuke from Prime Minister Malcolm Fraser when, a few weeks later, he delivered the inaugural Sir Edmund Barton Lecture at Sydney University. He condemned the bi-partisan move for a new Australian Constitution by 1988 as "one of the most divisive proposals that can be contemplated in Australia."

Responding to this criticism, Senator Evans, as reported in *The Age*, spoke to Michelle Grattan saying:

> The Prime Minister, Mr Fraser, was to the Australian Constitution 'what Attila the Hun was to the Roman Empire' and it was sickening to see Mr Fraser contemptuously dismissing high-minded efforts to generate debate about extensive constitutional reforms ... His own actions in 1975 were the most divisive in our constitutional history, and his government has resisted all subsequent attempts at rational reform on the key issues of Senate powers, Federalism and human rights.

Perhaps stung by the backlash against his outdated views and risking being left behind by his own party colleagues involved in the project, in early May 1982 the Prime Minister announced that he had invited the states to join in a new constitutional convention to be held in 1983, the first since the previous convention in Brisbane in 1978.

In supporting the need for such a convention, *The Age* editorial noted that in the past few years momentum for constitutional reform has built up, referring to the work of Standing Committee D's recommendations on the adoption of 24 previously unwritten conventions of constitutional practice. This committee was one of four specialist standing committees of Commonwealth and States parliamentarians at the first Australian Constitutional Convention held in 1973 in the NSW Parliament. The recommendations were referred to the Standing Committee of Attorneys General to ensure the abolition of 10 rules left over from our colonial past to ensure decisions on Australian matters were made here and not in Britain. In addition, *The Age* noted that the NSW Law Foundation had begun a massive research project on a range of constitutional problem areas.

As the project moved ahead, it soon became clear that there were so many issues to consider which then needed to be refined into a report, that the original year time frame was not going to work. The Foundation agreed to extend the project and allocated additional funds to meet the researcher's costs and to subsidise publication through George Allen & Unwin. It was also agreed that, to ease the burden on John McMillan, Senator Evans and Haddon Storey QC would become co-authors of the report with John.

The smaller Supervisory Committee was to meet regularly and work closely with the researcher contributing oral and written commentary on the drafts. Their dedication and diligence over a period of nearly two years was exceptional.

The Consultative Committee met with the Supervisory Committee and authors on four occasions, to review its shape and direction from time to time and to contribute ideas to the content of the book, while providing overall leadership for the project.

I must say that my role as convenor, trying to keep meetings moving having regard to the tight schedules of most of the participants, was not easy. On either side of me at the larger meetings were two legal giants in Evans and Sackville, whose egos matched their respective statures, and to whom I was clearly an irritant, needing to be swatted away. Nevertheless, the chemistry worked, and a great outcome was achieved.

Late in 1982, as the project's report was reaching publication stage and having had responsibility for many other Foundation research reports, I was confident this book would achieve the goals set for it. While comprehensive in terms of its coverage of the issues, it also met the Foundation's standard for lay directed publications in terms of its accessibility. It was a publication which a moderately well-educated and interested member of the public would find interesting as well as a useful resource for those curious to know more about our Constitution.

The book was divided into five parts. The first part was an introduction which began by providing some colourful examples of modern-day problems confronted by state and Commonwealth governments, by individuals, by businesses and the court system so that readers were helped to recognise Constitutional issues. This part also explained who were arguing for change. It finished with the referendum record, that is, a simple summary of the attempts to change the constitution and an explanation of what could be learned from that record.

The second part explained the meaning of Australian federalism, starting with a short history of the origins of the Constitution, and explained the division of legislative powers between the states and the Commonwealth and how it might be improved.

The third part described the institutions making up our national government, briefly referring to our British heritage, the roles of the Governor General, the executive government, the Parliament and parliamentarians and, finally, the role of the High Court.

The fourth part discussed rights and freedoms and the possible role of a Bill of Rights.

The fifth and last part focused on whether change was needed and a short summary of past changes.

The Book Launch

In light of the book's nearing readiness for publication, the issue of who might launch the book arose and Evans said that it might be good to see if the Governor General, Sir Ninian Stephen, might do so and that he would make inquiries.

With Malcolm Fraser announcing that the federal election would be held on 5 March 1983, the feedback from Sir Ninian's office was that he was interested but only after the election had been held. Once the election was out of the way, we were told that not only would Sir Ninian be happy to launch the book, but also to host the launch at Admiralty House, his Sydney residence looking across the harbour to the Opera House and Circular Quay.

Australia's Constitution: Time for Change? was published by Allen & Unwin and launched at 3.00 pm on Friday, 22 April 1983, a beautiful sunny autumn day, at Admiralty House by the Governor General, Sir Ninian Stephen, who spoke warmly about the book and the need for such initiatives. I am sure Gareth Evans and all those associated with this significant project were delighted with the timing of the launch, with the Australian Constitutional Convention, which Malcolm Fraser had arranged early in 1982, commencing in Adelaide the following Monday.

The launch took place about six weeks after the election of the Hawke government in front of many legal and political luminaries, including High Court Justice Lionel Murphy, as well as former Prime Minister Gough Whitlam. The project committee was hopeful the event would generate significant publicity. However, I was warned by Gareth just prior to the official speeches that it was likely to be overshadowed by an impending announcement in Canberra due at the same time the launch was to commence.

The competing event which grabbed the evening news headlines was that a Russian diplomat was being expelled due to inappropriate contact with former Labor Party executive, David Combe.

The story of the book's launch in the next day's *Sydney Morning Herald* carried a photo of Gareth Evans having a private discussion amongst the colonnades of Admiralty House with Gough Whitlam and Lionel Murphy, inferring that the project was a party-political activity.

Despite my concerns about negative press coverage, the book sold well and made *The Australian's* non-fiction best seller list a week or so later, and several editions were subsequently published due to demand. The book still has relevance today. *Australia's Constitution: Time for Change* remains arguably the best modern overview for non-specialist audiences of the strengths and weaknesses of our current governance processes, both federal and state.

After the Admiralty House launch event, those involved in the project later reconvened in the Foundation's Board room for follow up drinks. John Iremonger, the book's publisher with George Allen and Unwin who knew Evans well, gave him a present wrapped in gift paper. Around this time the press had started referring to Evans as "Biggles" because he had been in the headlines for ordering the Air Force to fly over the Franklin River in Tasmania. Evans had taken this novel step to get photographs of damage being done to Franklin River area by the Tasmanian government and its notorious Hydro Electric Authority.

When Evans opened the present and saw that it was a Second World War fighter pilot's leather helmet, he angrily threw it back at John, followed up by several colourful expletives. However, he soon saw the joke and happily wore it around as a badge of honour. In his 2017 autobiography Evans acknowledged a lack of discretion in the days following the spy flight as he notes that earlier in the week of our launch he said at a door stop with journalists about the spy flight, "Whatever you write about this, don't call me Biggles", which of course led to every cartoonist in the country having a field day for years thereafter.

Later in May, Professor David Kemp and a colleague from Monash University Department of Politics wrote letters to the press criticising the Governor General for "straying across the line into the area of political controversy by agreeing to launch the book". This immediately drew responses from myself and a joint response from Senator Evans and Haddon Storey. My letter, which was published in both the *Australian Financial Review* and *The Sydney Morning Herald*, dated 23 May 1983, made the following points:

> ... The accusation levelled at the Governor-General is that he made a "questionable error of judgment" in identifying himself with the authors' perspective of stimulating a serious national debate on the desirability and possibility of updating the Constitution.
>
> If they are correct, then surely any identification by the Governor-General with steps to reform the Constitution would also amount to "questionable political judgment" and therefore must apply to his Excellency's opening address

at the Adelaide session of the Australian Constitutional convention a few days after our book launch.

Similarly, it must also apply to Sir Paul Hasluck and Sir Zelman Cowan, who officiated at the openings of the 1973 and 1978 sessions of the Convention respectively, both of whom in their own way spoke in support of undertaking reviews of the Constitution.

Perhaps the real problem is that the Constitutional Convention only involves politicians and is therefore 'safe' whereas the Governor-General was indirectly encouraging wider public consideration of the Constitution which the professors see as "divisive and harmful" to national unity.

It is somewhat puzzling that Monash University, which no doubt treasures its academic freedom and objectivity, has two professors so unsympathetic towards discussion and enlightenment at a community level on such as significant topic.

The ultimate reception of the published work was a tribute to the considerable input by both committees, and the authors, but also to the credibility they all brought to the task.

27

CONSTITUTIONAL REFORM 3: THE CONSTITUTIONAL COMMISSION

The realities of Gareth Evans' appointment as Commonwealth Attorney General soon meant that constitutional reform was not high on his agenda and his 2017 biography *Incorrigible Optimist: A Political Memoir* confirms that his ardent enthusiasm for reform was not shared by his Cabinet colleagues preoccupied with reviving the national economy.

It was left to his successor Lionel Bowen to revive the government's interest in this issue, and I soon found myself being heavily involved in the work of the new Constitutional Commission he established in late 1985.

Prime Minister Bob Hawke, when announcing the establishment of the Constitutional Commission, said:

> We owe it to ourselves and to future Australians to do our very best to ensure that our constitutional framework is effective and well adapted to modern needs and circumstances. To do otherwise may consign us to wearing that 'boys coat' and making do with a rigidity in our governing institutions which holds back our development as a nation.

Hawke's reference to a "boy's coat" harked back to a famous speech by Thomas Jefferson arguing for the need for the proposed American Constitution to be flexible and capable of moving with the times, saying:

> ... we might as well require a man to wear the coat that fitted him as a boy, as civilized society to remain ever under the regime of their ancestors.

True to form, Professor Kemp and a colleague espoused the

traditional view of conservatives and criticised the need for such a review.

The members of the Commission were Sir Maurice Byers CBE, QC, former Commonwealth Solicitor General, Professor Enid Campbell OBE, constitutional lawyer from the Faculty of Law, Monash University, the Hon Sir Rupert Hamer KCMG, former Premier of Victoria, the Hon E G Whitlam AC QC, former Prime Minister, Professor Leslie Zines, Faculty of Law, ANU, and Mr Justice John Toohey AO of the Federal Court and later of the High Court.

Appointment to Chair Rights Sub-Committee

Not long after the Prime Minister's announcement, I received a call from the Attorney General's Sydney Office asking me to a meet with Mr Bowen. At the meeting he said he was in the process of making appointments to the five sub-committees of the new Constitutional Commission to be headed by former Solicitor General Maurice Byers QC. He wanted to know if I was able to accept an appointment as chair of the Rights Committee and, after learning about the aims of the committee, I was a bit overwhelmed by such an honour but had enough sense to readily accept the role. I did so, aware that the Foundation's Board was still interested in constitutional reform and would be supportive.

We then discussed how the committee would relate to the Commissioners and who else was being considered for appointment to the Rights Committee. I learned that they were hoping to appoint Tom Keneally, Ron Castan QC, Peter Garrett and Paolo Totaro. Later I was advised that several other people whom I did not know, but who they felt would bring diversity to the committee, had accepted invitations. These were Professor Eric Willmot, a professor of education at Townsville University, who had an Indigenous background, and Russell Clarke, a young journalist from Cairns.

The committee was later expanded following its first meeting when I raised the issue of the under-representation of women on the various sub-committees. This view was shared by the rest of the committee, and I was requested to take the matter up with Mr Bowen's office. This promptly led to the appointment of Rhonda Galbally, a prominent Victorian activist and community leader.

The committee was an interesting mix with people such as Tom Keneally having a wealth of relevant knowledge and being quite a star following the success of his recent best seller *Schindler's Ark* and the subsequent Hollywood blockbuster movie based on it, *Schindler's List*. Tom, however, remained a down to earth Homebush boy and a joy to work with. Peter Garrett was similarly low key and a great contributor to the work of the committee, aided by his legal training. Both he and Tom were later great drawcards when the committee went on the road for public hearings.

However, the real star of the committee was Ron Castan who, at the time, was heavily involved in the Mabo native title case slowly moving through the courts. Ron was a highly regarded Melbourne QC and his deep knowledge and practical experience of constitutional law, supplemented by his role as President of the Victorian Council of Civil Liberties, meant that with our allotted topic he was the expert we could rely on whenever we were at a loss to understand the ramifications of some issue.

Initially I felt somewhat uncomfortable by being appointed Chairman of a committee with such an eminent black letter lawyer as a member. However, Ron made it clear from the outset that he was more than happy not to have the additional organisational responsibilities of being the Chairman and having to report to the Chairman of the Commission and deal with the Commission's excellent support staff.

The membership of the other four advisory committees included:
- Australian Judicial System, was chaired by Mr Justice David Jackson and members included Professor James Crawford from Sydney University Law School and several judges including Mr Justice W M C Gummow, later member of the High Court.

- Distribution of Powers, was chaired by Sir John Moore and included Don Dunstan, Jack Ferguson, George Polites and Haddon Storey.
- Executive government, chaired by former Governor General Sir Zelman Cowan and included Professor Donald Horne, John Wheeldon, Professor George Winterton and Sir James Killen.
- Trade and National Economic Management, chaired by former Tasmanian politician and Judge Merv Everett and included businessman Mark Burroughs, Professor Michael Coper, retired Queensland politician Rex Patterson and ACOSS economist Phillipa Smith.

Being appointed chair of the Commission's Rights Committee began an intense 15 month period which started in January 1986 with settling the committee's terms of reference and then developing and publicising at short notice a discussion paper for public consumption.

This was soon followed by a series of 18 public hearings held around Australia over a couple of months in late 1986 in a context when the government's proposed Bill of Rights had stirred a lot of community resistance to our particular topic and resulted in many quite colourful public hearings. This in turn was followed by then having a few intense months to finalise our recommendations in a detailed report for the Commissioners to consider.

Allocated to assist our committee initially was a bright young lawyer, Marian Schoen, who along with Ian Cunliffe, the Commission secretary, ensured we received excellent support from the secretariat. Ian was an experienced senior lawyer with the Attorney General's Department. Later, we were assigned another young departmental lawyer, Greg McLeod, who stayed with us and made a great contribution to the committee's productivity.

At the first meeting of the new committee on 31 January 1986 the initial task was to settle the committee's terms of reference while distancing its role from the government's recent moves to introduce legislation into the Australian Parliament to create a Bill of Rights and Human Rights and Equal Opportunity Commission, both Bills having been passed by the House of Representatives, although the government had not taken them to the Senate.

According to the Attorney General, in a long article published in March 1985 in *Australian Law News,* the journal of the Law Council of Australia, the proposed Bill of Rights was intended to follow the recently adopted Canadian Bill of Rights and would be "a shield not a sword".

This legislative initiative had polarised large sections of the Australian community. A number of well-funded and quasi-religious organisations, some with links to the US, were vehemently opposed to a Bill of Rights. Many of our later public hearings were either the subject of protests or faced disruption during hearings by these groups.

This was the backdrop to the committee's establishment, which now looked distinctly like the Attorney General's Plan B in light of the impending withdrawal of the Bill of Rights legislation. The government reluctantly realised that there was little prospect of gaining public acceptance of such a Bill.

This situation resulted in an interesting discussion at the first meeting, with Ron Castan keen to see the committee avoid becoming embroiled in the political controversy surrounding the Bill of Rights issue. Both Tom Keneally and Peter Garrett had well known views in support of a Bill of Rights. They acknowledged that when dealing with the media they would not back away from their previous positions but emphasised that, when asked, they would emphasise that their responses were personal and did not reflect the views of the committee or the commission.

As a result, the committee was unanimous in seeking to avoid getting caught up in this polarising debate and discussion focused on settling the terms of reference. After considerable further discussion and to everyone's relief, as reaching a quick consensus seemed unlikely, Ron Castan offered to take on board the committee members' views and concerns and to distil them into a draft terms of reference and promised to circulate a draft within a few days for comment by the committee members.

Another matter which exercised the minds of the committee was the agreed inadequacy of the initial name given to it, namely Rights Committee, and eventually it was decided to seek the Commission's approval for the committee to be known as the Advisory Committee on Individual & Democratic Rights Under the Constitution.

Over the next couple of months further meetings were held with the settlement of the committee's terms of reference being the initial priority. The following terms were endorsed by the Commission:

- What is the best way to ensure and advance the individual and democratic rights of Australian people as citizens and as a society within the legislative, executive and judicial structure of Australian government?
- Should the Constitution spell out guarantees of individual and democratic rights?
- Are the guarantees already provided in the existing Constitution adequate for Australians today?
- Are we already sufficiently protected by existing laws and traditions, apart from the Constitution?
- If any Constitutional guarantees are desirable, which ones should be included, what form should they take, and who should be bound by them and who should enforce them?

Launch of the Issues Paper

With the terms of reference settled, the committee moved ahead with settling an Issues Paper. The drafting proceeded swiftly through a committee working party, aided by drafts prepared by Ms Schoen. Tom Keneally generously devoted time to enhancing the content and style of the final version of the paper ensuring that it would be interesting and readable by members of the public, with the finished product nicely designed and presented. The opening page was headed "The Debate" and quoted Bob Hawke's comments at the launch of the Commission as noted earlier, contrasting with the negative sentiments of Professor Kemp and his colleague.

The Commission's modus operandi was to generate public responses to the various issues papers by way of public hearings throughout Australia around each topic. This provided an opportunity for those interested to make oral presentations. Both the hearings and invitations to make written submissions were widely advertised.

The committee decided that it would launch the Issues Paper on Sunday 29 June 1986 with a public event held in Centennial Park on the site of the proclamation of the Constitution on 1 January 1901 by Lord Hopetoun. It was organised by the committee aided by Ian Cunliffe and prominent publicist Max Markson.

Max pulled all the levers and the event received excellent media coverage during the week leading up to it. We were very lucky with the weather with the public coming to see a re-enactment ceremony. After being called to order by the colourful Sydney Town Crier Graham Keating, the crowd hushed as actors Peter Sumner and Julie Lowe in Vice Regal garb played the roles of Lord and Lady Hopetoun. Peter re-enacted Lord Hopetoun's 1901 Proclamation of the Constitution in front of a crowd of some hundreds of people, including the Attorney General Lionel Bowen in mufti, according to one press report of the event, although we were not made aware of his attendance.

In the lead up to the event, a number of people called radio stations which had run the story of the launch in advance and told how they, as children, had attended the 1901 event. Others were calling because their parents or grandparents had attended, having received formal invitations, and some of these people were contacted and invited to come. They were seated prominently at the front of the crowd and treated by everyone as celebrities. This gave a real and nostalgic link between our launch and the original great event.

Hundreds of copies of our Issues Paper and other materials prepared by the Commission were distributed and good media coverage flowed from the event. It was probably the only issues paper launch which achieved such public recognition.

On the podium watching were a group of eminent Australians, including Jack Ferguson, former Deputy NSW Premier, Sir Rupert Hamer, former Victorian Premier and Constitutional Commissioner, Sir John Moore, former President of the Arbitration Commissioner, and Philippa Smith, both of whom were members of other expert sub-committees. Tom Keneally and Peter Garrett jointly launched the Issues Paper and addressed the crowd. *The Sydney Morning Herald* quoted Tom as saying:

> We are looking for new ideas to adjunct the Constitution, not to overthrow it, there are threats to our basic rights like freedom of speech, religion, association and property which are not guaranteed in tough times under the Constitution here as they are in the United States or France.

The Australian quoted Keneally at length, noting his point that questions of law and freedom are never glamorous or interesting until the law runs aground, adding:

> The Constitution was a living constitution – it must grow as Australia grows and it must do this for the good of us all ... the Australian people should not depend on High Court judges to make changes to the Constitution by way of 'sensible' legal decisions. It's we the Australian people who are the ones meant to make the adjustments to the remarkable political framework which today we are today justly celebrating.

Its report noted that rock star, Peter Garrett, was careful to distinguish the Commission's activities from the Bill of Rights legislation, saying:

> The only way the proposals for change can be adopted by

Australians is if it goes to a referendum, when we will say 'yes we want this' or 'no we don't want this'. The only way we can make up our minds is to enlighten ourselves.

To those going to the Swans game that sunny Sunday afternoon, whom he passed when driving to the event, he wanted:

> ... to explain to them that this thing that is very dull is very important ... we can and we do need to look at what things should be changed and improved.

It was a noteworthy event, with the committee's objectives in terms of widespread publicity achieved. On a personal level, my five children aged eight to 16 enjoyed the spectacle and seeing Peter Garrett and, for me it was one of the more exotic and memorable ways of marking the day, it being my birthday!

The press coverage was excellent, topped off by *The Sydney Morning Herald*'s editorial a few days later which some might consider 'damned it with faint praise'. It grudgingly admitted that the Issues Paper probably dealt with the issues appropriately but went on to question the government's motives for establishing the Commission. It categorised it as "yet another manifestation of the bicentennial binge", arguing that the history of constitutional reform was a record of unmitigated failure and totally ignoring that a number of vital changes had been adopted by the Australian people. It finished with the whinge:

> Despite the PR flair, therefore, the commission seems set to be yet another expensive ($4.5 million) tilt at the constitutional windmill.

While the Commission via its secretary Ian Cunliffe responded, defending its role and budget in a letter to the editor, I felt the need to also respond on behalf of the committee, both of which letters the paper published, with my effort being:

> Your editorial suggested the Constitutional Commission was tilting at windmills but you sat squarely on the fence. Freedoms and rights are the stuff of editorial writers-

racism and discrimination, freedom of movement, rights to life, to work, and to own property, freedom of political belief and from political detention and so on.

Australia scores fairly well on those questions. But none of the freedoms and human rights issues listed above is protected by the Constitution. However, this question is raised in the Constitutional Commission's issues paper on 'Individual and Democratic Rights'.

The Constitution can only be amended if the people of Australia vote at a referendum to change it. It won't be changed unless the people decide it needs updating.

Not long after the launch, much to the relief of the committee, the government announced the deferment of the Bill of Rights legislation, which decision we hoped would improve the prospects of generating responses to the Issues Paper.

Australia-Wide Hearings

The next stage in the committee's progress was to hold hearings around Australia at which members of the public or representatives of organisations could offer their comments on the Issues Paper. The committee settled the list of locations for hearings which were to take place in the major capitals of each state and territory and a number of other centres in most states. Fortunately, being an activity initiated under the auspices of the Commonwealth Attorney General's Department, the hearings were recorded by its court reporting service in each location.

Several committee members presided at each hearing, with them scheduled to commence in late September with hearings in Newcastle and Tamworth and due to be finished in Perth in early December. Most hearings were held on weekends to allow as many people as possible to either attend or make submissions with all meeting well publicised in advance and advertised in the press. The transcripts of each of the 18 hearings provided the committee, the government and future scholars with a record of every hearing and was an extremely valuable source of views and information about the relevant issues which ensured that the committee's final report was based on an extraordinary range of views.

It was an unprecedented process of public consultation about the source document underpinning the Australian Federation. The hearings revealed that the Australian Constitution's role was mostly well understood by those who responded to invitations to make submissions. Many people were passionate about participating in this opportunity to seek their views. Some of those attending were the descendants and heirs of the generation of Australians who battled for 15 years to make Australia an independent nation, starting almost exactly a century before these hearings.

As Chairman, I ended up participating in most hearings which meant that my family did not see much of me during those few months. However, they seemed to appreciate that I was on a journey for the greater good and that it gave me a chance to visit places and meet and hear the views of many hundreds of fellow Australians. This was very rewarding on several levels. Perhaps the most important was the realisation that so many thoughtful and experienced people around Australia held passionate views about the Constitution and most agreed with the need for its reform and modernising. There seemed to be a lot more like Thomas Jefferson than John Howard.

A secondary benefit, at a personal level, was that I was fortunate to be able to spend a lot of time in the company of some great Australians on the committee, all of whom had much to contribute to our task and were a happy, cohesive and productive group.

I was very fortunate to participate in several hearings with Ron Castan in Melbourne. Unlike the other states, the Melbourne power structure was on display with senior representatives of a number of major organisations being involved. The Confederation of Australian Industry was represented by a small entourage headed by Mr Brian Noakes. Its purpose was to disabuse the committee of the need for a Bill of Rights or to include a human rights head of power in the Constitution.

Such views were strongly countered by other presenters, including legal academics such as Professors Tony Blackshield and Peter Hanks, both of whom argued in favour of the inclusion of a range of such enforceable rights in the Constitution. Other presenters included Peter Sheldrake, speaking on behalf of the Australian Institute of Multicultural Affairs, Mrs Margaret Tighe representing Right to Life Australia, a Mr Goode from the Proportional Women's Group and lawyer Julian Gardner on behalf of the Council of Civil Liberties.

Ron's practical knowledge of constitutional law as well as his reputation as one of Melbourne's leading silks meant that I happily played the role of his junior counsel for the day. That outcome was not organised in advance as Ron was too nice a person to hog the limelight, but simply came about because of his knowledge of many of those presenting and of their proposals.

Unlike in other hearings where there was a mix of organisational representatives and individuals with some relevant experience or point of view, in Melbourne the list of proposed speakers quickly filled with those previously mentioned who had given prior notice of an intention to make presentations. As a result, little time was left for interested but less experienced individuals to be heard.

Ron's role in the Mabo Case should never be forgotten and, to me, it was ultimately more significant than Gough Whitlam's creation of land rights with his pouring of a handful of Wave Hill soil into Vincent Lingari's hand on 16 August 1975. Why? Because the Mabo decision provided a threshold and a legal foundation on which Paul Keating's government could then enshrine the recognition of native title into Australian legislation. Regrettably Ron's contribution to Australian law was cut short by his premature death and I am pleased to use this opportunity to remind readers of this humble yet creative and brilliant Australian lawyer who took on the might of the Queensland government to prove Eddie Mabo's right, and that of his fellow Murray Islanders, to their traditional lands.

Gough Whitlam Saves the Day in Sydney

When the caravan finally arrived in Sydney on 25 October 1986, initially the only members of the committee available were Paolo Totaro and me, as other committee members, who had all participated in hearings around Australia in the previous month, all had commitments. Professor Eric Willmot was in the process of taping his *Boyer Lectures*, Peter Garrett had a longstanding interstate commitment (I don't recall if it was a Midnight Oil gig!), Tom Keneally was otherwise engaged and Ron Castan was in Queensland and journeying to Cape York to gather evidence in the Eddie Mabo native title case in which he was lead counsel and which would ultimately result in the recognition of native title in the High Court's 1992 decision in that case.

However, in the Sydney Town Hall, at the last minute almost, we were fortunate in that Gough Whitlam, who only a few days earlier had returned to Australia from Paris having relinquished his role as Australian ambassador to UNESCO, had generously volunteered to open the Sydney hearing and spoke at length about the importance of the work of the Commission. Gough opened by explaining his long interest in and commitment to reform of the Constitution and describing various attempts to initiate both reviews and referenda to have changes made to the Constitution.

He shared some of his experiences and pointed out to those who were not in favour of individual and democratic rights in the Constitution that there were already three such rights embedded in the it. He spoke at length about how all three, because of the limitation of their wording or because they only applied to the Commonwealth sphere, had their effectiveness limited, and in one case, eroded.

The first was the right to a trial by jury for offences under Commonwealth law in Section 80 which, in his view, had been effectively bypassed and provided an extensive analysis how this came about.

The second example he referred to was the requirement in Section 51 paragraph xxxi which requires the Commonwealth to acquire a citizen's property on just terms. He pointed out this too was readily circumscribed because in many instances the Commonwealth delegated the task to a state and the states may or may not have a similar requirement. If they did, it could easily be repealed.

The third example he referred to was Section 116, which famously prevented the Commonwealth legislating to impose a religion or limit the practice a religion and, again, this limitation does not apply to the states.

He finished by stressing the importance of the work of the Commission and of its committees in helping Australians get a better understanding of the role of the Constitution. He emphasised the need for them to insist that the members of the Parliament be made to accept responsibility for taking the final step of legislating to hold a referendum, which is the condition precedent for Australian voters to have the opportunity to support or not support proposed changes.

Before Gough left to help Margaret set up home again, I gave an example of such power sharing by the Commonwealth, delegating responsibility to the states to manage the acquisition and subsequent allocation of land for soldier settlement farming. I had been told of the case of an elderly Australian ex-serviceman who, because he was of Aboriginal background, had been prevented by state law from participating in a state managed allocation of such farmland. When I heard that issue raised, I felt seriously embarrassed about this treatment of people who had more claim to the land than their white comrades, yet were denied such an entitlement. I was deeply shocked by this person's experience, but it was another injustice because of the shortcomings of our Constitution and the refusal of its drafters to consider the country's Indigenous people.

Despite the history of prejudice, discrimination and appalling treatment of the original inhabitants of this land by our governments and community, it was gratifying that in this Sydney hearing there were many presentations by organisations and individuals dealing with the status and rights of our Aboriginal citizens. Such sentiments were included in the presentations by representatives of the Catholic Commission for Peace and Justice, the Anglican Archdiocese of Sydney and the NSW Council for Civil Liberties.

On that day in the Sydney Town Hall detailed submissions were made by Aboriginal leader Paul Coe, who presented with Duncan Kerr, soon to become a member of the federal Parliament and later Minister for Justice in the Keating government. Their presentation focused on the lack of recognition of Aboriginal people in the Constitution and the need for positive discrimination in their favour, the need for a treaty or Makarrata between the Australian government and the Aboriginal people and the need for land rights reform.

Professor Richard Chisholm, then an academic at the UNSW Law School and later a Family Court judge, attending on behalf of the Law School's Aboriginal Law Centre, made a joint presentation with Professor James Crawford from Sydney University Law School, as well as being a member of the Commission's Judicial Committee. They also were strong supporters of the need for the Constitution to protect the rights of Aborigines and Torres Straight Islanders. They, and several others who presented, recommended that the committee study closely the provisions in the new Canadian Constitution dealing with the rights of native peoples. The committee was already aware of the relevant provisions, and it was seen as a possible model to follow.

Another presenter was Gavin Andrews from the NSW Aboriginal Land Council who put the case for constitutional recognition of land rights as well as full recognition of Aboriginal peoples in the Constitution.

A long day concluded with a curious group of individuals with some surprising expectations speaking, including the man representing the Unemployed Peoples Embassy and seeking constitutional protection for society's bottom rung from legislative and administrative abuse.

CONSTITUTIONAL REFORM 3: THE CONSTITUTIONAL COMMISSION

The hearing process was planned to be completed with a series of hearings in Queensland over four days, starting in Brisbane on Tuesday, 2 December 1986, and followed by Rockhampton, Townsville and Cairns. Tom Keneally, Russell Clarke and I, assisted again by Greg McLeod the Secretary to the committee, were attending which meant a number of intercity flights on small planes at the end of a day of hearings. This was a pretty arduous itinerary, but it was memorable because, periodically, on these flights Tom would entertain us with stories, some of which later appeared in his memoir *Homebush Boys*. These stories were all told with Tom's trademark twinkle and with Tom doing a great impression of a traditional Irish storyteller. It was a unique and unforgettable experience for those fortunate enough to be there.

With the hearings completed, the committee had a deadline to complete their report by the end of June 1987 and work commenced with the assistance of the Commission staff to absorb the key messages from the hearings and use them as the basis for preparing its report to the Commission. A drafting committee was established and met on nine occasions. It was a demanding role and I attended all meetings. However, with the co-operation of all those directly involved, including Greg McLeod and Ian Cunliffe from the Commission's staff, the final draft when finalised was readily supported by the full committee.

The work of finalising the report was also greatly assisted by the appointment of Stephen Odgers, then a constitutional law lecturer on the staff of the Sydney University Law School. Together with Greg McLeod, he prepared a number of research and discussion papers on specific matters raised by the committee's inquiries. The papers were invaluable as they covered several topics including the constitutional protection of rights in the US and Canada, protecting constitutional rights and constitutional rights during a public emergency.

Greg McLeod had also prepared detailed analyses of written and oral submissions dealing with the topics of democratic rights, direct democracy, and Aboriginal rights. In addition, he prepared a paper titled *Democratic Rights: An Examination of Proposals* which, together with those prepared by Stephen Odgers, enabled the drafting committee to move forward. With this support, the committee was confident that nothing relevant put forward to us via submissions or as the subject of consideration elsewhere was overlooked. This work was complemented by references to a wide range of articles, legal cases or other forms of legal commentary listed in a long bibliography in the report. These gave great confidence to the committee that it had left few, if any, relevant authoritative stones unturned when it was finalising its report.

Consulting the Chief Justice

One article we wished to cite was a paper by the then newly appointed Chief Justice, Sir Anthony Mason, which had come to the notice of Ron Castan. The paper appeared to be a review of prior constitutional decisions of the High Court which Mason considered to be in need of review, in other words his own personal reform agenda which appeared to support the committee's conclusions as to past interpretations of the Constitution by the High Court over many years. The paper had been published a few months previously in the ANU's *Federal Law Review*, under the title *The Role of a Constitutional Court in a Federation: A Comparison of the Australian and the United States Experience*. The paper had been delivered by Mason at one of the periodic meetings held in the US in that era during which the justices of both the High Court and the US Supreme Court met for discussions.

I was somewhat intrigued that there had been no press comment on the paper and the only reason one seasoned journalist, whose beat included the High Court, became aware of it was when I asked him at a legal conference a short time later why there was no press reaction to the paper. It was clear he had no idea what I was talking about, so I gave him the copy I had with me!

CONSTITUTIONAL REFORM 3: THE CONSTITUTIONAL COMMISSION

I had posed the question because I was aware that if a prospective Chief Justice of the US Supreme Court had published such a paper it would have quickly been the subject of a flurry of learned articles in leading law journals as well as academic conferences devoted solely to it. Such a paper would have also been the subject of intense Congressional scrutiny during hearings held to approve their appointment to the Supreme Court. This role, incorporated in the US Constitution, effectively gave the elected members of Congress the final decision on who would be appointed by the highest court in the land. In the circumstances, it struck me as a sad commentary on both Australian legal academics and the press that such an important statement had passed apparently unnoticed by legal commentators and the media.

As there were several very quotable quotes in Mason's paper, which we were keen to use in support of various proposals in our report to the Commissioners, Ron thought that it might be appropriate to seek a meeting with the new Chief Justice to give him "a heads up" of what we had in mind. At the meeting with the somewhat reserved Mason, Ron outlined our interest in the paper and our proposal to use some quotes from it in our report. We felt that it was important to know that our conclusions were not particularly radical. Mason said that as the paper had been published, he had no problem with it being quoted from and seemed to me pleased that we were interested in what he had to say.

The quote which was used as a lead in to Chapter 3, *Enshrining Freedoms in the Constitution: The Arguments in Favour* said:

> ... the common law system, supplemented as it presently is by statutes designed to protect particular rights, does not protect fundamental rights as comprehensively as do constitutional guarantees and conventions on human rights. The common law is not as invincible a safeguard against violations of fundamental rights as it was once thought to be.

The Committee's Report

When writing the report titled *Individual and Democratic Rights*, the committee saw its task as practical rather than theoretical, and it prepared what it believed to be a concise report accessible to the lay reader. It was not intended to be an academic document. The report dealt with those fundamental issues the committee thought were crucial to the maintenance of a democratic society and covered those matters essential for clarifying or justifying its conclusion.

The committee's report noted that in the Commonwealth sphere there is no constitutional power to pass laws relating to a wide range of individual rights. The government has to create the authority to do so by relying on international treaties and covenants to meet its obligations under such agreements. This has long been seen as a back door way of overcoming what are clearly shortcomings in the Constitution when a government needs to find authority to legislate on issues not found within the existing powers in the Constitution.

The report went into considerable detail discussing the views put to it for enshrining freedoms in the Constitution, noting those arguments in favour and those against enshrining them. The report noted that, apart from several submissions and witnesses seeking the inclusion of particular rights and freedoms in the Constitution, the majority focused on the inadequacies of the existing framework of protections for fundamental rights. Given the extent of public opposition to the earlier proposed Australian Bill of Rights, the committee was impressed by the breadth of arguments put to it for including protections in the Constitution.

The report unveiled a proposed framework for the protection of democratic and individual rights and, after taking into account the competing arguments, the committee concluded that the Australian experience was unique. Unlike the UK, we have our written Constitution with power divided between federal and state parliaments, with no single parliament being supreme. This meant that in Australia, freedoms, privileges and immunities have been entrenched in

CONSTITUTIONAL REFORM 3: THE CONSTITUTIONAL COMMISSION

the Constitution for nearly 90 years. It noted that, while it originally derived its force from the British Parliament, changes deriving from the *Statute of Westminster* and various *Australia Acts* passed by the parliaments of the Commonwealth and the states in the mid-1980s makes its British origins irrelevant.

The report set out the proposed draft wording for each of the protections the committee had identified. It recommended they be submitted to the people of Australia for adoption by referendum. Following adoption by referendum, the new provisions would be incorporated in the Constitution, assuming the conditions of Section 128 were met.

These arguments, however, fell on deaf ears and the Commissioners recommended the insertion of a comprehensive list of constitutionally protected rights and freedoms in a new Chapter V1A Rights and Freedoms which to the world at large looked like a Bill of Rights but with another name.

It was a great experience and a privilege to work so long and closely with the other committee members while being ably assisted by the staff of the Commission.

Having completed the report, the Commission's media advisers arranged for our report to be launched on 20 July 1987 by Tom Keneally, Peter Garrett and me on the Ray Martin *Midday Show* on Channel 9. It was an interesting experience, both for us and viewers, for such a popular programme to have a lively discussion regarding the Constitution on live television in front of an audience. It seemed to work, and we received a warm reception!

A report I wrote regarding the launch, which later appeared in the *Australian Law Journal*, showed our report being presented to a very different audience as it contained a half page photo of us being interviewed by Martin. I seem to recall that including a photo was a first for the editor, as the *Journal's* traditional content was learned articles on recent cases and legislation.

So ended my involvement with this grand initiative. The outcome was one more building block, along with the excellent reports of the other four committees, supporting the case for modernising the Australian Constitution. With the work of the committees finalised by the middle of 1987, it was over to the members of the Commission to sift through and consider the recommendations of the various committees.

The thoroughness of the exploratory work of the committees can be seen in the large number of recommendations for change eventually endorsed by the Commissioners in their final report submitted to the government in August 1988.

28

ADAPTING TO KEATING'S MICRO-ECONOMIC ERA

In early 1993, speaking at the policy retreat held for the Law Foundation's recently appointed Board members, the Attorney General John Hannaford, said:

> A body like the Law Foundation must know and understand the world it operates within. It must always be aware of the particular interests and concerns of its community of interest. More importantly, to be effective it must use that knowledge to map out the future. It was important that the thinking of the board needed to be five to seven years 'ahead of the pack'. I urge the Board to be in the vanguard as an agent for cultural change within the legal system.

Commenting on the event in the Foundation's 1993 Annual Report, I noted that the Board accepted this challenge and over the next few days of debate and discussion they arrived at a number of potentially far-reaching conclusions in keeping with the tradition of taking the long view when deciding to launch new initiatives. The Board accepted that the new priorities would require long-term support.

The Board's ability to take such a position was based on the confidence which flowed from the clear political support the Foundation had continued to enjoy during the previous decade from Attorneys General of both political persuasions, starting with Labor's Terry Sheahan and continued by the Coalition's John Dowd, Peter Collins and John Hannaford.

The proof of their support was clearly evidenced by the Foundation continuing to receive significant funding allocations from the Statutory Interest Account in the previous 10 year period.

These distributions also enabled the Foundation to make major distributions to the Law Society to support its own community service initiatives seen as falling within the Foundation's charter.

The issues which the Board considered as priorities for future attention, having been encouraged by John Hannaford's exhortation, included curial resolution of civil disputes and the alternatives, which was intended to put the spotlight on the costs and delay involved in the current system of resolving civil disputes with a focus on the adversarial culture of the legal industry. The Board also identified the need for new mechanisms which avoided the need for litigation, and the need for methods of resolution which were quick, cheap and fair for all parties. It was all extremely ambitious.

The Board saw the Civil Justice Research Centre as playing a significant part in investigating these various initiatives, potentially in conjunction with an appropriate external institution.

Under the priority of funding legal services, the Board noted, that with limited funds available for legal aid for those involved in civil disputes, the Foundation's longstanding interest in developing alternatives to legal aid should be accelerated. Following the meeting, considerable progress was made in developing a litigation disbursement fund model. Discussions were underway with both the Legal Aid Commission and the Law Society about the final shape such a scheme might take, with a view to it operating within the next 12 months or so. In time, the market produced its own solution with commercial class action litigation funders emerging.

With the increasing interest at that time, both from within governments and from consumers regarding the role of the legal profession, the Board recognised that this attention was, at least in part, due to the perception that the service standards within the legal profession were too often not acceptable. The Board was aware that both complaints against lawyers and claims against professional indemnity insurers were increasing. It believed that the Foundation, under the priority of the legal profession – standards and service, ought to see as a priority a way of assisting the profession to aspire to new standards of service.

The issue of micro-economic reform was then very topical, being driven by the Keating government. There was considerable pressure to achieve economies through micro-economic reform and sectors such as government trading entities, both federal and state, and according to Hannaford the professions were likely to be targeted in this national push for economic reform.

Responding to the Attorney's concerns, in no doubt he was aware of the pressure being put on state governments by Keating, the Board recognised that both the legal institutions and the legal profession needed to be contributing to this essential national reform initiative.

The four areas the Board identified where the Foundation's intervention might be rewarded with improvements in the cost effectiveness of the legal system and legal services were:

- an examination of reducing systemic cost through structural and procedural changes;
- analysing current legislation and procedures to ascertain where economies and efficiencies might be gained through appropriate reforms;
- promoting the Foundation's interest in plain language more widely to encourage solicitors to develop simplified documentation to reduce the cost of legal transactions, commercial or otherwise; and
- exploring ways of working with the NSW Parliament to ensure regulations and secondary legislation did not contribute to inefficiencies and inhibit economic growth.

The fourth issue later became a catalyst for often mindless deregulation by incoming governments with modest agendas keen to be seen to be doing something under the banner of reducing red tape!

Another relevant Board priority was for the Foundation to

continue its longstanding interest in the application of computer technology to the law under the heading, role of technology in legal access and courts, recognising the growing use of computers in the provision of legal services which provided opportunities for efficiency and costs reduction.

Following the retreat, I began to explore a possible role for the Foundation which, while primarily concerned with standards of service, would embrace several other priorities set by the Board at their retreat.

The result was that a few months later the Board accepted my recommendation that the Foundation support a new project to be known as the Legal Services Outreach and Access Project which would aim to develop a new legal services model and an expansion of the legal services market. My view was that the challenge facing the Law Foundation and the legal profession involved more than just lifting standards of service. It involved finding a way to help smaller law firms achieve a level of economic viability through greater efficiencies and offering an expanded range of cost-effective services to an expanded client base.

A key element of the project would focus on how computer-based information technology applications might assist in achieving these outcomes.

Trade Practices Act and the Legal Profession

The prescience of the Board at its 1993 retreat was borne out by developments confronting the profession later that year. The regulatory environment in which the profession operated found itself entering a period of major change and scrutiny at both the state and federal levels, triggered by the NSW *Legal Profession Reform Act*, the proposals contained in the *Trade Practices Commission Report*, the *Hilmer Report* proposals on a national competition policy and the contemporaneous move to establish a national legal profession.

The *Legal Profession Reform Act* was assented to and became law on 29 November 1993. It adopted the *Trade Practices Act 1974* through the insertion of a new Division 1AA within the *Legal Profession Act 1987*. Included in this new division was a new Section 38FC sub-clause (1), which stated:

> (1) The restrictive trade practices laws apply as a law of the State to the conduct of legal practitioners and of any professional association in connection with the provision of legal services.

This was revolutionary and done almost in "the still of the night", with the traditional status of the professions in society abandoned with no great resistance largely because there was probably little the legal profession could do about it politically. One also assumes the NSW government probably accepted the need for the professions to conform to the new micro-economic reform agenda and the need to co-operate with the federal government in the national interest.

Other radical changes meant that the traditional prohibition on advertising was also summarily removed, as was the restriction on who could be a partner in a legal practice through the new law mandating that barristers and solicitors were free to operate in a multi-disciplinary partnership. These changes made the Foundation's new focus all the more urgent and important, as we had planned to address a wide range of issues aimed at making the profession more able to cope with such changes and also able to take advantage of the new freedoms.

The focus of Stage One of the Legal Services Outreach and Access Project was mapped out by a working party which I convened. It included two consultants, one being Peter Truda, partner in charge of Management Consulting at KPMG, who had advised the Foundation on the establishment of the Civil Justice Research Centre, and lawyer Ronwyn North who, through her firm Streeton Consulting, had a long experience of consulting with private and public sector legal practices and had undertaken the first risk management study of NSW legal practices.

The initial step was to test the feasibility of establishing a cost competitive legal practice model, but as this stage progressed it became clear that while new approaches to increasing access to legal services were possible, the development of a new legal services model was premature. This was due to a number of barriers to the acceptance and implementation of any new model. These were the same barriers which were driving the federal and state government reforms of the legal profession.

During the second reading speech on the Legal Reform Bill in September, 1993 Attorney General Hannaford said:

> The purpose of the Government's reforms is to create a more competitive market for legal services, balanced by appropriate client protection … The application of competition policy to legal services will ensure maximum exposure to the market place. This, in turn, will lead to increased productivity and greater efficiency in the delivery of legal services.

While acknowledging the significance of these reforms, the working party nevertheless concluded, based on their various experiences of the provision of profession services, that merely changing the rules governing the legal profession would do little to achieve a new model which both improved access to legal services and expanded the market. There was no alternative but to find ways to help law firms adapt to this new competitive era.

The working party's recommendation was that the profession needed to take competition seriously and to do this it needed to enhance its capabilities in three specific areas:

- research into legal practice and into the market for legal services;
- managing innovation and change; and
- applying technology.

The first step to achieving this was to move to a position which addressed the immediate needs of practitioners, and in so doing to create an environment conducive to the adoption of the longer term changes needed. Having regard to the Foundation's charter, resources and long experience in project management, it was well equipped to assist legal practitioners to enhance their capabilities.

Accordingly, the working party recommended that the Law Foundation establish a new operating unit to:

- undertake research into legal practice and the market for legal services;
- foster innovation and support which enables legal practitioners to adopt new ways of doing things more often, more rapidly and more effectively; and
- establish and support a user-friendly communications facility dedicated to the needs of the legal practitioners.

The working party concluded that with Board members coming from the profession, the community, the government and the Opposition, and with the need for a body independent of the various institutional stakeholders, able to focus on ways of improving the community's relations with the law and the legal system, it was clear that the Foundation was the appropriate body to help address issues such as standards of service within the legal profession, micro-economic reform and the role of technology in legal access to the courts.

29

Tomorrow's Legal Services: A Plan of Action

The end result of the exploratory stage of the project described in the preceding chapter was a well-designed, 55-page report of the work undertaken and the conclusions reached, entitled *Tomorrow's Legal Services*.

It was supplemented by three significant appendices, the first describing the working party's approach to identifying opportunities in the market for legal services. The second identified opportunities for innovation in service delivery and more cost-effective use of practice capabilities, and included what was believed to be first attempt to flow chart processes involved in the sale and purchase of a residential property, in an attempt to see how greater efficiencies could be built into the most common legal transaction. The third explored opportunities for greater adoption of technology in the provision of legal services.

The report itself was the outcome of a nine-month feasibility study undertaken as the Legal Services Outreach and Access Project, which had been endorsed by the Board the previous year in response to the pressure put on the state government by Keating's micro-economic reform agenda.

With the completion of the report, the Foundation's Chairman, Robert Kelly, and I agreed that the significance of the issues covered by the report deserved an extended meeting of the Board. This took the form of a day-long meeting of the Board held on Saturday, 9 April 1994.

The importance of the project was acknowledged by all members of the Board. Those attending, included both the Attorney General

John Hannaford MLC and the Opposition representative on the Board, the Hon Ron Dyer MLC, the Law Society's current President David Fairlie and CEO Mark Richardson and Philip Greenwood representing the Bar. There were also five community representatives, headed by the Hon Gordon Samuels AC QC, Ms Sally Manion, Mr Greg Bartels, lawyer Philip Madden and Jeremy Kinross, a lawyer who represented the Attorney General at meetings.

Besides myself and Assistant Director, Dawn Wong, the other two members of the project's working party and authors of the report, Peter Truda and Ronwyn North, also attended.

Following the meeting's opening, the Chairman invited me to comment on the report and its recommendations. I outlined the history of the project starting with the priorities adopted by the Board at its policy retreat in February 1993, which established a project working party to investigate and report back on a number of issues, including:

- how the Law Foundation would reach law firms and involve them in the proposed initiatives;
- whether the proposed initiatives were "radical" enough to stimulate changes in the way legal services were delivered;
- possible competition from large firms following the establishment of the *First Class Law* communications network;
- the likely income generation potential of the project;
- the likely structure of the proposed research and development unit;
- Elements which indicated that the proposed communication network might succeed where others failed;
- the potential of transactional analysis to assist practitioners do business more effectively;
- the need to avoid duplication of effort and draw on relevant experiences from other Law Foundation projects; and
- the structure and levels of the proposed project budget.

The Attorney General reminded the Board of his recommendation to the policy retreat, that the Foundation should become more relevant to legal practitioners. He felt that this project would support smaller law firms to cope with "future shock" and to stay in the market. It was, he said, unlikely that such support would come from any organisations other than the Law Foundation, and it was essential that attention be directed to the needs of such firms over the next four or five years, otherwise he was concerned that many small practices would not survive in this new competitive era and disappear.

He felt that there was potential for joint venture agreements with computer companies in relation to the communications network, and that this might be an area where the Foundation should play a facilitating rather than a service providing role.

David Fairlie agreed with the Attorney General's comments and noted that the project would need to find ways of turning concepts into realities.

Members of the working party felt that much would be learned over the project's first year of operation in this regard. In particular, the new communications network could be used to demonstrate the benefits of technology to both practitioners and to the various institutions within the legal system. I commented on the potential of this initiative to help the Law Society in communicating with its members and its possible relevance to the Society's Community Assistance Department.

Robert Kelly then directed the meeting to the various recommendations in the report which included the establishment of a project board of management which could help address issues relating to the structure of the proposed research and development unit.

After some discussion the Board endorsed the proposal to establish a new operating unit within the Foundation, with a project board of management to be established. In terms of the amount of funding, there was discussion about whether a special allocation needed to be sought but the meeting ultimately agreed that the proposed operating costs for the first year of the project could be met out of the Foundation's current level of funding.

As to an ongoing commitment, the meeting took the view that the most appropriate course was to commit the level of funding requested for the first year, and to make a commitment to support the project, at a similar level to the first year, over the next two years, subject to satisfactory progress being made and availability of funds.

The possibility of approaching the federal government for a funding contribution to the project was raised, in the context of possible compensation relating to changes to the profession flowing from the *Hilmer Report*. The Attorney General indicated that, if the Foundation approached him with such a proposal, he would be prepared to raise it with the federal Attorney General.

However, the meeting noted that approximately $200,000 remained of the initial allocation of $300,000 made at the retreat for the feasibility stage of the project, which meant that the funding proposed for the establishment of the new unit could be met with a further allocation of $550,000.

The Board resolved that to achieve these goals, it would make a commitment to support the work of the new research and development unit for the first three years of its life and:

- make an allocation of up to $750,000 for the first year's establishment and running costs; and
- agree to support the project for a further two years at a similar level of funding subject to satisfactory progress being made and the availability of fund.

In the context of this meeting, the willingness of the Board to make such a significant commitment to address the very serious concerns about the viability of many small law firms was a necessary response to the Keating government's previously mentioned microeconomic reform agenda.

Launch of Tomorrow's Legal Services

Having made the commitment to fund this project, one of the largest in its history, at a function at the Law Society in late April 1994 the Board formally launched this new major research and development project and the initial report, *Tomorrow's Legal Services – Access and Competitive Success through Research, Innovation and Support*, and announced its initial three year commitment of $750,000.

Speaking at the launch of the project, the Attorney General John Hannaford said:

> I am delighted the Foundation is undertaking a project so practically focussed on assisting solicitors to cope with the challenges of competition and change that will be the hallmark of tomorrow's legal services.

Robert Kelly, said:

> Although the project involves a three-year time frame it is anticipated that the research will produce important results throughout the course of the project. The legal profession and other interested groups will be kept regularly informed of developments. The rapid flow of information is a key element in maximising the benefits of the project for consumers and the legal profession.

David Fairlie, strongly endorsed the project at the launch, saying:

> This is a unique opportunity to help the legal profession to develop a new model for the competitive delivery of legal services that will provide a significant increase in access for people with everyday legal problems.

Mr Fairlie, a strong supporter of the project, wrote in his President's message in the May 1994 edition of the *Law Society Journal*:

> Recent research, and a 1993 LEXPO seminar on the future of small practice, showed that many practitioners were struggling to cope with the current changes which they felt were likely to overwhelm their practices if left unchecked.
>
> On the other hand, practitioners in their thousands in

smaller law firms spread throughout the State are highly regarded in their local communities and their knowledge of the law and the legal system make them uniquely placed to help people with legal problems.

To answer those challenges facing legal practitioners the Foundation's new Tomorrow's Legal Services Research and Development Unit was intended to conduct three separate research and development programmes.

Programme 1 was *Research into Legal Practice and the Market for Legal Services*. The initial approach to this task was to retain former senior Foundation social researcher and lawyer, John Schwartzkoff, mentioned previously as the evaluator of the Community Justice Centres Pilot Program, and then a research consultant in private practice, to assist with the settlement of a research agenda for the project. Essentially the task would involve developing new and reliable sources of empirical data on legal practice which bring the legal services industry on par with other industry sectors.

Programme 2, *Fostering and Supporting Innovation*, was largely dependent upon the outcomes of research findings and transactional analysis. It was noted that it may well be some time before pilot programmes could be commenced within this programme.

However, one initiative to encourage innovation involved exploring ways to apply available computer technology to assist practitioners to handle matters more cost effectively and efficiently. The project team was confident that the then current technological advances would provide an excellent basis for the development of a new range of computer based legal tools for practitioners.

Programme 3, *A Communications Network for the Legal Profession*, was seen as a key element in the process of learning about practical information needs of the profession, as well as the gathering of appropriate information sources and presentation formats to meet those needs while relying on the latest communications technology.

This programme had a lengthy gestation period which the

Foundation monitored with the assistance of Bill Briffa, computer consultant to the Law Society and the Foundation. The feasibility of a data sharing network for the courts and the legal profession began in the early 1990s when Bill recommended a Canadian developed software programme, First Class. This proved to be a versatile, user-friendly communications facility which would meet the needs of the legal profession.

In October 1994 I delivered a paper entitled *Technology's Role in access to Legal Services and Legal Information* at a conference in London organised by Legal Action Group, a charitable trust focused on increasing access to the law. I also demonstrated how a number of features of the system worked and the feedback from those attending was very positive, although somewhat envious of what we had been able to achieve.

During the pilot phase, a core group of users was to be drawn initially from law firms who had indicated interest in being involved in the pilot and had appropriate communications capacity existing within their offices. These early adopters were being encouraged to suggest other firms, barristers, or clients, with whom they had regular contact, to participate in the pilot.

The Foundation maintained the host computer, "The Gateway", which supported a number of bulletin boards, the initial one providing up-to-date access to the daily court lists. It was hoped that in due course this would be accessed government agencies.

One of the keys to stimulating demand from users would be the range of information available through the network. A very enthusiastic response was received from the NSW Supreme Court, and in a national first, Supreme Court daily case lists were soon available on the network. The Law Society was considering the type of information it would make available on the network.

When fully operational, the network was to operate 24 hours a day, with customer support being available over the phone during business hours and via the network's help screen after hours.

30

Tomorrow's Legal Services: International Recognition

Over the years I had been fortunate to be able, periodically, to undertake study tours of North America and the UK, and as a result had attended a number of American Bar Association (ABA) Annual Meetings, which were extraordinary events by Australian standards. As a result, I had met many leading figures in the Association as well as participated in meetings with Bar Association representatives responsible for their Interest on Lawyers Trust Account Funds which met annually during ABA annual meetings.

The process of our Australian law societies generating income for public purposes from trust accounts began in the 1960s and soon travelled to North America, originally via Canadian Law Societies, and then across the border to local US Bar Associations, which for some reason I received the kudos for.

Because of these types of connections, I had been communicating with Bar contacts in the US about Tomorrow's Legal Services and it seemed that the issues we were addressing were common to both American and English lawyers alike. As a result, following my attendance at the annual ABA meeting in August 1993 as a part of the NSW Law Society delegation, the then ABA President Bill Ide III was keen to find a way of continuing the dialogue with me and Rodger J Pannone, the progressive President of the English Law Society at the time.

United States

Bill Ide's proposed strategy was to hold a future of the law conference in early May 1994. He suggested that we should, together with Cecilia Johnstone, then President of the Canadian Bar Association, attend this event to be held in the Lansdowne Conference Centre in Leesburg, Virginia. Rodger Pannone suggested, on the afternoon of the last day of the conference, we should all set aside some time to discuss establishing a process for the ongoing communication and exchange of ideas about the shared problems relating to the future of our legal professions and with our respective justice systems.

Following the launch of Tomorrow's Legal Services, I sent copies of the report air express to the other interested overseas parties and to Bill Ide and the others involved in organising the future of law event, as I was interested in getting feedback on our ambitious project from such well-placed commentators.

Having received and accepted Bill Ide's invitation to attend the Just Solutions Conference at Lansdowne as observers, David Fairlie and I arrived at the conference centre on Sunday, 1 May 1994, to attend what turned out to be an extraordinary event. The conference was attended by leaders of the US legal profession, members of the judiciary including the US Chief Justice and other members of the Supreme Court, together with a number of other leading judges from the federal and state courts, the then US Attorney General, Janet Reno, deans of a number of leading law schools, a number of Congressional leaders and state governors, representatives of foundations and public interest bodies, writers, business leaders, lawyers, journalists and a small number of foreign observers from the UK, Canada and Australia.

The range of speakers was very wide, with one memorable contributor being a very colourful Hawaiian academic who was a prominent futurist and, as I recall, shook up what was a fairly conservative audience with his predictions.

On the last day Janet Reno spoke, after which Bill Ide arranged for me to meet her and, during our brief discussion, I explained why I was there and mentioned Tomorrow's Legal Services, which she expressed an interest in seeing. Having a spare copy with me I presented it to her. She then asked me to meet two of her assistants separately and they were particularly interested in issues the Board had identified and the approach we were taking to address such issues and I corresponded with them on my return home.

Following the closing of the conference Bill Ide arranged for Rodger Pannone, Cecilia Johnstone and David and I, and several of their assistants, to meet in a small conference room where we spent several hours comparing issues and mapping out the ground rules for sharing information and keeping in touch. It was personally exciting to find that the issues confronting us were common to other jurisdictions and that they saw what we were doing as being in the vanguard and were keen to monitor our progress and be kept informed.

It was also encouraging that all those present at the meeting recognised that there was great value in developing some ongoing communication strategy. The value of this was made clear to the Americans when both Rodger Pannone and I were able to point out that many of the issues of concern to the delegates attending the Just Solutions Conference were issues that had been, or were in the process of being addressed in satisfactory ways, in some instances, in other jurisdictions. In particular, I told the gathering about the Model Court Project's impact, which had successfully addressed some of the more common issues raised by conference delegates concerning courts.

Before the meeting concluded, responsibility for keeping in touch was delegated to a number of senior representatives of the various organisations represented, including the executive director of the Canadian Bar Association, senior officers of the ABA who were in attendance, the Director of the Practice Department of the English Law Society and me, representing the Australian interests. A further step taken was that the nominated representatives would draft a communique to be circulated amongst the participant in the next few weeks. Bill Ide also decided that a special reference to this action would be included in the final report of the Just Solutions Conference.

England

Later in the year I was invited to speak at a conference in London organised by the Legal Action Group, an English charity established in 1971 to fund access to legal services for disadvantaged members of the community. The conference and the published papers were funded by the Nuffield Foundation. I made two presentations, one entitled *Technology's role in access to legal services and legal information* which provided an overview of the Foundation's long history of support for computer applications to the law and legal services. It also described the First Class Law computer network being developed for the profession as part of Tomorrow's Legal Services. I provided a demonstration of its features during a conference break.

The second paper I presented was entitled *Filling the void in civil litigation disputes – a role for empirical research* and was written jointly with Gillian McAllister, the Executive Director of the Foundation's Civil Justice Research Centre. It provided an overview of the type of research undertaken by the Centre since its establishment in the late 1980s and the benefits to policy makers and administrators which flowed from such applied research. While the Centre's research was carried out to the highest standards, I emphasised that it was never intended to be a pure research facility.

On my return, I got back into moving the Tomorrow's Legal Services Project forward and eventually, in consultation with the project management team, we concluded that undertaking the project in-house was not feasible having regards to the range of disciplines within the project's objectives and the level of specialist input needed. Drawing on our past experience we started to cast around for a likely partner, the most obvious being a local university that might be interested in providing a home for an innovative research centre which in turn could readily access the range of specialist disciplines required.

For various reasons we were attracted to the University of Western Sydney, which had recently opened a new home for its fledgling law school in Campbelltown, a locale likely to see a rapid growth in the numbers of solicitors servicing the growing new communities in south-western Sydney, access to whom we saw as an important requirement. Ultimately, the University was very enthusiastic about our idea and by later that year a detailed proposal had been prepared for the Foundation Board's consideration.

There were a couple of issues to be addressed before the end of the year, one being that the Board's term was coming to an end and the current Chairman, Robert Kelly, had indicated he did not wish to be re-appointed. This led to discussions being held within the Board with a view to encouraging Gordon Samuels AC QC to continue on the Board and be appointed as Chairman. Related to this was that my own term was up for renewal by May 1995.

I was reasonably confident of both goals being achieved in light of the enthusiasm of the Attorney General and the Law Society's representatives on the Board for the Foundation's major new project. This in turn was reinforced by them jointly endorsing the commitment of very significant funding for the project. With such a strong endorsement from John Hannaford and the Law Society representatives for this project, I could look forward to being re-appointed as a matter of course.

The recent, and very encouraging, international recognition of the significance of the scope of our new project was a real bonus.

31
A Politician's Assassination Changes My Life

My story has shown that, prior to and during my time with the Law Foundation, I enjoyed a reasonable amount of luck as well as the support of many good people who shared my enthusiasm for the work of the Foundation and its potential. However, just as the luck of John Newman, the Member of the NSW Parliament for Fairfield in Sydney's western suburbs, ran out on the night of 5 September 1994, when he was shot dead by a political rival, mine started to run out from the next day, 6 September 1994.

The Foundation's current Board's term was about to end, and Attorney General John Hannaford was due to table his proposed new appointees to the Board at the Cabinet meeting due to be held on 6 September 1994. Under the Foundation's legislation, the appointments of Board members were to be made by the Attorney General, but those running the Premier's Office had decided that all ministerial appointments had to be tabled at a Cabinet meeting. Normally such nominations, I was told, were rarely considered due to the Cabinet's workload.

However, the Cabinet meeting was being held in the country at Tamworth and the ministers had all arrived the evening before. Apparently, in light of the news about John Newman's murder, the Premier John Fahey and his Police Minister, Terry Griffiths, returned to Sydney early in the morning and the other ministers carried on but had time to read the various documents. I understand that the Attorney General's nomination of Gordon Samuels AC QC as Chairman aroused some interest amongst other ministers, who apparently held a grudge against him because of his role in the Neil Pickard affair.

A POLITICIAN'S ASSASSINATION CHANGES MY LIFE

This arose from Pickard's appointment as NSW Agent General in London in 1992, his seat in Parliament having been abolished, a role Pickard apparently approached with great enthusiasm to the extent that there was some discontent within the government about his activities

According to an obituary following Pickard's death published in *The Sydney Morning Herald* on 1 May 2007 and written by eminent QC Bob Ellicott:

> On October 27, 1992, a letter arrived from the new premier, John Fahey, dismissing him as agent-general, alleging failure to obey a ministerial travel directive. It was a devastating blow. Gordon Samuels, QC, who arbitrated the issue, found Pickard's dismissal not justified on any of the grounds relied on by the government and that he was entitled to substantial damages. He also found that media reports to the effect that he was 'enjoying some personal and unauthorised frolic around Europe at the taxpayers' expense' were nonsense.

Nevertheless, that put paid to Gordon's appointment and, for reasons I never understood, his replacement as Chairman was Supreme Court Justice Vince Bruce, who made it clear from our early encounters that he was not going to conduct himself as all previous Foundation chairpersons had done. He soon decided that Tomorrow's Legal Services was not a project he had any regard for and worse was to come.

Again, an accident of bad timing meant that this new Board would be deciding in the first half of 1995 whether I would be reappointed to a further term as Director. By late 1994 it was clear that he did not like me or my ideas or, for that matter, the Foundation's current roster of projects. He clearly wanted to put his stamp on the Foundation and, as one finds in any crisis, there are people you can rely on and those you can't.

Yet I was surprised that, with so much pressure on the legal profession to adapt to this new era of micro-economic reform and competition, the Law Society members particularly seemed unable to take on the new Chairman when so much benefit would flow to so many of its members struggling to survive in this new competitive era.

The ultimate irony was that the meeting held to deny me the opportunity to continue in my role was quickly arranged so that it could be held 17 hours before the new Carr government was to be sworn in. This was despite a personal approach by me to incoming Attorney General Jeff Shaw. He clearly did not want to have a fight with a Supreme Court judge on the eve of his being sworn in and declined to intervene as he would have been entitled to.

To compound my distress, a few days later Bruce was interviewed by *The Australian Financial Review* and made disparaging remarks about me which provided me with the grounds for a defamation action. In the absence of any compensation after 23 years of service and with comparatively modest superannuation, I felt I had little option but to commence proceedings against an impressive array of defendants which included the Attorney General, a Supreme Court judge, the Presidents of the Law Society and the Bar Association, the CEO of the Law Society, an eminent QC and several hapless community members who no doubt looked on in surprise.

Twelve months later the matter was settled, and I received a modest settlement. By then I had embarked on the next stage of my working life. Later, I learned from someone in insurance at a cocktail party, whom I did not know, but he obviously knew of me once we were introduced, that the settlement was paid for under some insurance policy, presumably a directors and officers liability policy protecting the Law Society's representatives on the Board. The Foundation's various Boards had never seen the need to take out such a policy.

A final note. Several years after my departure from the Foundation, Justice Bruce found himself being referred to the NSW Judicial Commission and in 1999 he resigned from the Supreme Court.

Postscript

I admit to being shocked and very distressed by the traumatic, unfair and long drawn out ending of my role at the Foundation and was very unsure about the future direction of my career. But I am the supreme optimist; nothing gets me down for too long, so I looked for other ways I could have an impact within the legal profession.

Dawn Wong was also shown the door and, having worked together for 12 years, we decided to start a business. Building on our strategic planning and project management experience, and on the philosophy behind Tomorrow's Legal Services, we started out in the suburbs, working with small law firms whose partners expressed an interest in improving their practice management.

Over an eight year period we supported numerous small to medium legal practices in enhancing their operational procedures. This included development of planning frameworks and implementation of policies and procedures covering staff recruitment and development, client communications, marketing and business succession.

We advised a number of firms on upgrading their then manual systems and procedures to take advantage of the fast moving developments in computerisation for law firms. This led to our guiding several firms through the process of obtaining Best Practice Certification, and in one instance to assisting a mid-size practice with a major conversion of its precedent system from one commercial computer application to another.

By late 2002, the rigours of convincing lawyers to change the way they managed their firms started to take a toll. Dawn and I, with Pat's encouragement, decided we knew enough about managing law firms to do it ourselves. Our consulting work had led us to identify an area of practice that had the potential to develop into a niche offering, namely estate planning. In mid-2003, RetireLaw Pty Ltd. opened its doors, operating under the recently introduced incorporated legal practice structure. This meant that Dawn, who at that stage had not been admitted to practice, could be a director of the practice.

We had invested heavily in building our skills and knowledge in estate planning, and retained an experienced practitioner to guide us during the first couple of years. Dawn set up Best Practice quality procedures and documentation to comply with the requirement that incorporated legal practices have "appropriate management systems" in place, while I started making contact with the many groups of potential referrers, particularly in the areas of financial planning and accounting.

Looking back on RetireLaw's key performance indicators, it is astonishing how quickly the practice took off. In the first six months, we opened over 60 matters, and the practice continued to grow strongly until the advent of the global financial crisis. It duly recovered and continued providing high quality estate planning services over the next dozen years or so.

In early 2020, just as COVID hit, Dawn and I decided it was time to wind down the practice with a view to retirement. We retreated to home offices and provided remote client services during COVID until, after nearly 20 years, RetireLaw finally ceased operating as an incorporated legal practice in June 2022.

I am proud of the high level of legal and management skills Dawn and I were able to apply to our practice. Our strong commitment to client communication and satisfaction is reflected in the fact that we are still fielding calls from clients expressing their appreciation of our services over the years.

A few updates on my personal life

In my chapters describing my Churchill Fellowship trip I mentioned my two daughters Anne and Jane, toddlers at the time, and rushing back to meet my son John who was born as I was leaving to return home.

Pat and I also had two more children, so a lovely family of

five. They are now wonderful adults with their own careers and families.

Anne is a senior NSW public servant. She lives in inner-city Tempe and has two teenage kids, Ruby and Henry.

Jane is a primary school teacher at Newport Public School and has two sons in their twenties, Sam and Alex. She recently re-married and lives with her husband Simon in Waitara.

John is a published author (*The Girl on the Page*, *The Lessons*) and lives with his wife Tamsin, a veterinary nurse, in Kent in the UK. He has two stepchildren, Ben and Isi, both in their twenties and living in Australia.

Matthew lives in Merriwa with his partner, Angela, a nurse, and they have three primary school age children, Olivia, Jack and Emily. He also has two daughters from his previous marriage. Kate just finished university and Mia is finishing the HSC. Matthew works in the Merriwa office of the Upper Hunter Shire Council and is the owner of the historic Fitzroy Hotel in Merriwa, which he is threatening to renovate.

Tim and his partner Claire are small business owners and budding DIY home renovators. They live in a lovely old cottage in Katoomba with their many cats and hope to start a family soon.

My wife Pat opened her own business when our youngest started school and had a children's shop called Wear it Again Sam, selling recycled clothing, toys, books, etc. for over 28 years.

After the kids left home, we bought a holiday house in Toronto on Lake Macquarie where we had some wonderful times with kids and grandkids. We are now enjoying retirement on the beautiful Northern Beaches of Sydney.

Acknowledgements

This book would never have been written without the multiple contributions of my wife and chief supporter Pat, who often worked alongside me and was a great sounding board for my ideas.

I also wish to record the generosity of my friend Dr David Clune who kindly read, reviewed and offered invaluable editorial advice and support, as well as recommending my book to his publisher Anthony Cappello of Connor Court.

More recently my longstanding friend and former business partner, Dawn Wong, has contributed much time in ensuring we met the publisher's requirements and I thank her for her valuable assistance.

Index

Aboriginal Affairs Department 186

Aboriginal Land Rights Act 217

Aboriginal Legal Service 67-8, 77, 287

Advisory Committee on Individual and Democratic Rights 313, 333

Advisory Council on Inter-Governmental Relations (ACIR) 303

American Bar Association (ABA) 77, 363

American Bar Foundation 77, 79, 146, 154

Anderson, Kevin 234

Anderson, Peter 222, 231-2

articled clerk 26-9, 123, 135, 150

Askin, Robert vii-ix, 139, 161, 163-6, 172, 174-81, 201-2

Athenaeum, The 131

Australia's Constitution: Time for Change? 313, 324-5

Australian Assistance Plan (AAP) 188

Australian Film Commission 190, 311

Australian Law Reform Commission 156, 160, 185, 200, 227, 239

Australian Legal Information Institute (AUSTLII) 285

Avery, John 281

Balmer, Colin 305, 308

Bamberger, Clinton 42, 86-8, 242

Barnard, Lance 183-4

Barton, Edmund 315, 321

Beale, Jack 166, 177-80

Beed, Terry 263-4

Bell, Virginia 250

Berrigan, Daniel 93-4

Berrigan, Philip 91, 93

Blacktown Local Court 257, 259

Blewett, Neal 211, 294-5, 321

Boudin, Leonard 92, 94-5

Bowen, Jan 248-9

Bowen, John 46, 143, 148, 150

Bowen, Lionel 149, 278, 293, 328-30, 334

Bramston, Troy 202, 293

Bresnahan, Kathleen 255

British Legal Aid 116, 118, 122, 142

Broadbent, John 46, 143

Bruce, Vince 369

Bureau of Indian Affairs 67-8, 71

Burns, Philp & Co 17-19, 22, 24, 131

Buttrose, Ita 247, 249

Byers, Sir Maurice 329

California Commission on Judicial Performance 242, 245

Californian Rural Legal Assistance 54

Campaign for Constitutional Change 192

Campbell, Ian 155-6

Campbelltown Youth and the Law Project 275-6, 278-9

Canadian Bar Association 113, 147, 363, 365

Carlin, Jerome 57-9, 63
Carr, Tom 78, 98, 114
Carter, Sir William 121
Cashman, Peter 89, 200, 238, 240, 265
Castan, Ron 329-33, 338, 340, 344-5
Castle, David 37
Catholic Anti-War Peace Rally 84
Catholic Education System 15
Chappell, Duncan 276-9
Christian Brothers High School, Lewisham 15-16
Churchill Fellowship ix, 19, 36-41, 44, 47, 52, 61, 64, 68, 72, 78, 98, 112, 132, 139, 144-6, 152, 155, 186, 194, 237, 251, 372
Churchman, Susan 157, 161
Civil Justice Research Centre (CJRC) 262, 268, 272, 350, 353, 366
Clark, Ramsay 92
Clean Waters Act 1970 177-8
College of Law 144-5, 147-54, 157, 252, 283
Committee on Computerisation of Legal Data 195
Commonwealth Public Service 25
Communications Law Centre 303, 309-12
Community Justice Centres 216, 234, 236-7
Community Justice Centres Pilot Project 233, 361
computerised legal information retrieval 113, 148, 285
Connery, Maxwell & Co 27-8
conscription 29, 182, 184
Constitutional Commission 8, 313, 328-9, 335-7

Consultative Committee on Computers and the Law 147, 199
Cook, Milton 49
Courtguide 259-60
Criminal Injuries Compensation Act 1967 169
Crook, Alison 254-5
Cunliffe, Ian 331, 334, 336, 343
Curtin, John 1, 294
Daley, Richard 62, 77, 81

Darling Harbour 217, 221
Datalex project 285
Davies, Anne 312
Day, Dorothy 84
De Witt, Paul 103
Dinebeiiina Nahiilna Be Agaditaher Inc (DNA) 68
Director of Public Prosecutions Act 1986 223
Disney, Julian 252
District Court Act 1973 174
Dougherty, Gerald 121, 126, 132
Douglas, Boyd 94
Dowd, John 253, 262, 349
Dusseldorp, Tjerk 157, 161
Dyer, Ron 357
dyslexia 11

Easson Michael 220, 223
Ebener, Pat 271
Ellard, Dr John 20, 143, 148, 150, 305
Ellicott, Bob 192, 369
Engel, John 280
English Law Society 79, 118, 153, 363, 365

INDEX

environmental protection 163, 177
Eslake, Saul 305
Ethnic Affairs Commission 212, 306
Evans, Gareth 192, 293, 303, 313, 320-1, 325, 328

Fahey, John 303, 368-9
Farquhar, Murray 243
Ferran, John 95-6, 98
First Class Law 357, 366
Fishwick, Elaine 281
Ford Foundation 107, 155
Fraser, Malcolm 187, 189, 191-2, 292, 294, 303, 308-9, 319-25
Fulham Road Legal Advice Centre 135
full text legal retrieval system 114-5, 199

Gamble, Helen 281
Garrett, Peter 329-30, 332, 335-6, 340, 347
Gates, Ronald 304
Gaudron, Mary 28
Gorman, Anne 273, 275
Grants Programme 251, 283, 285, 288-90
Great Barrier Reef Marine Park 191
Greenleaf, Graham 285
Gregory, Dick 84
Griffiths, Terry 368
Griswold, Dr. Erwin 45, 86, 88-90
Groppi, Jim 84
Guest, Chris 271, 278
Hadrian's Wall 130
Hand, Paul 75

Hannaford, John 349-54, 357, 360, 367-8
Harlem 103, 105-7
Harrisburg Seven Trial 86, 90-2
Harrison, Kate 309-12
Hatter, Terry 64-5
Haven, Leo 69
Hawke, Bob vii, ix, 133, 211, 221, 224, 291-8, 301, 303, 307, 309, 321, 325, 328, 334
Healy, Hank 103
Hensler, Deborah 267
Hidden, Peter 67-8
High School Education Law Project (HELP) 136, 157-8, 273
Hillyard, Simon 135
Hoffman, Tim 51, 55
Hogan, Michael 280-2
Hoover, Herbert 3
Hopetoun, Lord 315, 334
Howard, John 210, 292, 301, 338
Huge, Harry 95-6, 98
Hughes, Davis 165
Hulme-Moir, Bishop Francis 143

Intellectual Disability Rights Service 286-7
International House, University of Chicago 79, 102

Jackson, Rex 231, 274
Jarvis, Kenneth 109
John Sands Pty Ltd 22-5
Judicial Officers Act 1986 223, 244
Justice for All 125

377

Keating, Paul ix, 291-3, 296-301, 303, 339, 342, 349, 351, 356, 359
Kelty, Bill 296, 300
Kemp, David 326, 328, 334
Keneally, Tom 329-30, 332-3, 335, 340, 343, 347
Kennedy, Father Ted 34-5
Kennedy, Senator Ted 100
Kennedy, Robert 42-3, 101
Kerr, Sir John 189, 201
Kids in Justice Project 280-1, 290
Kingsford Legal Centre 286
Kirby, Michael 200, 239, 321
Ku-ring-gai College of Advanced Education 150

Land and Environment Courts 316
Law Foundation Act 215, 246, 283
Law Foundation of New South Wales vii-x, 47, 139, 161, 163, 234-6
Law Handbook, The 251
Law, Lawyers and the Community 155
law libraries 140-1, 147, 194, 253, 288
Law Reform Commission 134, 152, 156, 160, 163, 172-3, 176, 185, 200, 211, 239, 241, 281, 321
Law Society of England and Wales 43, 121
Law Society of NSW viii-ix, 124
Law Society's Associate Committee 35, 38, 103, 119
Law Society's Young Lawyers Section 35, 286
Lawyers Practice Manual, The 252
Leeds Area Office 121, 127

Legal Action Group 119, 362, 366
legal advice service 36
legal aid 35-6, 41-4, 51, 58, 68, 77-89, 103, 106, 108-12, 116-32, 136-8, 140-2, 145-6, 170, 185-6, 195, 216, 251, 258, 269, 350
Legal Aid Commission 216, 239, 241, 253, 350
Legal Aid Society of New York 103-6
Legal Eagle 158-61
Legal Information Access Centre (LIAC) 246, 252, 254-5
Legal Practitioners (Amendment) Act 1967 139, 162
Legal Resources Manual for Lawyers, The 251
Legal Services Corporation 89, 101
Legal Services Outreach and Access Project 352-3, 356
Legal Services Program 42, 51, 57, 89, 100-1, 109, 147
legal studies 136, 152-4, 157-8, 160-1, 273
Legal Toolkit 255
Lenzner, Terry 90-2
Leonora 2
Longstaff, Simon 288
Loxton, Allen 46
Lund, Sir Thomas 130

Mabo 299-300, 330, 339-40
Maddison, John viii, 143, 162, 166, 170, 174-7, 321
Maher, Michael 33
Mant, John 37

INDEX

Marsden-Smedley, Susan 119
Marshall, Thurgood 72
Martin, Ray 347
Mason, Sir Anthony 344-5
Maxwell Connery & Co 27
McAllister, Gillian 271, 366
McCann, Terry 98-9
McCaw, Ken viii, 134, 141-2, 148, 162, 166-9, 173-4, 176
McDonald, Barry 140, 162
McDowell, Norman 45-6, 143-5, 149-50
McMillan, John 321, 323
Medibank 186, 190
Mills, David 155
Mock Trial Competition 160
Model Court Project 256-8, 260-2, 365
Modesto 55, 60-2
Monument Valley 73
Morgan, Jenny 235
Morris, Milton 166, 180
Morris, Norval 80, 205
Mortlake Gas Works 4
Mowbray, Andrew 285
Muir, Alec 227, 230
Murphy, Lionel 87, 151, 184-6, 195-7, 199, 221, 325
Murphy, Tom 271

National Conference for a Democratic Constitution 192
National Conference on Legal Education 157
National Gallery 191
National Geographic 12

National Legal Aid and Defender Association 78
native title 299-300, 330, 339-40
Navajo Reservation 67-8, 72, 75-7
Nettheim, Garth 250
Newman, John 368
Nixon, Richard 50-1, 84-5, 88-91, 99-101, 123, 137
North Kensington Neighbourhood Law Centre 135
North, Ronwyn 353, 357
NSW Court of Appeal 167, 239
NSW Judicial Commission 244-5, 370
NSW Law Reform Commission 134, 156, 172-3, 176, 211, 281, 321
NSW Law Society 39, 79, 119, 140, 160, 363

O'Grady, Frank 47, 127
Oakes, Laurie 183
Oates, Kim 284
Occupational Health and Safety Act 219-20
OEO Legal Services Program 42, 51, 66-7, 91, 98, 100, 104-5, 242
Oerlemans, Robert 280
Ombudsman Bill 176
Ontario Legal Aid Plan 110-2, 124
Operation Compulex 114-5, 194

Pagan, Sir Jock and Lady 134
Panton, Alistair 131
Parole Review Committee 221, 226, 232
Pattern of the Islands, A 17

Periodic Detention of Prisoners Act 174

Perspectives on Small Business Assistance 156

Petre, Clare 256

Pickard, Neil 368-9

Plimpton, Francis 104

Pocket Guide to the Law, The 246-9

Pollock, Seton 117, 120-1, 136

Prices and Income Accord ix, 292

Probation and Parole Act 221

Profile of the Profession 156

Public Defenders Act 1969 172

Public Interest Advocacy Centre (PIAC) 89, 237-8, 280, 303, 309

Public Service Act 213-4

Purcell, Daniel and Edna 1-2

Quebec 109-10, 112, 317

RAND Corporation 262

RAND's Institute for Civil Justice 262, 264-8, 271-2

Reagan, Ronald 50, 61-2, 101

Real Property (Conversion of Title) Bill 167

Redfern Legal Centre 135, 246, 250-2, 256, 284

Redfern Legal Centre Publishing (RLCP) 246, 250

Redfern Pro Bono Legal Service 37

Reno, Janet 364

RetireLaw Pty Ltd 371-2

Rizzo, Concetta 200, 235

road safety 163, 177, 180

Robin Hood's Bay 129

Robinson, Jacklyn 155-6

Rough Justice 126

Royal Commission on Human Relationships 187, 210

Royal Humane Society 22

Russell Sage Foundation 107, 155

Samuels, Gordon 255, 311, 357, 367-9

San Francisco Neighbourhood Legal Aid Foundation 51-2

San Mateo Legal Aid Society 56-7

Sanctuary, Gerald 136, 153

Scarborough 128

Schell, Peter 258

Schoen, Marian 331, 333

Schwartzkoff, John 216, 235, 361

Scottish Legal Aid 132

Seale, John 23-4

Sells, Cato 70, 73, 75

Sexton, Michael 133-4, 136

Sheahan, Terry 35, 144, 179, 192, 221-4, 240, 243, 245, 258, 261, 278-9, 303-4, 349

Shriver, Sargent 42, 86

Shubert, Gus 264-5

Silverman, Leon 104-5, 164

Smith, Rod 280

Smithers, Kenneth (Ken) CBE 46, 107, 142-3, 148, 150, 152, 305

Solicitors' Fidelity Guarantee Fund 140-2

Sons of Gwalia 2-3

South Side Chicago 82-3, 85, 103

Speaker, Fred 90-1

INDEX

St James' Ethics Centre 288
Starke, J G x
State Emergency Services and Civil Defence Act 1972 181
State Library of NSW 254-5
Statutory Interest Account 139, 141-2, 145-6, 154, 216, 237, 240, 246, 258, 261, 349
Staunton, Jim 244
Steigler, Mayo 78-80
Stephen, Sir Ninian 324-5
Stewart, Russell 37, 149
Stone, Julius 45, 57, 88
Storey, Haddon 321, 323, 326, 331
Streetwize Comics 251
Supplementary Benefits Commission 124, 130, 132
Supreme Court Act 173, 176, 319

Tan, Lyn 161
Thornton, Brian 265
Tomasic, Roman 155, 208, 279
Tomorrow's Legal Services 263, 356, 360-1, 363-4, 366, 369, 371
Traill, John 199
Tresidder, Julia 281
Truda, Peter 263, 265-6, 353, 357
Turner, Roy 35

University of Chicago Law School 42, 77-9, 83, 154
UNSW Aboriginal Law Research Unit 287
Unsworth, Barrie ix, 201, 222-5, 244, 303
Utzon, Jorn 164-5

victimless crimes 175, 203, 205, 207, 211
Victims Compensation Act 1987 224
Vietnam War 48-9, 104, 137, 182
Vinson, Tony 208, 232

Walker, Frank 143, 162, 176, 203-4, 209-10, 213, 215, 226, 233-5
War on Poverty 30, 41-3, 48, 66, 101, 116
Washington DC 52, 57, 61, 77-8, 86, 89-90, 98-100, 114, 153, 196, 242
Waters, Peter 240
Weatherburn, Don 279
Webb, Peter 256
Western Center for Law and Poverty 64-5
White House Fellows Program 78, 86, 98
White, Margaret 161, 250
Whitlam, Gough vii-ix, 31, 37, 138, 148-51, 158, 164, 182-92, 194, 197, 199-202, 204, 207, 211, 213, 222, 224-5
Wilker, Murray 113, 147
Willis, Eric 166, 180, 201-2
Willis, Ralph 296, 311
Window Rock 70, 74-5
Wong, Dawn 247, 255, 280, 289-90, 357, 371, 374
Workers Compensation (Amendment) Act 170
Working Group on Intellectually Disabled Offenders 286

Wran, Neville vii, ix, 132, 142, 193, 201-13, 217, 219-24, 226, 249, 274
Wright, Pat 33

Young, Julia 275, 280

Youth Forum 273-5, 277-8
Youth Justice Coalition 280-1

Zah, Peterson 69
Zander, Michael 119, 125

www.ingramcontent.com/pod-product-compliance
Lightning Source LLC
Chambersburg PA
CBHW052055300426
44117CB00013B/2135